Made in Scotland

Made in Scotland: Studies in Popular Music serves as a comprehensive and thorough introduction to the history, politics, culture, and musicology of twentieth- and twenty-first-century popular music in Scotland. The volume consists of essays by local experts and leading scholars in Scottish music and culture, and covers the major figures, styles, and social contexts of popular music in Scotland. Each essay provides adequate context so readers understand why the figure or genre under discussion is of lasting significance. The book includes a general introduction to Scottish popular music, followed by essays organized into three thematic sections: Histories, Politics and Policies, and Futures and Imaginings.

Examining music as cultural expression in a country that is both a nation and a region within a larger state, this volume uses popular music to analyse Scottishness, independence, and diversity and offers new insights into the complexity of cultural identity, the power of historical imagination, and the effects of power structures in music. It is a vital read for scholars and students interested in how popular music interacts with and shapes such issues both within and beyond the borders of Scotland.

Simon Frith is Emeritus Professor of Music at the University of Edinburgh, UK.

Martin Cloonan is the Director of the Turku Institute for Advanced Studies (TIAS) at the University of Turku, Finland. He is also coordinating editor of Popular Music and sometimes sings in public.

John Williamson is a lecturer in Music at the School of Culture and Creative Arts, University of Glasgow, UK.

Routledge Global Popular Music Series

Series Editors: Franco Fabbri, Civica Scuola di Musica "Claudio Abbado," Milan, Italy, and Goffredo Plastino, Newcastle University, UK

The *Routledge Global Popular Music Series* provides popular music scholars, teachers, students, and musicologists with a well-informed and up-to-date introduction to different world popular music scenes. The series of volumes can be used for academic teaching in popular music studies, or as a collection of reference works. Written by those living and working in the countries about which they write, this series is devoted to popular music largely unknown to Anglo-American readers.

Made in Turkey: Studies in Popular Music
Edited by Ali C. Gedik

Made in Australia and Aotearoa/New Zealand: Studies in Popular Music
Edited by Shelley Brunt and Geoff Stahl

Made in Greece: Studies in Popular Music
Edited by Dafni Tragaki

Made in Taiwan: Studies in Popular Music
Edited by Eva Tsai, Tung-Hung Ho, and Miaoju Jian

Made in Poland: Studies in Popular Music
Edited by Patryk Galuszka

Made in Hong Kong: Studies in Popular Music
Edited by Anthony Fung and Alice Chik

Made in Yugoslavia: Studies in Popular Music
Edited by Danijela Š. Beard and Ljerka V. Rasmussen

Made in Germany: Studies in Popular Music
Edited by Oliver Seibt, Martin Ringsmut, and Davil-Emil Wickström

Made in Ireland: Studies in Popular Music
Edited by Áine Mangaoang, John O'Flynn and Lonán Ó Briain

Made in Finland: Studies in Popular Music
Edited by Toni-Matti Karjalainen and Kimi Kärki

Made in Nusantara: Studies in Popular Music
Edited by Adil Johan and Mayco A. Santaella

Made in Scotland: Studies in Popular Music
Edited by Simon Frith, Martin Cloonan and John Williamson

Made in Scotland

Studies in Popular Music

Edited by

**Simon Frith, Martin Cloonan
and John Williamson**

Routledge
Taylor & Francis Group

NEW YORK AND LONDON

First published 2024
by Routledge
605 Third Avenue, New York, NY 10158

and by Routledge
4 Park Square, Milton Park, Abingdon, Oxon, OX14 4RN

Routledge is an imprint of the Taylor & Francis Group, an informa business

Library of Congress Cataloging-in-Publication Data
Names: Frith, Simon, 1946– editor. | Cloonan, Martin, editor. | Williamson, John, 1949– editor.
Title: Made in Scotland: studies in popular music/edited by Simon Frith, Martin Cloonan, and John Williamson.
Description: New York, NY: Routledge, 2023. | Series: Routledge global popular music series | Includes bibliographical references and index.
Identifiers: LCCN 2023018268 (print) | LCCN 2023018269 (ebook) | ISBN 9781032161976 (paperback) | ISBN 9781032161983 (hardback) | ISBN 9781003247470 (ebook)
Subjects: LCSH: Popular music—Scotland—History and criticism.
Classification: LCC ML3492.7.S36 M33 2023 (print) | LCC ML3492.7.S36 (ebook) | DDC 782.4216409411—dc23/eng/20230517
LC record available at https://lccn.loc.gov/2023018268
LC ebook record available at https://lccn.loc.gov/2023018269

ISBN: 978-1-032-16198-3 (hbk)
ISBN: 978-1-032-16197-6 (pbk)
ISBN: 978-1-003-24747-0 (ebk)

DOI: 10.4324/9781003247470

Typeset in Minion Pro
by codeMantra

This book is dedicated to the memory of Stewart Cruickshank (1951–2015), a constant presence around and supporter of Scottish music.

Contents

Foreword

Popular music studies have progressed from the initial focus on methodologies to exploring a variety of genres, scenes, works and performers. British and North American music have been privileged and studied first, not only for their geographic and generational proximity to scholars, but also for their tremendous impact. Everything else has been often relegated to the dubious "world music" category, with a "folk" (or "roots," or "authentic") label attached.

However, world popular music is no less popular than rock 'n' roll, r&b, disco, rap, singer-songwriters, punk, grunge, brit-pop or nu-gaze. It is no less full of history and passion, no less danceable, socially relevant and commercialised. Argentinian tango, Brazilian *bossa nova*, Mexican *reggaeton*, Cuban *son* and *timba*, Spanish and Latin American *cantautores*, French *auteurs-compositeurs-interprètes*, Italian *cantautori* and electronic dance music, *J-pop*, German cosmic music and *Schlager*, Neapolitan Song, Greek *entechno*, Algerian *raï*, Ghanaian highlife, Portuguese *fado*, Nigerian *jùjú*, Egyptian and Lebanese Arabic pop, Israeli *mizrahit*, Indian *filmi* are just a few examples of locally and transnationally successful genres that, with millions of records sold, are an immensely precious key to understand different cultures, societies and economies.

More than in the past there is now a widespread awareness of the "other" popular music: however, we still lack access to the original sources, or to texts to rely on. The *Routledge Global Popular Music Series* has been devised to offer to scholars, teachers, students and general readers worldwide a direct access to scenes, works and performers that have been mostly not much or at all considered in the current literature, and at the same time to provide a better understanding of the different approaches in the field of non-Anglophone scholarship. Uncovering the wealth of studies flourishing in so many countries, inaccessible to those who do not speak the local language, is by now no less urgent than considering the music itself.

The series website (www.globalpopularmusic.net) includes hundreds of audio-visual examples which complement the volumes. The interaction with the website is intended to give a well-informed introduction to the world's popular music from entirely new perspectives, and at the same time to provide updated resources for the academic teaching.

The *Routledge Global Popular Music Series* aims ultimately to establish a truly international arena for a democratic musicology through authoritative and accessible books. We hope that our work will help the creation of a different polyphony of critical approaches, and that you will enjoy listening to and being part of it.

Franco Fabbri
Civica Scuola di Musica "Claudio Abbado," Milan, Italy
Goffredo Plastino
Newcastle University, UK
Series Editors

Selected Timeline of Key Events

1951

Hamish Henderson helps to establish the School of Scottish Studies at the University of Edinburgh and organises the Edinburgh People's Festival Ceilidh, thus launching the Scottish Folk Revival.

1952

First reception of BBC television broadcasts from Scotland.
    Scotland's best-loved trad band, the Clyde Valley Stompers, form in Glasgow.
    A group led by clarinetist Sandy Brown and trumpeter Al Fairweather put on a 'legendary' concert at Edinburgh's Usher Hall.

1957

Scottish Television (STV) is launched.

1960

Alex Harvey and his Big Beat Band support Johnny Gentle at Alloa Town Hall. Gentle's backing band is made up of John Lennon, Paul McCartney, George Harrison, Stuart Sutcliffe and Tommy Moore.
    A teenage Bert Jansch appoints himself unofficial caretaker of the Howff folk club on Edinburgh's High Street.
    Robin Hall and Jimmie Macgregor become featured performers on the BBC's *Tonight* programme.

1961

Jack Bruce graduates from the Royal Scottish Academy of Music and Drama where he had studied cello and composition.

1962

La Cave, an all-night restaurant /venue, opens in Glasgow.
    Jimmy Shand is made an MBE in the same year he is presented with a commemorative disc on the *White Heather Club* by his label, Parlophone, marking the occasion of him becoming the first Scottish artist to sell 250,000 albums.

1963

The Beatles play their first show with Ringo Starr at the Two Red Shoes Ballroom in Elgin on 3rd January. On the subsequent nights they play in Dingwall, Bridge of Allan and Aberdeen.

Alex Harvey and His Soul Band move to Hamburg, recording an album for Polydor (released in 1964) later in the year.

1964

The Athenians release what is widely considered the first Scottish 'beat' single, *You Tell Me/ Little Queenie*, in aid of Edinburgh Student Charities Week.

Lulu reaches the top ten with her debut single, 'Shout,' the start of a career that spans seven decades.

1965

Radio Scotland, an offshore pirate station, begins broadcasting (on 31 December). It stays on air until August 1967 and the passing of the Marine Offences Act.

1966

Clive Palmer opens an all-night folk venue, Clive's Incredible Folk Club on Glasgow's Sauchiehall Street. The Incredible String Band is the resident group.

1967

Scottish Arts Council established.

The first of Bruce Findlay's record shops, Bruce's Records, opens in in Falkirk.

1969

Marmalade becomes the first Scottish group to top the UK charts – with 'Ob-La-Di, Ob-La-Da.'

Scottish Tourist Board established.

Seventeen-year-old Tiger Tim Stevens, the nearest thing Scotland has had to a Personality DJ, starts work at the Electric Garden on Sauchiehall Street. He would go on to have a show on Radio Clyde that ran, with only occasional breaks, from 1973 to 2000.

1970

The Scottish Blues and Progressive Rock Festival takes place at Telford Street Park in Inverness, featuring Atomic Rooster, Taste and Brinsley Schwarz. The first outdoor festival of its type in Scotland.

1972

Guitarist Les Harvey dies after being electrocuted on stage at Swansea's Top Rank Suite while performing with Stone the Crows, the band he formed with Maggie Bell in 1969.

1973

Radio Clyde, the first Independent Local Radio station outside London, is launched. (Radio Forth followed in 1975 and Radio Moray Firth in 1982.)

The first edition of Sandy Bell's *Broadsheet* is published from Sandy Bell's folk club/bar in Edinburgh.

Glasgow Apollo opens for business (it will close in 1985).

Ivan Tiefenbrun establishes Linn Products, a manufacturer of high-grade hi-fi and audio equipment (and, later, a record company).

1974

Glasgow's Grand Old Opry opens at Paisley Road Toll.

Brian Young launches CaVa Sound, a recording studio in the west end of Glasgow.

1975

The Bay City Rollers top the UK charts twice in a year at the height of Rollermania with 'Bye Bye Baby' and 'Give A Little Love.'

Billy Connolly's first appearance on the BBC's *Parkinson* show.

The Average White Band release 'Pick Up the Pieces.'

1976

The Who – supported by the Sensational Alex Harvey Band – play Parkhead: the first large-scale stadium show in Scotland.

1978

BBC Radio Scotland is launched.

Barry Wright and Pete Irvine form Regular Music which goes on to become Scotland's largest concert promoter in the subsequent decades.

Scotland qualify for the Football World Cup finals in Argentina

1979

A referendum on devolution produces an insufficient majority for change. 51.6% of those who voted supported the proposal but with a turnout of only 64% this represented only 32.9% of the registered electorate which was less than the 40% required.

Regular Music promote the Edinburgh Rock Festival at the Royal Highland Showgrounds in Edinburgh featuring Van Morrison, Talking Heads, Steel Pulse and The Undertones.

The first of two Loch Lomond Rock Festivals takes place in the Cameron Wildlife Park in Balloch. The Stranglers, Boomtown Rats, Average White Band and The Skids are among the performers.

1980

Alan Horne's Postcard label releases its first record, Orange Juice's 'Falling and Laughing.'

Altered Images play their first John Peel session.

1981

First Shetland Folk Festival.

1982

Alex Harvey dies on his way back from a show in Belgium.

1983

Glasgow's Barrowland Ballroom (originally opened in 1934) reopens as a gig venue with three nights of shows by Simple Minds.

1985

Jesus and Mary Chain release their debut album, *Psychocandy*.
   Scottish Exhibition and Conference Centre (SECC) opens. The Clyde Auditorium (the Armadillo) will be opened in 1997 and the SSE Hydro in 2013.

1986

Aly Bain and Phil Cunningham meet and play together for the first time (in London).
   Gordon Campbell launches a Music Management course at West Lothian College with associated student-run record label, Different Class.

1987

The Proclaimers make their television debut on *The Tube*.
   First Glasgow International Jazz Festival.
   Sub Club opens in Glasgow.

1989

Poll tax is introduced in Scotland (a year before its introduction in England). To mark this, a *Rock Against The Poll Tax* concert is held at the Usher Hall in Edinburgh featuring Wet Wet Wet, Texas, Deacon Blue and Hue and Cry.
   Slam All-Nighter at the recently reopened Tramway in Glasgow attracts thousands (and the riot police). Line-up includes Inner City, 808 State and DJs Mike Pickering and Graeme Park.

1990

Glasgow is European City of Culture
   Deacon Blue headline to an estimated 150,000 people on Glasgow Green at the end of 'The Big Day,' a free, all-day event produced by Channel 4 as part of Glasgow's City of Culture celebrations – the largest audience ever for a gig in Scotland.
   Runrig, Hue and Cry and Dick Gaughan are among the performers at *A Day For Scotland*, organised by the Scottish Trades Union Congress (STUC) at Fallen Inch Field in Stirling. Over 30,000 attend an event that was foundational in the revived campaign for a Scottish Parliament.

Both King Tut's Wah Wah Hut and the Glasgow Concert Hall open as venues.

Teenage Fanclub release their debut album, *A Catholic Education*.

1991

The Arches opens in Glasgow (it will close in 2015)

Rhumba Club nights launched at Roxanne's, Perth

The development agencies Scottish Enterprise and Highlands and Islands Enterprise are established.

The Scottish Fèis movement, Fèisean nan Gaidhal, is launched.

Gaelic rock band, Runrig, play to 50,000 people at Loch Lomond, eighteen years after forming as the Run Rig Dance Band on the Isle of Skye.

Frankie Miller's version of 'Caledonia' (a song written by Dougie MacLean in 1977) is featured in a TV ad for Tennent's lager.

1992

The Lemon Tree opens in Aberdeen.

Primal Scream wins the first Mercury Music Prize.

Electric Honey is launched as a student-run record label on the HNC/HND Music Business Administration course at Stow College

The National Youth Jazz Orchestra of Scotland is established.

Craig Tannock opens The 13th Note in its original Glassford Street location in Glasgow. He would later lose control of this venue but went on to open the vegan café/bar venues Stereo, Mono, the Flying Duck, The Old Hairdressers and 78.

1993

Irvine Welsh's novel *Trainspotting* is published (the film version will be released in 1996).

1994

Edinburgh's Festival Theatre opens for business.

The first T in the Park festival is staged in Strathclyde Park in Lanarkshire. The headliners are Primal Scream, Rage Against the Machine, Del Amitri and Björk.

Celtic Connections is launched.

Wet Wet Wet's cover of 'Love Is All Around' spends fifteen weeks at number 1 in the UK sales charts.

1995

The first Edinburgh Mela is held at Meadowbank Stadium. (A Glasgow Mela had been staged in the Tramway in 1990 as a City of Culture event.)

Braveheart gets its cinematic release

The Delgados release their first single, 'Monika Webster,' on their recently formed Chemikal Underground label. It goes on to release key records by Mogwai, bis, Arab Strap, Interpol and many others.

1996

The Royal Scottish Academy of Music and Drama launches its new BA (Scottish Music).

1997

The devolution referendum produces a definitive majority for change – almost 75% of those who voted.

The Scottish Parliament sits with the first devolved Scottish government. Labour politician Donald Dewar is the first Minister.

The Fence Collective comes together in Anstruther in the Kingdom of Fife.

Texas release *White on Blonde*. It will go on to reach UK sales of 1.8 million (or six times platinum).

Chem 19 recording studio opens just outside Hamilton.

1998

Jazz drummer Tom Bancroft launches Caber Records (it survives until 2005).

2000

The new Scottish government repeals Section 28 (UK wide legislation restricting gay rights).

2002

The Jazz Bar opens in Edinburgh while club life in the city is seriously disrupted by the Cowgate fire.

2003

Scottish Enterprise publishes *The Value of the Music Industry in Scotland* by John Williamson, Martin Cloonan and Simon Frith.

2004

Franz Ferdinand win the Mercury Music Prize.

Time Magazine compares Glasgow to 1960s Liverpool and Detroit.

2006

Snow Patrol have the UK's biggest selling album with *Eyes Open*.

2007

The first Scottish National Party government is elected.

Sunshine on Leith, the Proclaimers' jukebox musical opens (the film version will be released in 2013).

MLitt degrees in Popular Music Studies, the Music Industries and Creative Practice are launched by Martin Cloonan at the University of Glasgow.

2008

Glasgow is named a UNESCO City of Music.
    BBC Scotland's Gaelic language station BBC Alba is launched.
    The Scottish Music Industry Association is formed.
    Calvin Harris tops the charts for the first time as a collaborator on Dizzee Rascal's 'Dance Wiv Me.'

2009

The Royal Scottish Academy of Music and Drama launches its new BMus (Jazz) programme.
    Susan Boyle is runner up in *Britain's Got Talent*. Her debut album, *I Dreamed a Dream*, is the biggest selling record in the world that year, eventually reaching sales of over 9 million.

2010

Creative Scotland, a merger between the Scottish Arts Council and Scottish Screen, is established.

2012

The Offensive Behaviour at Football and Threatening Communications (Scotland) Act is passed, making the terrace singing of sectarian songs a criminal offence.
    Aidan Moffat and Bill Wells' *Everything Is Getting Older* is the first winner of the Scottish Album of the Year Award.

2014

A referendum on Scottish Independence produces a small majority (55%) against change.
    Young Fathers win the Mercury Music Prize.

2019

Last Night from Glasgow, not-for-profit independent 'patronage' label established.

2017

TRNSMT festival (an urban replacement for T in the Park, which ended the previous year) takes place on Glasgow Green.

2018

The exhibition *Rip It Up: The Story of Scottish Pop* opens in the National Museum of Scotland.

2016

Sixty-two per cent of Scots vote Remain in the UK's Brexit referendum.

2022

Gerry Cinnamon plays two sold-out shows at Hampden.

Introduction

Simon Frith, Martin Cloonan and John Williamson

In 2002 the editors of this book were commissioned by an economic development agency, Scottish Enterprise, to survey systematically music businesses across Scotland. Our report, *Mapping the Music Industry in Scotland*, was published in 2003. When we began the work we knew each other as fellow popular music researchers, teachers, journalists and activists but this was the first time we had got together to consider what made *Scottish* music practices and interests distinctive. Our collaboration had a lasting effect on our subsequent academic work, leading for example to Williamson and Cloonan's study of the history of the British Musicians' Union and Frith and Cloonan's three volume history of live music in Britain, but we have not until now thought systematically about the best way to explain Scottish music to people who don't live here.

The Routledge *Global Popular Music Series* is designed to introduce students to music "largely unknown to Anglo-American readers" and to be written by scholars "living and working in the countries in which they write … mostly, but not exclusively from outside the Anglophone world". How, then, do we three Anglophones justify including in the series a book on music made in Scotland, a good deal of which is well known internationally?

Implicit in the rationale of this publishing project is a critique of the Anglo-American hegemony in popular music studies, a hegemony reflected not only in the genres and topics studied but also in the terms in which other countries' popular music is discussed: through its influence on US rock or UK dance music, for example, or with the indiscriminate use of the term 'world music'. The issue here is not just a condescending account of music in non-English speaking communities but also a blinkered view of how popular music works. Questions about musical power and the making and unmaking of music as national expression are neglected; the meaning of concepts like 'folk', 'community' and 'identity' are taken for granted. What's missing in many popular music studies is any exploration of what Michael Denning calls "audiopolitics", a politics of listening that does not privilege Anglo-American conventions or assume fixed musical hierarchies.[1]

This is our reason for contributing a book on music made in Scotland to this series. Our starting point is that Scotland is both a part of and apart from Great Britain. Scottish male and female footballers, for example, compete in the Olympics as members of the GB team; they compete in the World Cups as members of Scotland teams. To examine Scottish music is to address the complexity of cultural identity, the impact of historical imagination and the effects of musical power structures. These issues are important for all studies of popular music.

DOI: 10.4324/9781003247470-1

We don't have the space here to document Scotland's historical relationship to England. Part of the same landmass, the countries were for many centuries separate kingdoms with ever changing boundaries and overlapping kinship ties. Scotland and England have shared a monarchy since 1603 and been embedded in the same class structure and pattern of landownership for longer. Lords of the Manor and Lairds of the Glens and their various dependents have long collaborated in staffing the institutions of the British ruling class: military regiments, universities, the Church, etc. Anglo-Scots remain a recognizable social group. The Act of Union in 1707 merged these interests in formal governmental terms: the English Parliament voted to merge with the Scottish Parliament; the Scottish Parliament voted to merge with the English Parliament. The new fused Parliament was sited in Westminster, previously the seat of English parliamentarians.

What was an initially an uneasy formalization of the British power structure became over the next two centuries a profitable partnership in the development of colonialism, the slave trade, imperialism and industrial revolution. By the early twentieth century the Scottish urban proletariat had developed a decidedly international rather than national ideology, with a particular commitment to socialism and communism. All that being so, however, Scots never lost the knowledge that Scotland was *not England*. There were still distinctly Scottish institutions— the law, education and banking, for instance. Arguments for political devolution and/or independence continued to be heard. Few Scots were content to regard their country as a British region; many continued to refer to a loosely imagined Scottish nation.

The problematic interplay of Scotland as region and Scotland as nation is illustrated most clearly from a musical perspective by the history of broadcasting. From its foundation in 1922, the London-based, state-funded British Broadcasting Company, autocratically run by John Reith, the Scottish son of a Presbyterian minister in Stonehaven, treated Scottish broadcasting as just one of its local services. Radio Scotland, in charge of all Scotland's local radio outlets, was not established until 1978, and the management of BBC Television Scotland (broadcasts began in 1952) primarily meant organizing the transmission of London-made programmes to Scottish audiences. Scottish broadcasting executives could only ever negotiate small budgets and limited time slots for locally focused output: a few minutes local news at the end of the nightly national news bulletin, for example. To attract bigger budgets to make Scottish programmes that might be shown across the UK was always an uphill task.

For BBC bureaucrats Scotland was just one of four National Regions and even today, post-devolution, programming and commissioning power is cosseted in London; few Scottish-made shows are nationally networked, and viewers and listeners in Scotland mostly consume the same shows as everyone else in the UK. Lip service has always been paid to the development of 'local talent', by both the BBC and commercial broadcasters (Scottish Television (STV) was established in 1957) but what this has meant in practice is that the Scottish-made music programmes shown UK-wide have been those that celebrate particular kinds of Scottishness: Hogmanay parties, for example, and other *faux* local get-togethers like the *White Heather Club*, featuring Scottish country dancing and sentimental Scottish folk songs performed by kilted comic-entertainers like Andy Stewart.[2] By far the longest running Scottish-made BBC radio show in Scotland itself is *Take the Floor*, a showcase for Scottish dance bands that has been broadcast weekly since the 1930s, and there's little doubt presently that more locally made new music is performed on the BBC's Gaelic stations—BBC Alba and Radio nan Gàidheal, than on its Scottish ones.

In other Scottish music worlds the local BBC is less supportive. Writing about jazz, for example, Alison Eales compares the lack of support the Glasgow International Jazz Festival received from BBC Scotland with BBC Radio 3's generous sponsorship of the London Jazz Festival.[3] Writing about folk, Sean McLaughlin shows both how much the career of a Scottish folk artist is boosted by winning a Radio 2 Folk Award and how little Radio Scotland (primarily a speech station) helps them get such attention.[4] Mark Percival has documented the importance for the 1990s Scottish indie scene of *Beat Patrol*, Peter Easton's weekly hour-long Radio Scotland programme. Percival also points out, though, that for young bands in Scotland then, as for young bands then in the rest of the UK, what mattered far more was to get played on John Peel's London-based Radio 1 show. Peel's was the musical community to which admittance could mean a 'real' musical career.[5]

The BBC's historical approach to Scotland reflects the power structure of British broadcasting across the UK: programming decisions for the whole country taken in London; Scotland given limited resources to produce 'distinctively Scottish' material. It is unsurprising that the BBC became a loathed target for devolution and independence campaigners. But the BBC concept of 'national region' can also be understood as a bureaucratic solution to a problem that faces many Scottish musicians at the beginning of their careers: how to be both Scottish *and* British? If Scotland is where musicians are from, Britain is the space in which they need to be. In the summer of 2018 the National Museum of Scotland devoted an exhibition to 'The Story of Scottish Pop'. *Rip It Up* was designed "to explore the musical culture of the nation" but it was noteworthy how much of the illustrative material was actually made in England. This was Scottish Pop as seen on *Top of the Pops*.

The tension here is apparent in other musical institutions, in the Musicians' Union, for example, or PRS for Music. Such organizations have Scottish branches and officials but policy-making power resides in London, and just as Scottish musicians have to look south of the border for the infrastructure and investment they need to support their careers so do Scottish music entrepreneurs. Take the case of Alan McGee, perhaps the most celebrated Scottish businessman in British indie mythology. His career took off after he relocated to London, where he opened a club, The Living Room. The Living Room was profitable and McGee followed it up with a record label, Creation, to showcase the groups he liked. McGee, as David Cavanagh writes, "was one of the few London promoters willing to book unsigned guitar bands", and in 1993, Creation (by then half owned by Sony) signed a guitar band, Oasis.[6] McGee's successful career could therefore be said to be essentially English and yet his Scottishness was never in doubt. He managed both Primal Scream and the Jesus and Mary Chain and it was key to his legend that he discovered Oasis when he happened to drop into King Tut's in Glasgow on the right night.

Another way of approaching the issues here is through the history of Scottish arts and cultural policy. For its first twenty years The Arts Council of Great Britain included Scotland in its remit. In 1967, however, when its charter was renewed, the Council's office in Scotland became autonomous and in 1994, as part of the process in which British arts funding was reorganized following the creation of the National Lottery, the Scottish Arts Council (SAC) was formally established as a separate body altogether. In 2010 the newly devolved Scottish Parliament set up a new body, Creative Scotland, a merger between the SAC and the film development agency, Scottish Screen.

Unlike BBC Scotland, then, Creative Scotland has behind it fifty years' experience of acting as a national rather than a regional organization, acting indeed much like arts councils in other small European countries. Its policies, that is to say, are focused on and by the political economy of cultural import/export. This approach has led to a variety of popular music-related activities.

Investment in Talent and Infrastructure

The aim here has been to give local musicians sufficient local business support that they don't have to leave Scotland or sign to London-based managers, lawyers, publishers and record companies.[7] Unlike the Arts Council in England, for example, the Scottish Arts Council set up a recording fund, which supported recording studios and record companies as well as artists, and Scottish arts policy makers led the way in rethinking arts policy as cultural industries policy, working, for example, with local authorities and enterprise boards in developing music business networks.

Promoting Tourism and Music Markets

The aim here has been to promote a distinctly Scottish musical culture as an attraction for visitors and incomers, whether holiday makers or new businesses. This has meant aligning arts policy with the work of tourist boards and inward investment brokers.[8] Hence, for example, the importance of festivals in Scotland, whether for Edinburgh as a Festival City or in the summer rollout of Highland Games, whether the Glasgow Jazz Festival or the Shetland Folk Festival. And hence too the policy importance of Glasgow being chosen as European City of Culture in 1990 and as a UNESCO City of Music in 2008. Scotland the brand is, from this perspective, as financially important for arts policy boards as it is for the busking pipers and tartan shops on Edinburgh's Royal Mile. It is equally reflected in export activities, in the promotion of Tartan Days and state support of music trade fairs: providing funds for Scottish groups to perform at South by South West in Texas, for example, and sponsoring Showcase Scotland at Celtic Connections in Glasgow. The aim here is to take Scottish music and musicians directly to the world, not just to or via London.

Preserving Culture

A concern for Scotland's heritage—its musical crafts and traditions, its audiences and performing conventions—is as significant a strand of arts policy in Scotland as in any other small country, not least because of its tourist value. But an equally important strand in Scottish arts policy has been a concern for cultural geography, an understanding of the undue economic and political dominance of the Central Belt cities of Edinburgh and Glasgow and the continuing cultural importance of the historical cities of Stirling, Dundee, Aberdeen and St. Andrews, the Highlands and Islands, the Borders, Dumfries and Galloway, of oil and fishing and crofting. The SAC pioneered tour support, funding both bands to play around the country and venues in small places not just (as in England) for art music audiences but for popular music fans too.

We have been making a contrast here between the SAC/Creative Scotland, treating Scotland as a nation, and the BBC, treating Scotland as a region, but our point is that it is the tensions between different kinds of cultural identity that help to make Scotland's music world so interesting. For a start it is obviously difficult to escape the imbrication of Scotland as brand in any account of Scottish identity. The comic character that Harry Lauder (1870–1950) developed on the stages of early-twentieth-century music halls (he was Britain's first global pop star) is a version of the comic Scot that has been familiar ever since, as has the use of tartan—by the Bay City Rollers most enthusiastically. The use of such signifiers is not unproblematic. Rod Stewart, for example, also known for his tartan scarves and passionate support of the Scottish football team, was born (to a Scottish father and English mother) in Highgate in London and has never lived or recorded in Scotland. On the other hand, music is certainly made in Scotland by people who are not, by this kind of blood definition, Scots. In the lead up to the 2014 Independence Referendum, vociferous Scots-by-blood not living in the country claimed that they had as much if not more right to a vote than non-Scots on the electoral register. Scottishness—and the necessary signs of Scottishness—are matters of dispute.

We suggested earlier that in career terms musicians in Scotland are obliged, in effect, to be both Scottish and British. A key role in the history of Scottish popular music has therefore been played by what one might call national/regional power brokers, people who help music-makers to operate in two cultural worlds at once. This was the role played, for instance, by Nod Knowles and Ian Smith, the music officers of the Scottish Arts Council and Creative Scotland between 1998 and 2016, both of whom were originally English.[9] And we can point to equally pivotal figures in broadcasting.

Andy Park, for example, a graduate of the Glasgow School Art who began his career as a school teacher while running a jazz band, went on to write music for BBC Scotland's television drama department and the Citizens Theatre before becoming head of entertainment for the newly launched Radio Clyde in 1973. Clyde was Scotland's first commercial radio station and in his five years there Park made the station a resource for local musicians, exploiting the regulatory demand for local content. In 1978 he moved on to do a similar job at the new Edinburgh commercial station, Radio Forth, before being recruited, in 1982, to be Channel 4's first (London-based) music commissioning editor. In 1985 he returned to Glasgow to be Head of Light Entertainment for BBC Scotland where, among other things, he produced *Tutti Frutti*. In an interview with the *Glasgow Herald*'s Andrew Young, Park said:

> At the moment, I think there are too few boxes, containing game shows, and quizzes, music and concerts. I think we should have more boxes. I'd like to break down the edges a bit. I would like to see the prime movers of some of these Scottish bands who are now world famous people, get four or five of them together and see what happens. Within the past few years Scotland has produced a number of bands the quality of which makes them the equivalent of that whole Liverpool scene of the 1960s. These bands are at the centre of world popularity and they all come from this wee country. I would really like to offer them an opportunity to make something that their record company can't allow them to do and the bands they are in cannot do either. We could have a great forum for ideas.[10]

Stewart Cruickshank (who died in 2015) was a radio producer for BBC Scotland for more than thirty years, having joined the company as a music librarian in 1980. He was involved in these years with a range of music programmes, covering folk (*Travelling Folk*), rock (*Beatstalking*, a history of Scottish rock music presented by Muriel Gray), indie (*Beat Patrol*), classical (John Purser's history of *Scotland's Music* from the Bronze Age), jazz (*Be-Bop to Hip-Hop*) and the various versions of the *Iain Anderson Show*, featuring Scottish and American folk, country, blues and singer songwriters (Anderson had begun his presenting career under the mentorship of Andy Park at Clyde). Cruickshank worked on the live broadcasts from the early *T in The Park* festivals and the radio series that spawned *Celtic Connections*, and his connections weren't confined to Scotland. He worked with rock acts on both sides of the Atlantic and made numerous programmes for the BBC's UK-wide Radio 2.

To understand Scotland's music culture is to understand the importance of figures like Park and Cruickshank (many more such people will feature in this book) and their ability to treat Scottish music as simultaneously local, national and international and to ease musicians' movement between different networks and expectations.

Made in Scotland is divided into three sections.

The first part addresses the *history* of music made in Scotland since 1955. There are essays are on the musical institutions that are significant for popular music in any country: television, record companies, venues, festivals and clubs. Other essays reflect on issues that are particular to Scotland: the lineage of Scottish jazz, the importance (and neglect) of women's pop voices and the changing place of Gaelic and Scots song in Scottish musical culture.

The second part addresses the *politics* of Scottish music, looking at 'Scottishness', at Scottish hip-hop and at the role of popular music in the independence campaign, and Scottish music *policy*, looking at the campaign for a music centre (and a statue of AC/DC's Bon Scott!) in the small town of Kirriemuir, at the evolution of the Glasgow International Jazz Festival and at music education.

The third part addresses continuities and changes in the ways in which Scotland is imagined in music, with essays on popular music in Scottish fiction and on the musical impact of the country's increasingly diverse population, and an interview in which Alasdair Robertson reflects on his song-writing career.

We end the book with a reflection by the editors on Scottish music as 'world music' and the thoughts of a variety of Scottish musicians on what the future holds.

To round out this introduction, however, we should say something further about who we are and what we bring to this project, especially (to return to the point we made at the outset) as we are clearly from and, indeed, well established in the mainstream Anglophone world of popular music studies. Two of us (Martin Cloonan and Simon Frith) were born and educated in England, where we started our academic careers. Frith moved to Scotland in 1987 and Cloonan in 1997; between us we taught for fifty years across four Scottish universities—Strathclyde, Stirling, Glasgow and Edinburgh. John Williamson was born and bred in Scotland and before becoming an academic had a varied and successful career in Scottish music as a journalist, retailer, promoter and venue and band manager, roles which meant dealing with political, cultural and commercial issues across British, European and global borders.

We have known each other for almost as long as we have all lived here and have worked together in settings which cover almost every aspect of Scottish music and music-making, whether academic, political, critical or commercial; we come to this book as both insiders and outsiders. From this perspective, our advice to readers who don't know Scotland well is keep in mind three of its distinctive characteristics.

Language

None of the editors of this book and few of its contributors read or speak Scottish Gaelic. But then unlike the other countries covered by books in this series (with the partial exception of Ireland) Scotland is not a nation based on a distinct language. The 2011 Census found that 93% of the people then living in Scotland spoke only English at home (around 1% spoke Scots and Polish, around 0.5% spoke Gaelic, Urdu or Chinese). These statistics are, though, in some senses misleading. For non-linguists the differences between Scots as a language and Scots as a dialect—between Scots and Scottish English—are not necessarily clear. The question not answered by the census is what proportion of the Scots who speak English at home does so in a Scottish accent, uses Scottish dialects and Scottish words. Two of us, that is to say, sound English and are recognized and treated as such, one of us not only sounds Scottish but recognizably comes from the Glasgow area. It is precisely because Scotland is essentially an English-speaking country that the everyday politics of language matters culturally: what musicians' voices *sound* like is a significant strand of Scottish audiopolitics. This is obvious in stand-up comedy, with which music shares cultural space. Think of how Billy Connolly and Frankie Boyle deploy their (different) ways of speaking Glaswegian.

Movement

Scotland, like Ireland, is a country with lasting cultural memories of forced migration. People moved elsewhere from Ireland because of potato blights and famines from the 1840s; they moved elsewhere from Scotland following a new regime of land management and the clear-ances of the Highlands and Islands from the 1750s. This movement of Irish and Scottish fami-lies added new dimensions of geography and history to the performance of traditional Irish and Scottish music. When *Celtic Connections* was launched in Glasgow in 1994 it was presented as the celebration of "Celtic music and its connections to cultures across the globe". Three years later *Celtic Colours* was launched on Cape Breton Island in Nova Scotia: "whether it's Gaelic singing, Cape Breton fiddling, local dance traditions, or an afternoon of world-class bagpiping, you can tailor your musical experiences to suit your tastes".[11]

Self-consciously Scottish music *not* made in Scotland is certainly easy enough to find. In 1987 the 78th Fraser Highlanders Pipe Band from Canada became the first of various overseas bands to win the main title at the World Pipe Band Championships (staged annually in Glasgow since 1947) and Scottish Country Dance clubs can be found in such unexpected cities such as Moscow, Tokyo and Buenos Aires. In his musical history of Detroit, Mark Slobin notes that its St Andrews Society was founded as early as 1844 and formed a Kiltie Band in 1849. In 1932 this was renamed the St Andrews Highlander Ford Kiltie Band and Henry Ford was determined that it should be authentically Scottish. Its members had to have been born in Scotland and served in British pipe bands during the First World War; their uniforms were ordered from Scotland. The band's competitive success—in 1939 it won the group and individual golds at the USA and Canadian national piping championships—was, for Ford, the "triumph of a Northern white sound". Scottish songs in US school and home songbooks throughout the nineteenth century were, writes Slobin, set off from "grotesquerie" of African American music.[12]

Given the role of Scottish music in American racial politics it is, perhaps, not surprising that in the early 2000s Scottish journalists and broadcasters got excited when Willie Ruff, dis-tinguished jazz bassist and a Professor of Music at Yale, proclaimed that he had discovered the "true" roots of African-American gospel music. Scotland, not Africa, was the source of black music style in America. Scottish Gaelic precented psalm singing ('lining out') was, it seemed, the origin of call and response, the DNA of all African-American music. Alas, this suggestion did not survive ethnomusicological investigation.[13]

A different kind of connection can be drawn between the sounds, tunes and ballads that Scots settlers took with them to the USA and the Appalachian folk music that fed into American Old-Time performance and Bluegrass. The Scottishness of American country music is certainly assumed in Scotland itself. Glasgow's Grand Ole Opry (opened in 1974) is always described proudly as "the biggest country and western club in Britain if not Europe" and the links be-tween Scottish folk and American traditional music are celebrated by *Transatlantic Sessions*, an annual television show launched by BBC Scotland in 1995. In these programmes a house band, organized around fiddler Aly Bain, accordionist Phil Cunningham and the American dobro player Jerry Douglas, is joined by folk, bluegrass and country musicians from both sides of the North Atlantic.

One feature of these various transatlantic music ties—as the recurring reference to Celts suggests—is the assumption that the Scots and the Irish share a musical culture that can't be described as British (*Transatlantic Sessions* is co-produced by the Irish state broadcaster, RTE). This belief has been reinforced over the years by the steady movement of people from Ireland to find jobs in Scottish industries such as shipbuilding. These migrants not only had a major effect on Scotland's religious and secular politics, but also reinforced the experience of Scot-tish and Irish folk music and musicians as essentially intertwined. Dick Gaughan, for example, "Scotland's most passionate troubadour" (in the words of the Scottish Traditional Music Hall of Fame), came from a family of Highland Gaelic speakers and singers on his mother's side and Irish fiddle players on his father's.

In contemporary Scotland, however, the most significant movement of people is back and forth across the Scottish/English border. Non-Scottish students, for instance, play a part in music scenes in all Scottish university towns and for many professionals—in the academy and the media, in commerce and publishing, in cultural institutions such as art galleries and orchestras—careers routinely mean relocating from one country to the other and back again. Consider the example of Louise Mitchell, an important figure in Scottish music first as head of Glasgow Concert Halls for thirteen years and then as the initial director of Glasgow UNESCO City of Music. Before coming to Scotland she had worked at the Barbican Centre and for the London Philharmonic Orchestra; in 2011 she moved back to England to be the Chief Executive of Bristol Music Trust, running the Colston Hall (and managing its change of name to the Bristol Beacon).

Such career moves in the music world are so routine that both *people who stay* and *people who come back* become particularly interesting figures in Scottish music culture. In some cases musicians have such a specifically Scottish appeal that their music doesn't travel. A current example is the punk/ folk music act from the Isle of Lewis, Pete and Diesel. The group is beloved in Scotland and sells out Barrowlands but means little in the rest of the UK. Such an act, one could say, celebrates *being Scottish*, and the shared sensibility of band and audience in live performance is palpable and difficult to sustain by performers touring in and out of Scotland. Even for the Proclaimers, a band like this that does travel successfully, gigs are very different atmospherically either side of the border. A more common route to international fame is Billy Connolly's. The popularity of his routines in Scotland, which began as between-song stories in folk clubs, only translated to the rest of the UK when he was presented on the BBC1 prime time *Parkinson Show* as if talking about *them* rather than *us*.

A decision to stay may also be the effect of being committed to a particular space: a studio, a venue or a shop. Bruce Findlay, for example, started out in his family's music retail business in Falkirk in the 1960s before opening his own record shop, Bruce's in Edinburgh, setting up a successful small label, Zoom, and managing one of Scotland's biggest rock acts, Simple Minds. Craig Tannock started with a Glasgow recording studio, Tower, before opening a series of vegan pub/café venues, among them 13th Note, Mono, Stereo, 78 and the Flying Duck. Such local entrepreneurs are essential to the ecology of music-making in Scotland, as are promoters like Mark Mackie of Regular Music and musicians like Stephen McRobbie (aka Stephen Pastel of the Pastels), who also runs a record shop, Monorail, and Emma Pollock (from the Delgados), who is also involved with Chemikal Underground Records and the Chem 19 recording studio.

The best example of the impact of someone coming back is jazz saxophonist Tommy Smith. A youthful prodigy from the Wester Hailes estate in Edinburgh, he was given a scholarship by Berklee College in Boston in 1983 when he was sixteen. He flourished there, joining Gary Burton's band and signing to Blue Note but in the mid-1990s he began to centre himself in Scotland again, signing to Linn Records and then establishing his own Spartacus label and forming the Scottish National Jazz Orchestra (in 1995) and the Tommy Smith Youth Jazz Orchestra (in 2001). In 2009 he became director of the jazz programme at the Royal Conservatoire of Scotland.

Size

Scotland is a small country. Its population in 2019 of around 5.45 million meant that it had a few less people than Finland and but a few more than the Republic of Ireland. Its size means that Scottish music scenes are actually micro scenes but also that it's usual to know and work with people from quite different social worlds.

Scottish micro scenes have been focused on *venues*, such as the County Hotel in Perth, home of the Blue Workshop, a jamming club that ran fortnightly on Sunday nights from 1964 to 1967, brought together a variety of young and established soul, jazz, rock and R&B players and from which emerged the Average White Band. And such scenes have been organized around particular players: Lau and Inge Thomson; the Fence Collective of "musicians, artists, craftsfolk, chancers and slackers based in the East Neuk of Fife"; R. M. Hubbert and his DIY Glasgow friends. And they have been organized round college or conservatory courses: the Scottish Music degree at the RSAMD from 1996 to 2002, the Creative and Music Industries course at Stow College from 2009 to 2011. There have been genre specific microscenes: the resident deejays at the Sub Club since 1987, the jazz musicians on Tom Bancroft's Caber Music label from 1998 to 2006. It is indicative of how such Scottish scenes work that Bancroft is now a member of the Pathhead Music Collective, "15 professional musicians living in a small Midlothian ex-mining village" and, with Martin Green from Lau, curates PIE, a series of improvised, experimental concerts in the village hall.

But perhaps the best indication of the way different worlds overlap in Scotland is the fact that we know and have, between us, worked with almost everyone named in this introduction. For Cloonan and Frith, moving to Scottish universities from English ones, it was startling how easy it was as academic researchers to make contact with performers and policy makers and to be taken seriously by them. One consequence of what we are describing here, then, is that popular music studies in Scotland has a respect from music practitioners that is unusual elsewhere. Another is that to be a popular music scholar in Scotland is necessarily to be engaged in music politics, whether dealing with such bodies as Creative Scotland, Highlands and Islands Enterprise and the Scottish Parliament's Cross-Party Music Group or, like Williamson, chairing the judges of the Scottish Album of the Year Award, as he has since it was established by the Scottish Music Industries Association in 2011, the same year that Cloonan and Frith published a *Music Manifesto* to stimulate debate in the Scottish Parliamentary Election campaign.

The Brazilian musicologist Martha Tupinambá de Ulhôa, exasperated with British scholars' questions about the Brazilianness of Brazilian rock, has argued that Brazilianness is "between the lines"—inhering in indirect musical, poetic, and topical cues obvious to Brazilians but missed by non-Brazilians and in the linguistic nuances in rock lyrics that are often undetected by non-native Brazilian Portuguese speakers.[14]

To be such a 'native speaker' in Scotland is to have a particular cultural rather than linguistic sensibility, a grounded sense that music made in Scotland reflects the cultural duality which is the essence of both Scottish music history and the social, political and ideological networks in which musical lives are lived. This book is about such lives.

Notes

1 Denning (2015).
2 See Williamson (2021). In her memoir of growing up on the Ayrshire coast Janice Galloway (born in 1955) writes: "Most things we watched [on television] without complaint, the exception being *The White Heather Club*. I had never met anyone who liked *The White Heather Club*". It was "endured" because it "was somehow Scotland's fault and sticking it out was penance" (Galloway 2012, pp. 9–10).
3 Eales (2017).
4 McLaughlin (2012). The Young Trad awards for the Gaelic music community are shown on BBC Alba.
5 See Percival (2009). *Beat Patrol* ran from 1990 to 2000; Easton's previous show, *Rock On Scotland*, was broadcast from 1984 to 1990.
6 See Cavanagh (2000, pp. 57–63).
7 There is little evidence that this policy objective has yet been achieved.
8 It should perhaps be noted here that the Scottish Tourist Board was not established until 1969. Previously holiday makers were enticed to Britain by British Travel and Holidays Association, itself first created in 1929 as the Travel

Association of Great Britain and Ireland. By the 1980s the STB was claiming that tourism was Scotland's biggest employer.
9   Knowles was the music officer from 1998 to 2005, Smith from 2005 to 2016.
10   *Glasgow Herald* December 4 1984, p. 4.
11   Quote taken from the Inverness (Cape Breton) visitor website: https://invernesscapebreton.com/music-culture-arts/celtic-colours-international-music-festival/.
12   Slobin (2019, p. 146).
13   See Miller (2009).
14   This summary of Martha Tupinambá de Ulhôa's argument is taken from Wallach (2020, p. 480).

References

Cavanagh, D. (2000) *The Creation Records Story. My Magpie Eyes Are Hungry for the Prize*, London: Virgin.

Denning, M. (2015) *Noise Uprising: The Audiopolitics of a World Musical Revolution*, London: Verso.

Eales, A. (2017) *Bunting and Blues: A Critical History of Glasgow International Jazz Festival, 1987–2015.* Unpublished Ph.D. Glasgow: University of Glasgow.

Galloway, J. (2012) *All Made Up*, London: Granta.

McLaughlin, S. (2012) *Locating Authenticities: A Study of the Ideological Construction of Professionalised Folk Music in Scotland.* Unpublished Ph.D. Edinburgh: University of Edinburgh.

Miller, T. (2009) 'A Myth in the Making: Willie Ruff, Black Gospel and an Imagined Gaelic Scottish Origin', *Ethnomusicology Forum* 18(2), pp. 243–259.

Percival, J.M. (2009) 'Scottish Indie Music and BBC Radio's *Beat Patrol*', *Popular Music History* 4(1), pp. 23–28.

Slobin, M. (2019) *Motor City Music*, New York: Oxford University Press.

Wallach, J. (2020) 'Global Rock as Postcolonial Soundtrack', in A. Moore and P. Carr eds. *The Bloomsbury Handbook of Rock Music Research*, New York and London: Bloomsbury, pp. 469–485.

Williamson, J. (2021) 'The Kilt Is My Delight? Popular Music on Early Television from Scotland', *Journal of Popular Television* 9(1), pp. 105–122.

PART I

Histories

John Williamson

We begin this book with the topic of Scottish popular music history and our starting point is that such a history does indeed exist. Scotland's popular music history, that is to say, can and should be considered in its own right and not just as a footnote in global, UK-wide or genre-based histories.[1] In his introduction to a special issue of *Popular Music History* on the significance of locality for popular music cultures, Paul Carr notes the importance of local scenes for certain kinds of "collective identity, in a series of competing narratives that are often hidden from mainstream history" (2019: 5), but although there are elements of this in Scotland's popular music history, as a nation Scotland cannot really be considered simply as just another setting for "local popular music making in the UK" or as a popular music "scene" equivalent to, say, Liverpool or Manchester.

In Scotland itself Scottish pop already has many histories. These are increasingly ubiquitous and all-encompassing, and they have been around since there was enough of such history to warrant writing, producing or curating. Such histories began to appear in the 1980s, twenty-five to thirty years after two oft-cited starting points for Scottish pop: Lonnie Donegan's 'Rock Island Line' making the UK top ten in 1955 and Alex Harvey winning a competition in the *Sunday Mail* to find 'Scotland's Tommy Steele' the following year.

Regardless of where this kind of mediated pop history begins, the BBC was pivotal in the production of the subsequent narratives. Its 1981 two part-television series, *Jock 'n' Roll*,[2] could be viewed as the start of a story that has subsequently and repeatedly spanned radio as well as television, film as well as print. A more detailed account thus followed in the form of Radio Scotland's 1986 series *Beatstalking,* which was part of a BBC Scotland 'Rock Week' and billed itself "the history of Scottish Rock Music".

Revealingly, the radio series began with a Scot who had lived most of his life in England (Donegan) and ended with an Englishman living in Scotland (Lloyd Cole), but more importantly it was part of the BBC in Scotland's recognition that, circa 1986, something newer and bigger was afoot. It located the history of Scottish pop in amongst a range of programmes that featured new acts spanning both the independent charts (Jesus and Mary Chain, Primal Scream, The Primevals) and the pop charts (Wet Wet Wet, Del Amitri and Deacon Blue), acts which in turn became a focal point of subsequent histories, enjoying bigger sales and greater longevity than the bulk of their predecessors.

Both programmes predated the first extensive written accounts of Scottish popular music (Wilkie, 1991; Hogg, 1993), which billed themselves as "scenes from the secret life of Scottish rock music" and "the History of Scottish Rock and Pop" respectively – the latter being the more thorough and wide-ranging of the two, and heavily in debt to *Beatstalking*.[3] The stories and characters within them have remained a source of fascination subsequently for both journalists (Kielty 2006; Galloway, 2018) and the protagonists who have written their own versions of

DOI: 10.4324/9781003247470-2

events, from Lulu (1985) to Les McKeown (2003), Donovan Leitch (2005) and, most recently, Bobby Gillespie (2021).

Television in Scotland has subsequently given us further, updated variations on the general story in the form of *Och Around The Clock*[4] (1998) and *Scotland's Greatest Albums*[5] (2011) before a run of more focused and niche documentaries on particular eras, genres or genders of Scottish pop like *Rip It Up*[6] (2018) or *God Save The Quine*[7] (2021) as well as a number of documentaries on individual artists. Meanwhile, Radio Scotland has been broadcasting Davie Scott's series on *Classic Scottish Albums,* which began with Orange Juice's *You Can't Hide Your Love Forever* in June 2018 and had reached its 43rd album, Strawberry Switchblade, by November 2020.

These more fragmentary approaches can also be seen developing in other media: in the documentary films of Grant *Big Gold Dreams* and *Teenage Superstars,*[8] in the fictionalised representation of the mid-1990s Scottish rave scene, *Beats,* and in recent CD box sets *Big Gold Dreams*[9] and *C'mon, C'mon,*[10] which offered an interesting progression from precedents like EMI's *The Best Scottish Album in the World...Ever'.*[11]

As we passed the sixtieth anniversary of Donegan's chart breakthrough, the last decade, has undoubtedly seen an intensification and institutionalisation of this kind of Scottish popular music history. The past of Scottish pop, in its various forms, is no longer considered as a curiosity or the focus for affectionate jokes as programmes like *Jock'n'Roll* and *Och Around The Clock* once suggested, but rather as a source of pride and nostalgia for fans and musicians alike. Tellingly, and unlike the bulk of the musicians from the first thirty years, most of those who achieved success in the 1980s are still around, having had lengthy and viable careers rather than fleeting stardom. With most at various stages of comeback or ongoing success, 'classic' Scottish pop and rock musicians are only too happy to remind us of their past exploits. To this end, *Rip It Up,* 'the story of Scottish pop' exhibition at the National Museum of Scotland in 2018 and its aforementioned media offshoots, was something of a pivotal moment in the official institutionalisation of Scottish popular music histories, marking their ever-closer links to the heritage industry.[12]

In spite of the oft-repeated misgivings about the merits of such establishment histories of popular music (see Baker 2018) the point here is that they are generally popular among participants, public and press alike.[13] And, with its extensive resources the media-museum complex is able to shape these histories in a way that individual writers and producers can't. After *Rip It Up,* the main question is where such histories of Scottish popular music can go now. The curatorial decisions, it seems, have been taken and the die has been cast.

This is the context for our approach in this section. We are *not* attempting to provide our own history nor to rewrite any existing ones. We seek neither to fossilise nor to celebrate Scottish popular music. Rather we offer a mixture of archival research, oral history, memories, personal reflections and discussions that recognise the importance of history for popular music in Scotland while at the same time problematising, challenging and hopefully supplementing the most often told stories. The chapters that follow cover the familiar and unfamiliar and a deliberately wide cross-section of eras, genres and languages.

First, John Williamson looks at the role of television in Scotland in shaping the notion of Scottish popular music, largely through an analysis of the BBC's first pop series from Scotland, *Stramash!,* that was broadcast in 1965/1966.

Robert Anderson and Kenny Forbes then tackle aspects of the dominant music industries in Scotland: the former considering the role of independent labels, the latter re-examining the familiar narratives around the country's most mythologised venue (The Glasgow Apollo) and festival (T in the Park).

The closing chapters shift the focus from academic research to the musicians, producers and promoters who contribute in different ways and in a cross-section of genres, to the history of Scottish popular music.

In 'Fascinating Rhythm – The Life of Scottish Jazz', Alistair Braidwood argues the uniqueness of jazz in Scotland with the emphasis on contemporary acts like Fat Suit and Fergus McCreadie while, in Chapter 5, Carla J. Easton reflects on her journey as both songwriter and filmmaker, mapping in the process the story of all-girl bands in Scotland from the 1960s onwards.

Chapter 6 tells the story of the first decade of the electronic music festival, Riverside, in the words of its promoters, Dave Clarke and Mark McKechnie, and Chapter 7 is an interview with the Gaelic singer, educator and television presenter, Joy Dunlop. In it, she paints a picture of the challenges and opportunities for those working in a minority language.

Notes

1 As it was in the 2016 British Library *Punk 1976–78* exhibition and still is in the British Music Experience museum in Liverpool, in which one can find "The Ultimate History of British Rock and Pop".
2 Jock 'n' Roll was hosted by B.A.Robertson and features the likes of Alex Harvey, Lonnie Donegan, Maggie Bell and John Martyn. https://www.youtube.com/watch?v=LByWVVxSngc
3 Hogg acknowledges that the book 'started in 1985, inspired by the BBC Radio series, *Beatstalking*' (1993: 8).
4 https://www.youtube.com/watch?v=blYsthcsdAM [accessed 11 May 2021]
5 This was an STV show where viewers could vote for their favourite Scottish album from each decade.
6 *Rip It Up* on BBC 2: https://www.bbc.co.uk/programmes/b0bbbv4w
7 *God Save The Quine* on BBC Alba: https://www.bbc.co.uk/programmes/m000qsmj
8 These centred on the Edinburgh post-punk scene of the early eighties and the Bellshill indie scene of the late 1980s respectively.
9 Subtitled 'A Story of Scottish independent music 1977–1989', released on Cherry Red Records in 2019.
10 Subtitled 'The Rocking Sounds of Glasgow, Edinburgh, Aberdeen, The Orkneys and beyond', released by Particles in 2020.
11 This managed the not inconsiderable feat of combining the music of Harry Lauder, Jimmy Shand and the Corries with that of The Waterboys, The Blue Nile, Edwyn Collins and the Proclaimers.
12 An early portent of this was the 'Electric City' exhibition at The Lighthouse in 2001, celebrating Glasgow's music scene; most recently, in 2021, the V&A in Dundee has hosted an exhibition Designing Club Culture' that draws heavily on Scottish clubs and designers.
13 For the response to *Rip It Up*: https://www.nms.ac.uk/national-museum-of-scotland/things-to-see-and-do/past-exhibitions/rip-it-up/rip-it-up-reviews/

References

Baker, S. 2017. *Community Custodians of Popular Music's Past*. London: Routledge.
Carr, P. 2019. 'Introduction to the Special Issue', *Popular Music History*, 12(1), pp. 5–14.
Galloway, V. 2018. *Rip It Up: The Story of Scottish Pop*. Edinburgh: National Museum of Scotland.
Gillespie, B. 2021. *Tenement Kid*. London: White Rabbit.
Hogg, B. 1993. *The History of Scottish Rock and Pop: All That Ever Mattered*. Enfield: Guinness Publishing.
Kielty, M. 2006. *Big Noise: The History of Scottish Rock'n'Roll as told by the People Who Made It*. Edinburgh: Black and White.
Leitch, D. 2005. *Hurdy Gurdy Man*. London: Cornerstone.
Lulu. 1985. *Her Autobiography*. London: Harper Collins.
McKeown, L. 2003. *Shang-a-Lang: Life as an International Pop Idol*. Edinburgh: Mainstream.
Wilkie, J. 1991. *Blue Suede Brogans*. Edinburgh: Mainstream.

1

Stramash! When Pop Music Television Comes to Scotland

John Williamson

'Scotland is contributing an explosive new show to the network – *Stramash!*' proclaimed *Radio Times* a week ahead of the show's launch onto BBC1's evening schedules across the UK in October 1965.[1] Helpfully, the magazine explained to its readers in the rest of the UK that 'the word means riot' and revealed that 'during its thirteen-week run', the show would 'feature rhythms (sic) and blues, spirituals, jazz, folk and pop' (Anon, 1965a: 3). Later in the same issue the low-key hyperbole for the show continued: although it was produced in Scotland, *Stramash!* 'will be international in its appeal and as "with-it" as the modern pop scene requires' (Anon, 1965b:23).

For all its ambition and indeed achievements, few who have read this far will have heard of this obscure and long-forgotten pop television show. This is partly because, like many shows of the time, no recordings were kept, it had a relatively short time on national television and had limited impact outside Scotland itself. It is, therefore, understandable *that Stramash!* Warrants, at best, a passing mention in histories of pop music on British television (Evans 2016: 98), when placed alongside other better-known shows from the same era like *Top of the Pops, Ready, Steady, Go!* and *The Beat Room.*

This chapter will use archive material[2] to describe, recontextualise and argue the show's importance, if not in such a broad context certainly in the specific environs of the BBC, television from Scotland and the formative years of a Scottish music business. This is also to highlight the importance of localised accounts of music television for a scholarly field which usually offers a more global perspective. To do this, I will first paint a picture of the show itself, the politics behind it and its main contributors, before placing this in relation to popular music on early television generally, in Scotland particularly and on the BBC in Scotland specifically. I will argue that *Stramash!* had several positive impacts on television from Scotland when viewed from the perspectives of internationalisation, broadening representation, musical careers and the music industries.

Stramash! The Big Noise from Scotland

Stramash! first appeared on BBC1 on Monday 4th October 1965, beginning a run of thirteen weekly shows. Initially these were broadcast across the UK but on its conclusion a further five shows, now on Friday evenings, were broadcast in Scotland only, as an 'opt-out' from the network. After the final show, on 11th February 1966, *Stramash!* was consigned to history, despite earlier press suggestions that 'the word from the BBC is that the winning team is going to be given another chance at the big leagues' (Gibson 1965:5).

DOI: 10.4324/9781003247470-3

The show itself combined several elements that would have been familiar to viewers of pop shows on British television at the time, offering a similar 'club rather than theatre experience' (Frith 2002: 285) to *Ready, Steady, Go*. But *Stramash!* was also original in ways that are worthy of note.

It followed a rigid and tightly rehearsed pattern,[3] aiming to be a fast-paced musical and tele-visual spectacle with, according to producer David Bell, '45 people on stage and 14 numbers in 29 minutes and 45 seconds' (quoted in Gibson 1965:5). This was achieved by having a core of regular performers, who were supplemented on each show by two special guest acts. Of those who appeared on every show, the majority were local to Glasgow, where the show was filmed in the BBC's recently opened studios at Queen Margaret Drive.[4] These were Sol Byron and the Senate,[5] Chris McClure,[6] and two groups of dancers, The Stramashers and some recruited from the Lindella Dance Club in the city. All of these were little known beyond Scotland. The other regulars on the show, Peter London[7] and The Three Bells,[8] came with some experience as they had played similar roles on BBC2's London-based *Gadzooks! It's All Happening.*[9]

None of these acts would have attracted a large audience or BBC interest from outside Scot-land, which made the show's other bookings integral to its success. Initially, much of star qual-ity was provided by Lulu and The Luvvers.[10] Lulu was important for two reasons: she was the first major international star to emerge from Scotland in the 1960s (though she had moved from Glasgow to London prior to the success of her debut single, *Shout*, in 1964) and she was already a regular fixture on both British television networks, on shows like *Top of the Pops, Gadzooks* and *The Beat Room* for the BBC and *Ready, Steady, Go!* for ITV.

The guests on *Stramash!* included other Scottish acts of the era: The Beatstalkers, Dean Ford and the Gaylords (who in 1966 became Marmalade), The Poor Souls and Linda Flavell, for ex-ample, as well as artists from the rest of the UK and beyond. Elkie Brooks, Tom Jones, Herman's Hermits, The Hollies and Sandie Shaw came from other UK nations, while visiting Americans included Paul Simon and blues and soul singers Patti Labelle and the Bluebells, Jimmy Wither-spoon, Doris Troy and Fontella Bass.

The scripts for the show held in the BBC archive reveal that *Stramash!* was a revue show, bookended by the house acts and dancers, usually performing a well-known song of the period to open the show[11] and with the full cast on stage for the finale. The two guest acts played two songs each, interspersed by more contributions from Byron, London and McClure supported by the dancers.

None of this may appear particularly radical in the light of television's previous dalliances with the new forms of pop music over the previous decade. Many of Stramash's component parts – young people, dancing, house bands and the unashamed promotion of new records – were influ-enced by and familiar from shows like *Oh Boy, Ready, Steady Go* and *Gadzooks*. In this respect, *Stramash!'s* main innovation was the absence of a compere, which Bell explained was because audiences were now 'so familiar with television that it is no longer necessary to have identifying shots for every change made. It is possible to switch about from one act to another without a la-borious introduction at one end and a thank you speech at the other' (*quoted in* Gibson 1965: 5). Instead, the show and its guest stars were simply announced using a taped voice over.

Popular Music on Early Television

Having offered a brief description of *Stramash!*, I will now provide a wider background for the show from three perspectives: in relation to pop music on television generally during the 1950s and 60s; in the context of television in Scotland; and by reference to the BBC in Scotland spe-cifically. I will argue that the BBC's commissioning of *Stramash!* can be related to the arrival in Scotland of commercial television.

Academic work on the emergence of popular music on television covers several themes that provide clues as to the demands and challenges facing TV producers working in the field at the time. Much of this work focuses on the relationship between, and synchronous growth of, the television and pop music industries and the problems this presented. For example, Jon Savage notes that 'it's not entirely an accident that both the television and music industries expanded into their present forms at about the same time – the late 1950s' (1982: 20) and Richard Peterson claims that 'television, more than any other technological development, shaped the advent of rock music' (1990:102). This theme is examined in more detail by Forman (2012) and Kenton (2020), the former making the case that popular music's presence on television pre-dated any notional 1955 watershed. For Forman, 'popular music was a prominent consideration among television producers' going back to the 1930s and 1940s (2012: 13), and he provides evidence of this in his consideration of the place of black and Latino musicians on early television in the USA. Similarly, Kirstin McGee reflects that jazz musicians who had 'established their versatility and star personalities profited from television' before 1955 (2016:80).

As will become apparent, both the timescale and types of popular music appearing on television were markedly different in Scotland than in the USA even though the technical and aesthetic challenges of aligning early television and contemporary popular music as detailed by Frith (2002) were largely the same across the decades and geographic boundaries.

Television in Scotland

In turning attention to how this played out in Scotland, it is essential to remember the constitutional status of the nation and how this has impacted on broadcasting policy. Both pre- and post-devolution, broadcasting policy has been decided in London by the Westminster administration.[12] Ewen Cameron describes this situation as one in which 'sovereignty and authority are located at a United Kingdom level' while 'suggestions of Scottish autonomy or semi-independence are cultural or political, rather than constitutional or legal' (2012: 620).

The case of television illustrates this. Initially, the BBC was granted a monopoly on all broadcasting in the UK under its 1926 Royal Charter, which was maintained until the Television Act of 1954. The first television broadcasts took place in London in 1936 but a further sixteen years elapsed before *Television Comes to Scotland,* the first television broadcast from Scotland (on 14th March 1952).[13] Faced with the slow take up of television and very small budgets for programmes (Walker 2011: 179) little of note, especially in the field of Light Entertainment,[14] was produced in the first five years of BBC television from Scotland.

This started to change around the time competition for the BBC in Scotland arrived in the form of Scottish Television (STV) in 1957.[15] A space was now opened for Scottish-made programmes featuring popular music but this was perpetually constrained by the politics of the two networks and the initially very limited resources available to them. In the BBC this was the 'Programme Allowance' granted from London to the controllers of the then six BBC regions[16] while for the ITV franchises programme-making autonomy was largely determined by their success in generating advertising revenue and network commissions.

This presented two dilemmas for television producers in Scotland. At both networks decisions had to be made whether to produce programmes intended for Scottish-only audiences or UK-wide ones, and at the BBC in Scotland producers had to decide whether to follow the more populist leanings of its new competitor or remain tied to the Reithian values of informing and educating as well as entertaining. The attempts to resolve these dilemmas underpin much of the Light Entertainment output from Scotland over the subsequent decades, and *Stramash!* was part of that process.

Popular Music on Television in Scotland before Stramash!

As it was on television channels around the world, music, and especially popular music, was an important part of the initial output of the Scottish based broadcasters.[17] The BBC had two orchestras in Scotland, initially designed to provide radio output, which were increasingly co-opted to television shows during the early years of the medium.[18] STV appointed the band leader, Geraldo, as its musical director in 1957 and his orchestra provided the accompaniment for a number of shows in the station's early years, including for its gala launch show, *This is Scotland*. However, what was popular in Scotland at the time was not necessarily congruent with the tastes of the rest of the UK, and to sell popular music to the network both stations had to present a certain image of Scottishness to the rest of the country.

I have argued elsewhere that one consequence of this was that the first pop stars to emerge from Scotland, accelerated to fame by television, were the unlikely trio of Kenneth McKellar, Jimmy Shand and Andy Stewart rather than a Scottish equivalent of Elvis, or even Cliff Richard (Williamson 2020:119). To a large extent these three *were* Scottish popular music in the late 1950s and the fact that these safe and obviously clichéd Scottish acts – in both appearance and sound – were dominant at the outset of television in Scotland was down to four connected factors.

The first was the deeply conservative nature of Scottish society in the post-war era. This was exemplified by the biggest event of 1955 being the All-Scotland Crusade by the American evangelist Billy Graham, who spent six weeks in the country, attracting huge crowds and preaching to almost half the population of the country (Roy 2013: 179). Later in the year, the Conservative Party won an outright majority of votes in Scotland in the General Election – the only time this has happened, and the only occasion on which the party won a higher share of the vote in Scotland than it did in the rest of the UK. Reporting on the campaign, Alistair Cooke visited Glasgow and wrote of the city that 'a vast Presbyterian pall descends on Glasgow early on Saturdays' which 'shoos the sparking couples out of Kelvingrove Park half an hour after sunset, closes down the pubs at 9.30, blackens the dance halls at midnight and leaves the world to darkness' (1955:1).

A second factor was the slow take up of television across the country. With only one channel and limited transmitter coverage, coupled with high costs, there was little incentive for the wider Scottish population to consider buying or renting a television until after the launch of STV. In 1956, there were just 348, 152 TV licences in Scotland, covering less than a quarter of all households (BBC 1957: 124), a number which would more than double to 750, 891 by the end of the decade[19] (BBC 1960:224).

The two final factors were the demands of the television networks and the backgrounds of the producers, particularly in the case of the BBC in Scotland, which was particularly constrained both financially and editorially by decisions made in London. In 1956, Scotland across all departments, produced only 58 programmes for the national network (BBC 1957: 205) of which a small proportion were in Light Entertainment – largely shows for Burns' Night, St. Andrews' Day and Hogmanay. In terms of producers, the BBC's Light Entertainment department in Glasgow was dominated by two men, Eddie Fraser and Iain MacFadyen, neither of whom were of a background or outlook that made them receptive to new types of popular music. Fraser joined as a variety producer in 1950 having spent years as an actor and producer in amateur theatre companies in the West of Scotland while MacFadyen arrived from radio. He joined the BBC in 1943, moving to television when asked to produce the 1957 Hogmanay Show.[20] The variety theatre and radio backgrounds of these men cast a long shadow over the popular musical output of the BBC in Scotland until their retirement in 1971 and 1980 respectively.

These four factors meant that, put simply, Scotland generally and television particularly were not ready for jazz, skiffle, rock 'n' roll or any new or ground-breaking form of popular music on television around 1955.

This changed slowly with the arrival of STV in 1957. While some of its initial music offerings (like *Jig Time*) borrowed inspiration from and sometimes shared star turns with the BBC, it was not long before they began targeting younger audiences with formats and artists that were less burdened by entrenched notions of Scottishness. This was visible in various shows across the station's early years. First was *Dance Party*,[21] a 1958 show reported by *Disc* as featuring 'rock, jive, skiffle and all modern music trends' (Gauld 1958: 6), which was at one stage on four nights a week. It was a precursor of three important (if also largely forgotten) early 1960s series – *Studio Downbeat, One Night Stand* and *Dig This!* Each of these built on its predecessor and was important in different ways, notably in the promotion of new talent (in both the music and television industries) and the broadening on television of Scotland's musical palate.

Studio Downbeat (1962–1963) was a 'jive and jazz' show directed by David Bell and hosted by Raymond Boyd which combined formation dancing with pop guests.[22] *One Night Stand* (1964) ran for fourteen weeks and gave the first television exposure to many Scottish acts (including Lulu) and to beat groups like Sol Byron and the Impacts and Dean Ford and the Gaylords. Like *One Night Stand*, *Dig This!* was hosted by Pete Murray,[23] but during its second weekly run in 1964 widened the ambition of STV's pop music coverage. Its producer, Liam Hood, explained that 'this time it is a magazine programme instead of a purely beat show' (Irving 1964:8). The show now mixed news items with performances by touring and visiting acts including The Zombies, The Kinks, The Merseybeats and The Pretty Things as well as by Scottish talent in the form of The McKinleys, The Alex Harvey Soul Band, Lulu and Barry St John.

These specialist music shows were not the only outlets for pop music on STV, with other programmes like the youth magazine show, *Round Up*, featuring interviews with visiting bands, including famously, The Beatles, in 1963 and 1964. A one off special, *Scots Pops*, in 1965, also hosted by Raymond Boyd, acted as a showcase for local acts The Poets, The Senate and The Golden Crusaders.

Elsewhere, the newer franchises also got in on the act: Grampian's *Teenbeat* featured both local and touring acts in 1963, while Border produced three series of *Beat In the Border*, offering similar magazine fare in 1962 and 1963.

If the nature of popular music on STV changed quickly after its inception, the same could not be said of the BBC in Scotland, and the origins of *Stramash!* must therefore be traced to the experiments in popular music on the rival station. Here STV's influence on the thinking at the BBC in Scotland could be seen in two ways. STV's pop output showed that Scottish skiffle, jazz and beat groups could be successfully represented on the small screen and that well-known and popular acts from south of the border could be imported to perform to Scottish television audiences. Further, in the context of the BBC, shows with acts from outside Scotland were more likely to be networked.

Arguably, however, the major influence of STV on the BBC, was in creating a new, younger cadre of television workers. In the case of *Stramash!* this could be seen in the team that produced the show, all of whom had their start in television at STV. Bell began as a trainee cameraman 'in the days when they were taking cameramen off the streets' (Gibson 1965: 5) before quickly graduating to being a floor manager and director, moving to work for the BBC in London, before returning to Glasgow to launch a 'beat show'.[24] STV had effectively both trained the behind-the-scenes staff and given the first opportunities to many of the artists on-screen, thus making it possible for the BBC to bring a Scottish pop show to prime-time television across the whole of the UK.

At the same time, Light Entertainment at the BBC in Scotland was also still relying on tried and tested formulae. In 1965 David Gibson noted that the BBC was 'much more maidenish in Scotland than anywhere else' (1965:5), so it is unsurprising that, for the first half of the decade, its popular music output remained devoid of the type of youthful rumbustiousness seen on its rivals (or even in London-based BBC shows). This meant more tartan, more country dancing, more *White Heather Club*[25] and more *The Kilt Is My Delight*, though *The Hoot'nanny Show* (1964), a folk music show based around The Corrie Folk Trio and Paddy Bell, did give a first hint of a widening of outlook: it had several guests from beyond Scotland and a significant lack of tartanry.[26] It remains the case, however, that by the end of 1965 pop music, as it was represented elsewhere on television, had barely entered the thinking of the BBC in Scotland.

Conclusion / Rethinking Stramash!

To draw the chapter to a close I return specifically to *Stramash!*, first to discuss the contemporary response to the show, then looking at its significance using a much longer lens.

The former was underwhelming. Journalists were unimpressed: *The Evening Times* described it as less of riot 'and more of a mild disturbance of the peace' (Brown 1965: 8) and *The Reading Evening Post* went further, describing it as 'a resounding miss', with 'a complete lack of top pop stars' that 'gave the programme only a limited appeal to those of us who live outside Glasgow' (Unger 1965: 2). Largely it passed without making much impact but there was some posthumous recognition of its achievements. Lulu has acknowledged Bell's influence in being the first person to book her for television (2002:50); Mike D'Abo told *Rave* magazine that it was 'the only fast-moving show I have seen in recent years' (quoted in Grant 1967:53) and in a review of Granada's *Discotheque* James Towler asked 'wasn't the BBC in Scotland doing this far better five years ago with *Stramash!* – a pop show which, for my money, has never been equalled?' (1969:12).

If this suggests a limited legacy, I will end by highlighting four significant ways in which *Stramash!* is worthy of re-evaluation. These relate to parochialism, representation, careers and industry.

Stramash's first achievement was to be not only the first 'Scottish show for the network without kilts, bagpipes or Jimmy Shand' (Millar 1965: 5) but also the first from BBC Scotland Light Entertainment to be genuinely outward-looking.

Its second was to bring groups that had been largely excluded from the BBC's Light Entertainment output in Scotland to the screen: women, people of colour and young people. This was reflected in Lulu being the 'star' of the show, in the relatively large number of women on stage across the series; in the presence of McClure as one of the residents[27] and in the number of black American singers (and songs) featured. Compared to other BBC output from Scotland at the time, it was inclusive, forward-thinking and internationalist in an otherwise parochial environment.

Thirdly, *Stramash!* had an impact on the record industry by showcasing Scottish musical and television talent to the rest of the country, thereby reaching, if briefly, a large UK audience (unlike its STV antecedents). Some of the Scottish acts involved went on to release records on major record labels[28] and many sustained careers of varying levels of success and longevity after appearing on the show, though it was far from a passport to fame for all.

Finally, the show played a significant role in developing a television profession in Scotland. Director David Bell went on to have a successful television career, being promoted to senior roles at STV and London Weekend Television (LWT) before his death in 1990. McClure and

Rae continued to work for the BBC in Scotland and, importantly, *Stramash!* via STV also helped bring a new generation of personnel into television in Scotland, people who came from neither theatre nor radio backgrounds.

In short, the show was something of an anomaly in the localised context of Scotland: both behind the times (coming a decade after similar pop shows began to appear elsewhere) and ahead of them (two decades would pass before the BBC in Scotland produced another pop series for the network).[29] This chapter has sought to redress the lack of attention paid to it and re-evaluate its cultural and industrial importance, but in doing so it raises some wider questions about the study of popular music on television.

Andreas Fickers describes television as a medium 'accompanied by a revolutionary rhetoric but in fact developed in a framework of conservative patterns' (2012:52). This resonates on a transnational level and could certainly be applied to the early years of pop music television across Europe. The case of *Stramash!*, however, suggests that there is considerable value in the detailed study of local television stations and shows. The most revolutionary programming is not always the best remembered or most voluble.

Notes

1   *Radio Times* is a weekly television listings magazine, published by the BBC from 1937 to 2011. It was then sold to Immediate Magazines and continues to appear.
2   Primarily from microfiche copies of the scripts for the show held at the BBC's Written Archive Centre (BBC WAC) and from contemporary newspapers and television/ theatre trade publications.
3   Rehearsals took place in various halls around Glasgow for four days prior to the day of recording.
4   Although the BBC had bought the former Queen Margaret College in Glasgow in 1936 with a view to building its own television studios in Scotland, the first broadcast from Studio A did not happen until February 1964.
5   Sol Byron was a Glasgow based soul singer.
6   McClure at the time was in a band called The Fireflies; he subsequently made records as the Chris McClure Section on Polydor, before carving out a career on the Scottish theatre, cabaret and television circuit as Christian.
7   Previously known as Peter M. Cooke – he changed his name to avoid confusion with the actor. London was the show's musical director.
8   The Three Bells were three sisters from Liverpool.
9   *Gadzooks! It's All Happening* had run weekly on BBC2 for three short seasons through 1965, the last show going out just six weeks before *Stramash!* Although BBC2 launched in London in 1964, it was not immediately available in many parts of the country. It was only available in Scotland from July 1966.
10   Lulu was the main attraction on seven of the eighteen *Stramash!* episodes.
11   Examples include *Will You Still Love Me Tomorrow, Barbara Ann, Land of a Thousand Dances* and *Somewhere Over the Rainbow*.
12   Although a Scottish Parliament was re-established in 1999, broadcasting continues to be a reserved power of the UK Parliament.
13   The show was broadcast from the Edinburgh studio of the BBC and featured mainly speeches by politicians and BBC officials although there was also a segment of Scottish country dancing, a precursor of what was to follow.
14   All non-classical music was deemed Light Entertainment; the BBC in Scotland had a separate music department for dealing with the orchestras.
15   This was the Central Scotland franchise of the Independent Television (ITV) network which was launched two years earlier under the auspices of the Independent Television Authority (ITA).
16   At this point Scotland, Wales and Northern Ireland were viewed by the BBC as regions rather than nations.
17   As well as the BBC and STV, the smaller ITV franchises, Grampian and Border began broadcasting in 1961.
18   For example, the BBC Scottish Variety Orchestra appeared as the musical accompaniment in the Kenneth McKellar vehicle, *A Song for Everyone* in 1957.
19   With the exception of Northern Ireland, this was still the lowest percentage of households (49%) in any of the six BBC regions.
20   MacFadyen went on to produce the Hogmanay output for the BBC for until 1980 and was known as 'Mr Hogmanay' or, later as the 'Ayatollah Hogmanay' (Young 1983).
21   This was initially called *Dance Party Roof* and was recorded at the STV studios at the Theatre Royal in Glasgow. At other points it was called *Monday Dance Party, Tuesday Dance Party* and *Friday Dance Party* and was hosted by Rikki Fulton and Andy Stewart.
22   *Studio Downbeat* ran for two seasons spanning 1962 and 1963. Lionel Blair judged the dancing.

23 Murray was one of the hosts of *Six Five Special* and was a regular on British television and radio from the 1950s onwards.
24 Bruce McClure (choreographer) and Helen Rae (designer) – the other members of the team – had both also started their careers in television at STV.
25 In total, there were ten seasons of *The White Heather Club*, and it was broadcast across the UK from 1960.
26 It boasted an impressive range of special guests that included Ewan MacColl, Shirley Collins, Martin Carthy and Peggy Seeger.
27 McClure is Scottish and of mixed race with a black American father.
28 For example, Chris McClure on Polydor and RCA; Marmalade on CBS and Decca; The Beatstalkers on CBS.
29 FSD ran for two series of six episodes in 1986 and 1987 in Scotland and was repeated around the UK.

References

Anon. 1965a. "Stramash!", *Radio Times*, 30 September, p.3.
Anon. 1965b. "Also Tonight", *Radio Times*, 30 September, p.23.
BBC. 1957. *BBC Handbook 1956*. London: BBC.
BBC. 1960. *BBC Handbook 1960*. London: BBC.
Brown, H. 1965. "My View", *Evening Times*, 5 October, p.8.
Cameron, E. 2012. "The Stateless Nation and the British State since 1918", in T.M. Devine and J. Wormold (eds.), *The Oxford Handbook of Modern Scottish History*. Oxford: Oxford University Press, pp.620–634.
Cooke, A. 1955. "Temptation for Transplanted Socialists", *The Manchester Guardian*, 23 May, p.1.
Evans, J. 2016. *The Story of Rock & Pop on British TV*. London: Omnibus Press.
Fickers, A. 2012. "The Emergence of Television as Conservative Media Revolution: Historicising a Process of Remediation in the Post-War Western European Mass Media Ensemble", *Journal of Modern European History*, 10:1, pp.49–75.
Forman, M. 2012. *One Night on TV is Worth Weeks at the Paramount*. Durham, NC and London: Duke University Press.
Frith, S. 2002. "Look! Hear! The Uneasy Relationship of Music and Television", *Popular Music,* 21:3, pp.277–290.
Gauld, M. 1958. "Over the Border", *Disc*, 5 July, p.6.
Gibson, D. 1965. "The Big Three Who Put on The Big Noise", *Glasgow Evening Times*, 28 December, p.5.
Grant, M. 1967. "This Is Where It's At", *Rave*, 1 July, p.53.
Irving, G. 1963. "Ray's Double Life", *The Viewer*, 29 June, p.4.
Irving, G. 1964. "Pete Murray Invites You to Dig This", *The Viewer*, 27 June, p.8.
Kenton, G. 2020. *Transmission and Transgression: The History of Rock'n'Roll on Television*. New York: Peter Lang.
Lulu. 2002. *I Don't Want to Fight*. London: Time Warner.
McGee, K. 2016. "Jazz in 1950s American Variety Television", in B. Heile, P. Eldson and J. Doctor (eds.), *Watching Jazz: Encounters with Jazz Performance on Screen*. Oxford: Oxford University Press, pp.73–104.
Millar, B. 1965. "Telenews", *Evening Times*, 4 October, p.5.
Peterson, R. 1990. "Why 1955?", *Popular Music*, 9:1, pp.97–116.
Roy, K. 2013. *The Invisible Spirit: A Life of Post-War Scotland 1945–75*. Edinburgh: Birlinn.
Savage, J. 1982. "Young Lovers: 60s Pop TV", *The Face*, March, pp.20–22.
Towler, J. 1969. "Points That Please in Pop Show", *The Stage and Television Today*, 2 April, p.12.
Unger, M. 1965. "On the BBC's New Autumn Shows", *Reading Evening Post*, 5 October, p.2.
Walker, D. 2011. *The BBC in Scotland: The First Fifty Years*. Edinburgh: Luath Press.
Williamson, J. 2020. "The Kilt Is My Delight", *Journal of Popular Music Television*, 9:1, pp.105–122.
Young, A. 1983. "BBC's Iain MacFadyen Dies at 56", *Glasgow Herald*, 29 April, p.7.

Archives

BBC Written Archive, *Stramash! Scripts*, microfiche.

Television Programmes

American Bandstand (1952–89, USA: ABC)
Beat in the Border (1962–63, UK: Border)
The Beat Room (1964–65, UK: BBC)
Dance Party (1958, UK: STV)

Discotheque (1969, UK: Granada)
FSD (1986–88, UK: BBC)
Gadzooks! It's All Happening (1965, UK: BBC)
The Hoot'nanny Show (163–64, UK: BBC)
Jig Time (1958–61, UK: STV)
Oh Boy! (1958–59, UK: ITV)
One Night Stand (1962–63, UK: STV)
Ready Steady Go (1963–66, UK: ITV)
Round Up (1963–64: UK, STV)
Stramash! (1965–66, UK: BBC)
Studio Downbeat (1964, UK: STV)
Teenbeat (1963, UK: Grampian)
This Is Scotland (1957, UK: STV)
Top of the Pops (1964–2006, UK: BBC)
The White Heather Club (1958–68, UK: BBC)

2

Doing It for Themselves

A Brief History of Scottish Independent Record Labels

Bob Anderson

There has always been a labels scene in Scotland.

(EKOS 2014: 48)

This chapter aims to provide a brief history of Scottish independent record labels founded before 2000 (and therefore initially releasing material before the arrival of digital distribution). While a small number of these labels, such as Postcard and Fast Product, have received considerable attention within popular media, this chapter highlights the plethora of music genres that Scottish labels encompass and, in so doing, explores the meaning of the term 'independence' for Scottish record companies. It considers the notion of 'indie' as both a form of industrial organisation (with a specific focus on independent distribution) and as an ethos or aesthetic approach to producing music (Fonarow 2006). The chapter also highlights the ways in which Scottish labels developed as an entrepreneurial activity from enterprises separate from the various artists on their rosters to vehicles for artists themselves to release their own music.

The chapter is divided into three sections. The first discusses the various labels that were operating in Scotland before 1977. Though ostensibly focused on Scottish traditional music, these labels were also responsible for releasing Scottish original beat music (among other genres), and include long-running labels such as Lismor, and The Corries' own Dara label. I then go on to examine the ways in which labels in Scotland developed into small artist-operated ventures with the advent of punk and post-punk in the late 1970s. Here, the labels discussed include Zoom, which initially released music by Simple Minds, and the aforementioned Fast Product. These labels were both outward-looking and, in the case of the latter, focused on releasing material from non-Scottish artists. The chapter concludes with a discussion of the impact that labels such as Postcard Records had on Scottish popular music (by creating a demand for Scottish artists from major labels) and a brief examination of the profusion of commercially successful independent labels that were operating in Scotland in the 1990s.

The Sound of Auld Scotland

There is an extensive history of recordings made and produced in Scotland that long pre-dates the post-punk independents. One of the first known record labels to be based in Scotland was BOB, which dates back to as early as 1913. The printed label on the discs indicates that the

DOI: 10.4324/9781003247470-4

records were made for a shop at 4 Howard Street, Glasgow (Early 78s n.d.) and the label name appears to have derived from the fact that the price of the record was a shilling (commonly known as a 'bob'). Surviving examples of music issued on this label include a version of a ragtime tune, 'The Cubanola Glide', and a march by Wagner played on accordion. The accordion was also a feature of another label based in Glasgow ten years later. The Waverley label featured a well-known accordion player, William Hannah, and the music issued on the label from 1923 onwards included popular songs of the day and strathspeys (ibid). In the same year, Beltona Records released its first catalogue of 250 records. Though not based in Scotland, Beltona played an important role in the promotion of Scottish popular music throughout the early part of the twentieth century. By 1929, 75% of the label's releases comprised of Scottish repertoire, and 92% of its artists were from Scotland (Dean-Myatt 2004, 2009).[1]

Scottish-themed music continued to be released in the late 1950s by a second Waverley record label operating in Edinburgh. This Waverley label (sometimes also known as Waverley Records) put out records until 1981, with a focus on Scottish country dance (Lyons 2006) but also releasing discs encompassing a variety of genres, including Scottish folk, classical, and even jazz (Discogs 2021). In the 1960s (and through to the 1970s) many other Scottish record labels emerged and became known for releasing Scottish country dance and folk music. Such labels included Scottish Records and Norco Records (both based in Aberdeen); Grampian Records (based in Wick); ALP Records (based in Dundee); and Gaelfonn and Thistle Records (both based in Glasgow). As with Waverley, all these labels also issued recordings in a variety of genres. Norco Records, for example, released what could be considered the first Scottish 'beat' record, a version of *I'm a Hog for You* (AB 102) by Johnny & The Copycats in 1964. Similarly, ALP Records in 1966 released singles by both folk group The John Husband Scottish Sound and beat group Poor Souls. While the overtly named Scottish Records had a catalogue more evidently built around Scottish country dance, it also released recordings with titles such as *Brecht with Music* (D'ART 12-6) and *Children's Songs* (SRHA). Even the Gaelfonn label, which specialised in Gaelic language recordings, released titles such as *Hebrew Songs And Cantorial Items* (HRC 907) and a 7" single by Norrie MacFarlane And The Esquire Jazz Band.

The above-mentioned labels were all small entrepreneurial enterprises. Although Independent in nature, a number of the labels had relationships with the major UK record labels. Parlophone manufactured the 78 rpm discs for the original Waverley label and the later Waverley label had a 'close association with EMI' (Lyons 2006). Similarly, the ALP label had a distribution deal with Polydor Records (Strachan 2020). The label took its name from its founder, Andy Lothian (Productions), who also worked as an agent and promoter. He started the label as his 'venture into the recording industry' (ibid). In the same way, Norco Records was an expansion of the LCB Entertainment Agency, run by Albert Bonici in Elgin (Scotbeat 2021). Gaelfonn too was not a stand-alone company – its founder, Murdo Mackenzie Ferguson, also ran Caledonian Music (a publishing company). In addition, the later Waverley label provides a good example of the vertical expansion of a business. Its founder, Thomas Bryce Laing, had become the managing director of a furniture shop, Geo. Jeffrey Ltd., in Edinburgh. Laing at first added a record department to the premises, then a two-track recording studio, and then a record label to release the music recorded there (Lyons 2006). This was a strategy reminiscent of one followed by Polk Brockman, thirty-five years earlier in Atlanta, Georgia. While working in his family furniture store, Brockman opened a department selling phonograph record players (alongside records to be played on them). He then acquired the local dealership for the Okeh Record Company and became a talent scout for the company. This brought him into contact with Ralph Peer, who was later instrumental in bringing both Jimmie Rodgers and the Carter Family to public prominence (Peterson 1997). Though Laing and Waverley Records were perhaps not so influential in Scotland, a number of popular Scottish traditional musicians did record for the label, including Jimmy Shand and folk duo The Corries.

The Corries provide an early example of Scottish-based musicians releasing their music on a label they owned, or rather part-owned, Pan-Audio/Dara. Their most popular track, 'Flower of Scotland' (PA or SPA-003) was released on Pan Audio in 1974. The band also set up their own distribution company, CML Distribution. However, here again the label was an extension of a previous enterprise, in the sense that Pan Audio had developed out of a radio and TV commercial production company with its own recording studio in Edinburgh (Lyons 2009). In 1976 the label changed its name to Dara but continued to be mainly a vehicle for releasing music by The Corries. Other releases in the label's catalogue include albums by various Scottish traditional and folk musicians, including Mike Whellans, Iain MacIntosh, and Mary Sandeman.

According to the Discogs website, one of the last albums The Corries issued through Dara was *The Compact Collection* (LIDC 6032) in 1990. As the catalogue number indicates this was not on the Dara label as such but was licensed to Lismor Recordings, who released it in cassette format. Like the previous labels mentioned, Lismor Recordings developed out of other commercial activities, namely record shops. Peter Hamilton, who owned a number of record shops in Glasgow, started the label in 1972. Symon (1997: 213) views Lismor as 'one of the most commercially successful record companies involved in traditional music in Scotland'. Initially, its output focused on traditional Scottish music and Gaelic language material, including albums by the Gaelic poet Norman MacLean and singer Peter Morrison. While the former released a version of 'Flower of Scotland' (LISP 2002), one of the label's few singles, the latter would go on to release material on Decca and have a career on TV. Lismor also released music in other genres, including rock/pop and country. Significantly, in 1978, it released *Play Gaelic* (NA 105), the first album by folk-rock band Runrig, who later released music on Chrysalis and continued to have commercial success up until their split in 2018.

In 1980 Ronnie Simpson, who had worked as an agent and promoter, took over as managing director of Lismor and further expanded and diversified its catalogue. Expansion involved, among other things, acquiring Iona Records in 1990. In the same way that The Corries had started Pan-Audio/Dara, Iona Records was founded by folk band Ossian in 1978 as a means of releasing their second album *St. Kilda Wedding* (IR001). In the twelve years the label operated before the Lismor takeover it released a number of albums by the band as well as individual projects by its members.

In 1992 Lismor established Iona Gold as a sister label to Iona. The focus of this new label was music of a more contemporary nature and through it Lismor released albums by a number of Glasgow artists and bands more known for rock/pop than traditional music. These include *Za Za's Garden* (IGCD 204) by The Pearlfishers, *Littledeath* (IGC 206) by Love and Money, and *The Last Supper* (IGCDM 207) by the Kevin McDermott Orchestra. This is not to say that Lismor Recordings has forsaken its identity as a label of Scottish traditional music. Writing in 1997, Symon (213) notes:

> The company's marketing strategy exploits the 'tartan and castles' image of Scotland. Lismor has an annual turnover of around £1,000,000, one third of which is earned by exporting its back catalogue of around 380 titles to 'Scottish shops' in north America and the former British colonial countries, and another third from gift shops catering to the tourist market in Scotland. The remaining revenue comes mainly from other sales in Scotland.

Lismor Recordings is not the only independent Scottish traditional music label that has made a long-term success of selling Celtic music. Scotdisc (alongside several subsidiary labels, including Country House Records) was founded in 1978 by Dougie Stevenson and Bill Garden. The pair have been so successful that their label was the subject of a BBC documentary in 2018 (*The Scotdisc Story*). Though the Scotdisc label trades on its traditional Scottish music image – one of its best-selling albums is Tommy Scott's *Pipes and Strings of Scotland* (CD ITV 362) – its catalogue contains a large number of releases encompassing a variety of genres, country music being foremost. The label's first release was *Country Class* (BCG 164) by Helen, and one of its most prominent artists is Sydney Devine, who released a number of albums and singles on the label over a twenty-five-year period and (according to *The Scotdisc Story*) selling over a million records (BBC 2018). Besides focusing on the label's long association with Devine, the documentary also highlights Garden's and Stevenson's business acumen. They explain that they did not want the major record labels in the South to know how big the market was for albums like *Pipes and Strings of Scotland*. The album sold over 100,00 copies but Scotdisc avoided these sales being included in the charts. In addition, the label has products in over a thousand outlets and has even handled the distribution of Lismor Recordings' products to retailers, via an arrangement with Scotdisc's fulfilment house.[2]

Everybody [Should Be] on Top of the Pops

Arguably, the independent labels discussed so far have all operated within the system of mainstream cultural production, with the goal of maximising revenues. To this end, most of these labels were established as an extension of other commercial activities. Some, as noted, were not completely autonomous from the mainstream music industries but relied, for example, on the mediation of the major record companies for distribution. In one sense of the term they were, then, not truly independent (Passman 2009: 67). With the advent in the late 1970s of new popular music genres, such as punk and new wave, and new technologies, which made small-scale recording more affordable, Scotland (as elsewhere) witnessed a growth in do-it-yourself (DIY) record production. The new labels that arose were not necessarily an extension of previous business activity, and for the greater part could be considered as 'small scale operations usually run from private addresses by one or two individuals who undertake all the tasks necessary for a commercial release of a recording themselves' (Strachan 2007: 247). Aside from possible commercial motives, they were also borne out of a desire to promote music to a wider audience. In this sense, in 1977, a number of independent labels vied for the distinction of producing Scotland's first independent punk record. Among them were Boring Records, which was established to release The Exile's *Don't Tax Me: E.P.* (BO 1); NRG Records, which brought out The Drive's 'Jerkin' (Re 46); Zoom Records, which released 'For Adolfs' Only'/'Robot Love' by The Valves (Zum 1); and Sensible Records, which issued the first single by the Rezillos, 'I Can't Stand My Baby' (Fab 1). Both Boring Records and NRG Records exemplify the notion of the DIY independent record label, as they were essentially used as vehicles by the bands to self-release their own records. However, in mediated discourses around the advent of punk in Scotland, they are largely ignored in favour of the other two labels which received greater critical and commercial success.

Zoom Records was founded by Bruce Findlay, who owned a chain of record shops called Bruce's Records.[3] Though independent in the broadest sense of the term, the label shared many of the same characteristics as the labels discussed in the last section. Findlay already made a living from music retail, had previously been a talent scout for Island Records and had then moved into artist management, initially with the Edinburgh-based band Café Jacques. In founding Zoom Records, however, Findlay articulated many of the arguments used by other independent labels to position themselves against the 'music industry' (Strachan 2007: 250). In particular, he viewed himself as being an important participant in an interconnected UK independent music scene:

> this was the start of a proper music business revolution, where the majors would get put to one side and be major distributors for the independent labels, where every town would have one or two small labels, with 200, 500 labels across the U.K., all friendly, a network of people with local knowledge who would be involved with the local bands, nightclubs, fanzines.
>
> (quoted in Welsh 2020)

Findlay also saw the rewards of running an independent label in non-commercial terms: 'My kick will come from the artists' success as opposed to the label's cleverness at advertising gimmicks' (Zoom press release n.d.). However, in 1978 Zoom Records signed a manufacturing, marketing, and distribution deal with Arista Records (Lyons 2006) and so moved further away from the position of an 'independent'. Zoom only released thirteen singles and one album before Findlay moved on to manage Simple Minds.

Sensible Records, also based in Edinburgh, was founded by Lenny Love, who had been an A&R person for Island Records. Love and Findlay knew each other and it was Findlay who advanced Love £500 to record and press the afore-mentioned Rezillos' single (Glen 2016). Although only two singles were released by the label, it was notable for the Rezillos' release, which resulted in the band signing a contract with Sire Records in 1978 (Lyons 2006).

Another Edinburgh-based label, launched in 1978, was Fast Product, founded by Bob Last and Hilary Morrison. Last had also worked with the Rezillos and apparently turned down the opportunity to release a record by The Cramps. Fast Product has been hailed as the label that defines the DIY ethic of 'British indie' (Simpson 2016). Between 1978 and 1980 the Scottish label released singles by non-Scottish artists The Mekons, Gang of Four, and The Human League (among others). Tony Wilson, the founder of Factory Records, cites Fast Product as an influence: 'at the time we began, the really cool, arty independent label was Fast Product. Bob Last would send out little plastic bags with samples of dried potato in them. Now that's arty' (quoted in Maconie 1991). Though independent in both the aesthetic sense and in terms of distribution (through Rough Trade), Last reflected in 2005 that

> At our height, we were probably producing about one record per month. But it was never our intention to be anything but at the heart of the industry, we didn't want to be outsiders. We were quite commercially minded.
>
> (quoted in Wilson 2005)

Last (with Morrison) would go on to start another label, Pop: Aural, before going into artist management full-time, with The Human League, Heaven 17, and ABC.

The Rezillos also have an indirect connection with another Scottish independent label, one that has not received the same attention as Zoom or Fast Product. Klub, like Zoom, was started in 1977 (in Glasgow by Peter Shipton and Clem Dane), but has a very different catalogue to any of the punk/new wave labels mentioned so far. Its most commercially successful release was 'Ally's Tartan Army' by Andy Cameron (KLUB-03), which got to Number 6 in the UK charts in 1978 (Lyons 2006). Along with its subsidiary labels Klub has released material by a wide variety of (mainly Scottish) artists across several genres, from comedy (Hector Nicol) to folk (The Whistlebinkies), to Scottish traditional (Scottish Power Pipe Band), to pop (Rikki Peebles).

Though 'independent' in the industrial sense of the term, at least for its first two years, it was quite far removed from an 'indie' aesthetic. The loose connection between this label and the Rezillos is through the band Chou Pahrot, which released both a 7" EP, *Buzgo Tram Chorus* (K.E.P.101), and a live album, simply entitled *Live* (KLP 19), through Klub. The band's website describes them as being favourites of the Rezillos, whom they had supported at Glasgow's Apollo theatre in December 1978.

Chou Pahrot had been performing live in Glasgow, playing original material, since the early 1970s but by 1978 Glasgow bands that had begun as covers bands, playing 'pub rock', were also beginning to play self-penned songs (and seeking to promote them). Both Underhand Jones and Sneeky Pete are examples of bands from a non-punk background who released singles on their own or their manager's labels. While neither of these bands went on to have wider success outside Scotland, The Cuban Heels (like the Rezillos before them) did sign to a major label (in their case Virgin) after releasing singles on independent labels. In 1978 they brought out a version of 'Downtown' (JY 1) on the Edinburgh-based Housewives Choice label; in 1981 they released 'Walk on Water' (DRINK 1) on Cuba Libre, a label started by Ali McKenzie, the band's drummer.

Friendly Pop and Abraded Pop

In February 1980, Orange Juice released their first single, 'Falling and Laughing'/'Moscow' (80-1*)*, on Alan Horne's Postcard Records of Scotland label. This was the first of three singles they released that year. Much has been written subsequently in the media about the Postcard label and its influence on DIY independent music production (see, for example, Campbell 1986, Didcock 2009, Petridis 2010).

However, much of this acclaim was retrospective. At the time, in 1980, Adrian Thrills provided this brief overview of independently produced Scottish singles:

> A remarkable range of new Scottish bands announced their arrival via independent singles in 1980, only to be casually lumped together as part of some unwieldy and unwelcome Tartan Scene by some observers The activities of Alan Horne's Postcard set-up – Orange Juice, Josef K, The Go-Betweens – have been well documented, but the Glasgow label's half dozen singles are really only the tip of the iceberg, drops in an ocean which engulf bands as diverse as FK9, The Cuban Heels, TV21 and The Hollow Men. Glasgow's Cuban Heels transformed themselves from a dodgy modish bunch into a far more original funk-inclined group on 'Walk on Water' (Cuba Libre).
>
> (1980: 44)

Aside from suggesting that Postcard had been receiving a disproportionate amount of attention from the music press, Thrills' comments also highlight a tendency by the media to reduce Scottish popular music to narrowly defined categorisations. Certainly, in the immediate years following Postcard's first release, the number of DIY self-released records by Scottish artists greatly increased (too many to discuss in this brief chapter). However, as noted above, there were many examples of such DIY activity before Postcard and its real achievement was to focus the media's attention on this practice. While the label, and many of the subsequent independent releases by artists on their own labels, can be described as 'indie', in both the aesthetic and industrial meanings of the term, Alan Horne (like Bob Last) was keen to point out that this model of independent production was not a rejection of mainstream commercial success. Interviewed in the *NME*, Horne stated that:

Music should always aim for the widest possible market. The charts are there. I consider that we're the only punk independent because we're the only ones doing it who are young. Everybody else has come from the back of a record shop or are businessmen. We started with no money and just built it up from Orange Juice's first single.

(quoted in Morley 1980: 24)

His comments acknowledge the extent to which independent labels in Scotland had previously been an extension of other commercial musical activity, but it also highlights his own ambitions for commercial success. In Glasgow, at least in the years immediately following the demise of Postcard, the number of DIY independent releases declined. This may in part have been due to the recession which took place in the early 1980s, but it was also the case that this was the period during which major record labels became more interested in Scottish artists. By attracting major record deals, Scottish bands could by-pass the need to release independently on their own or other's labels. Richard King in *How Soon is Now* (2012: 73) attributes this interest directly to the national radio airplay that Orange Juice's second single, 'Blue Boy' (Postcard 80-2), received because suddenly 'The Sound of Young Scotland' was being taken seriously as a commercial proposition. A&R men, seeing Orange Juice being profiled as a new, friendly pop sensation, started flying up to Glasgow in search of the next young thing'.

In 1986 a new label was started by Stephen McRobbie (of The Pastels), Sandy MacLean (of Fast Forward), and David Keagan (of the Shop Assistants). 53rd and 3rd took its name from a Ramones' song and its catalogue reflects a turn in the latter half of the 1980s in Scottish independent music towards a more rudimentary style of performance and composition. Speaking of his own band, McRobbie explained 'we knew we would get laughed at because of our musical ability, but we didn't care. We wanted to stand up and represent something quite different' (BBC 1990). In opposition to the 'friendly pop' sensations being signed to the major labels, bands exemplified by Wet Wet Wet, the releases on 53rd and 3rd reflected a shared interest in a more 'lo-fi' approach. Hogg (1993) describes the first single, 'Safety Net' by the Shop Assistants (AGARR 1), as being 'abraded pop' (305) and 'E102' by The BMX Bandits (AGARR 3) as having an 'aural amateurism' (306), which was in keeping with The Pastels' ethos. In addition to this 'indie' aesthetic, the label used Fast Forward for distribution (Fast Forward had developed out of the distribution arm of Fast Product, once it had stopped releasing material as a record company, and was part of the independent UK-wide distribution network The Cartel).

While the collapse of The Cartel network at the end of the 1980s had an impact on some of Scotland's independent labels – both 53rd and 3rd and Egg Records stopped releasing material – the 1990s witnessed a considerable increase in the number of independent record labels operating across Scotland. These included Soma Recordings Ltd. (1991), Electric Honey (1992) Creeping Bent (1994), Chemikal Underground Records (1994), Vesuvius (1995), Modern Independent (1995), Rock Action (1996), Flotsam and Jetsam Records (1996), Fence Records (1997) and Benbecula Records (1999). The majority of these labels were started by musicians, looking to release their own music but also that of fellow artists: Chemikal Underground was founded by The Delgados, Vesuvius by a member of the Yummy Fur (along with others), Modern Independent by Urusei Yatsura, Rock Action by Mogwai, Flotsam and Jetsam by members of El Hombre Trajeado/The Poison Sisters/The Amphetameanies, Fence Records by King Creosote and Benbecula by Phase 6/Beluga. In a similar vein Soma Recordings was founded by electronic music duo Slam and Dave Clarke, Electric Honey by Alan Rankine (of The Associates) as Stow College's in-house label, and Creeping Bent by Douglas MacIntyre. MacIntyre however, underplays the commercial aspect of his label: 'We've never tried to be a proper record company in terms of business. At one point it did become full time, with everything that entails, and I didn't like that' (quoted in Cooper 2014).

There are several reasons for the growth in Scottish independent labels in the 1990s. By 1995, Scotland (and the rest of the UK) was emerging from an economic recession (Sentance 2010) and, following the growing professionalisation of the music industries in the 1980s, local popular music was a focus for entrepreneurial effort. In a newspaper article in 1993, David Belcher interviewed four Scottish businessmen – the aforementioned Ronnie Simpson and Bruce Findlay plus Barry Wright and Brian Young.[4] They took the view that, although the economic recession of the early 1990s had taken its toll on Scottish bands, Scottish labels were in a much better place to succeed. The article pointed to a variety of factors, including the development of a business infrastructure in the country and the fact that 'chequebook label-management has led up a blind alley: there's more of an opportunity [now] for those labels which have of necessity remained attuned to fresh sounds' (Belcher 1993).

Conclusion

The media narrative may still privilege the notion that independent record production began in Scotland in the late 1970s but Scottish independent record labels were operating for many decades before then. This chapter has argued that the relationship between these labels and the UK's major labels has always been nuanced, depending on the particular circumstances of each label and the commercial motives of the label owners. Early examples of Scottish labels were not usually independent in the full sense of the term, as they relied on the majors for manufacture and/or distribution. Even when independent distribution was possible, commercial motives would often lead a label to develop an association with a major in order to access wider distribution or greater marketing opportunities. This could be the case even when the label owners had initially positioned their label as separate from, if not in opposition to, the mainstream music industries.

Many of the Scottish labels discussed in this chapter developed as a result of entrepreneurial decisions taken by pre-existing music businesses. In the 1990s, as the number of labels greatly grew, such entrepreneurial decisions were increasingly being taken by the artists themselves, rather than by managers/agents/producers, as had often been the case in previous decades. In addition, many of the labels that I have discussed shared an openness towards releasing music across different styles (and even genres) of music. This was particularly the case with the earlier labels but was also a feature of the labels that began in the 1990s. Generally, the Scottish labels that have enjoyed the greatest longevity (for example, Lismor, Scotdisc, Klub, Soma, Creeping Bent, and Chemikal Underground) are also the ones that have a variety of musical styles in their catalogues. In addition, although it is difficult to detect a shared ideological position across the different labels, most of them do share a business-like attitude towards the decisions they have needed to make in order to continue to operate in a small market geographically distanced from the mainstream music business.

Notes

1   Beltona was based in London but run by a Scots family, the Murdochs, who came from a village near Perth.
2   Two other record companies can be added to the Scottish labels discussed in this section: Temple Records, founded in 1979 by Robin Morton "to create an outlet for the superb Scottish (and Irish) music which was being ignored by the mainstream labels" (Morton had been a member of the Irish traditional band Boys of the Lough) and Greentrax, founded in 1986 by former police inspector and Edinburgh-based folk promoter Ian Green.
3   In the 1950s Findlay's mother had opened and managed McDougalls, a record shop in Falkirk, so in a sense he was developing a family business.
4   Barry Wright ran the promotion company Unique Events, Brian Young ran the recording studio Ca Va.

References

BBC *Glasgow A Go Go* (1990). BBC Radio 1, 24 July.

BBC *The Scotdisc Story* (2018). BBC Scotland, 3 January.

Belcher, D. (1993). "The Recession's Rock-On Effect". *The Herald*, 18 February [Online]. Available at: <http://www.heraldscotland.com/sport/spl/aberdeen/the-recession-s-rock-on- effect-1.771768> [Accessed: 13 November 2021].

Campbell, A. (1986). "STILL ORANGE". *Cut*, November, p. 12.

Cooper, N. (2014). "No Time to Be 21? The Creeping Bent Organisation 20 Years On". *The Quietus*, 28 January [Online]. Available at < https://thequietus.com/articles/14316-creeping-bent-20th-anniversary > [Accessed: 1 December 2021].

Dean-Myatt, W. (2004). *Beltona Records and Their Role in Recording Scottish Music.* [Online]. Available at: <https://www.mustrad.org.uk/articles/beltona.htm> [Accessed: 28 January 2022].

Dean-Myatt, W. (2012). *Scottish Vernacular Discography, 1888–1960 Introduction.* [Online]. Available at: <https://www.nls.uk/media-u4/1056583/introductions.pdf> [Accessed: 28 January 2022].

Didcock, B. (2009). "The roots of Orange Juice". *The Herald*, 18 January [Online]. Available at: <http://www.heraldscotland.com/the-roots-of-orange-juice-1.834673> [Accessed: 23 November 2021].

Discogs (2021). [Online]. Available at: <https://www.discogs.com/label/113994-Waverley> [Accessed: 4 December 2021].

Early 78s (n.d.). [Online]. Available at: <http://early78s.uk/b/ and http://early78s.uk/w/> [Accessed: 6 December 2021].

EKOS (2014). *Music Sector Review: Final Report for Creative Scotland.* Glasgow: Ekos Limited.

Fonarow, W. (2006). *Empire of Dirt: The Aesthetics and Rituals of British Indie Music.* Middletown, CT: Wesleyan University Press.

Glen, A. (2016). "Kilty Pleasures". *Record Collector*, 6 January, pp.56–62.

Hogg, B. (1993). *The History of Scottish Rock and Pop: All That Ever Mattered.* London: Guinness Publishing.

King, R. (2012). *How Soon Is Now?* London: Faber and Faber.

Lyons, R. (2006). [Online]. "WAVERLEY". Available at: <https://www.7tt77.co.uk/WAVERLEY.html> [Accessed: 5 December 2021].

Lyons, R. (2009). [Online]. "PAN-AUDIO". Available at: <https://www.7tt77.co.uk/PAN_AUDIO.html> [Accessed: 5 December 2021].

Maconie, S. (1991). "Anthony Wilson: Renaissance Manc". *New Musical Express*, 30 November [Online]. Available at: <https://www.rocksbackpages.com/Library/Article/anthony-wilson-renaissance-manc> [Accessed: 5 December 2021].

Morley, P. (1980). "The Sneer That Says Wish You Were Here". *New Musical Express*, 4 October, p. 24.

Passman, D. (2006). *All You Need To Know About the Music Business*, 6th Edition. New York: Free Press.

Peterson, R. (1997). *Creating Country Music: Fabricating Authenticity.* Chicago, IL: The University of Chicago Press.

Petridis, A. (2010). "Orange Juice: Coals to Newcastle". *The Guardian*, 4 November, p. 9.

Scotbeat (2021). [Online]. Available at: <https://scotbeat.wordpress.com/2014/05/15/norco-records/> [Accessed: 5 December 2021].

Sentance, A. (2010). "Getting Back to Business". *Economic and Financial Computing*, 20 (4), pp. 181–198.

Simpson, D. (2016). "Cult Heroes: Bob Last – Subversive Scottish Post-Punk Label Creator". *The Guardian*, 9 Feb [Online]. Available at: <https://www.theguardian.com/music/musicblog/2016/feb/09/cult-heroes-bob-last-subversive-scottish-post-punk-label-creator> [Accessed: 5 December 2021].

Strachan, G. (2020). "Dundee Showbiz Boss Speaks of Regret That Folk Duo Didn't Walk the Tay Road Bridge to Success". *The Courier*, 27 August [Online]. Available at: <https://www.thecourier.co.uk/fp/past-times/1531822/dundee-showbiz-boss-speaks-of-regret-that-folk-duo-didnt-walk-the-tay-road-bridge-to-success/ > [Accessed: 26 November 2021].

Strachan, R. (2007). "Micro-independent Record Labels in the UK: Discourse, DIY Cultural Production and the Music Industry". *European Journal of Cultural Studies*, 10(2), pp.245–265.

Symon, P. (1997). "Music and National Identity in Scotland: A Study of Jock Tamson's Bairns". *Popular Music*, 16(2), pp.203–216.

Thrills, A. (1980). "The Pulse of Confusion". *New Musical Express*, 20 December, pp.42–44.

Welsh, J. (2020). "Into Scottish Creatives: Interview with Bruce Findlay – Part One". *into creative*, 24 December [Online]. Available at: < https://intocreative.co.uk/interview-with-bruce-findlay/> [Accessed: 4 December 2021].

Wilson, M. (2005). "My Launch Pad to Success". *Sunday Times*, 30 January [Online]. Available at: <https://advance.lexis.com/document/?pdmfid=1519360&crid=c318be4d-e99f-4bd6-b92b-48bc2c7e8b54&pddocfullpath=%2F-shared%2Fdocument%2Fnews%2Furn%3AcontentItem%3A4FDB-PG70-00GN-Y0KF-00000-00&pdcontent-componentid=332263&pdteaserkey=sr12&pditab=allpods&ecomp=xbxnk&earg=sr12&prid=27af856c-cc3a-4938-8741-ef719be8a96> [Accessed: 4 December 2021].

3

Scottish Live Music History

The Conflict Between Culture and Economics

Kenny Forbes

Introduction

The claim made by Fabian Holt (2021) that "everybody loves live music" may be knowingly all-encompassing but it can be readily applied to Scotland. Scottish live music audiences have long been renowned for their exuberance, their ability to raise the emotional capacity of the live concert experience. Numerous artists (including the Rolling Stones) have cited Scottish gigs as representing the highlight of their touring schedules (Williamson *et al.* 2003: 27).

Regular reiteration of such "best audience" accolades by artists, promoters, and the media through the decades (accolades which have, of course, been willingly embraced by Scottish audiences themselves) serves to both emphasise and idealise the sense of place that prevails within such scenarios.

If a live concert can be regarded as an "experiential good" (Cloonan 2020: 58), then it is apparent that the commodification of these sentiments has undergone numerous transitions historically, as promoters determine the most efficient way to accommodate changing demand (Jones 2012: 36). In the post-war period in Scotland the emphasis gradually moved from locally managed traditional and/or adopted venues (such as cinemas and ballrooms) to arenas and festivals, which can better house large audiences and attract major global artists. As I will discuss, such developments inevitably rely upon economics of scale, which are exploited most effectively by live music conglomerates, most notably, Live Nation Entertainment and AEG Live.

This process was galvanised in the late 1960s by the realisation among the more astute promoters that live rock music had the capacity to appeal to a mass audience. Since then, the Scottish live music sector has evolved from a rudimentary foundation, becoming more professionalised as it expanded even as, at the same time, the extent of local control within the Scottish live sector greatly diminished.

This chapter argues, then, that the recent history of Scottish live music has involved what initially could be understood as an implicit conflict between the local and global, as the stakes increased to commodify fully the local demand. However, these developments also indicate that a compromise between economics and culture has been reached, whereby traces of local identity remain in the course of the sector's everyday dealings, even if its overall ownership by live music conglomerates such as Live Nation serves to nullify this process.

The discussion to follow illustrates my argument by focusing on two case studies. First I explore the history of the Glasgow Apollo theatre (1973–1985), a former "super cinema", a locally run venue in its initial stages which became for a time the leading traditional live venue in the

DOI: 10.4324/9781003247470-5

UK. Then I examine the *T in the Park* festival (1994–2016), which evolved as one of the UK's major events but which relied extensively on its Scottish promoter's conglomerate owners and non-local partners. Overall, these cases serve as a basis for understanding the global dimensions of the current live environment as well as the local foundations from which it emerged.

The Glasgow Apollo (1973–1985)

Prior to the Glasgow Apollo's opening in 1973, the organisation and commodification of the live music experience in Scotland had, despite the enthusiasm shown by local audiences, been limited by the country's size, location, and largely rural dimensions; the country being both too small economically and too large logistically. Even Glasgow had a limited live music ecosystem with few local promoters. At the same time, the absence of a large local state venue, meant that that the city rarely featured on the nationwide tours organised by UK promoters from the early 1960s (Frith *et al.* 2013: 117). This scenario was further compounded by Glasgow's geographical location, which diminished its economic viability for touring artists.

Nationally, the UK live music sector during the 1960s was positioned firmly within its "glorious amateurism" phase (Frith 2007: 3). It was spearheaded by a small group of major London-based promoters who relied upon a network of regional promoters and agents (Frith *et al.* 2013: 191). When The Beatles first toured Scotland, in 1960, as the backing group for the Larry Parnes act Johnny Gentle, Parnes relied upon Galashiels-based promoter Duncan MacKinnon to handle their Scottish dates (Lewisohn 2013: 318). Likewise, when the group toured Scotland in 1963 and 1964, Elgin promoter Albert Bonici acted as the agent for their Scottish schedule (McNab 2012: 93). At that point regional agents like Bonici and Eddie Tobin and Ronnie Simpson of Glasgow-based Music and Cabaret possessed a certain amount of gravitas within the limited dimensions of the Scottish live sector. However, the power base of this regional cartel began to fade as live rock became increasingly popular and many of these promotional companies had folded by the late 1960s (Hogg 1993: 102).

Recognising that Glasgow lacked a large venue suitable for live rock, local night-time entrepreneur Frank Lynch took over Green's Playhouse, a large, once-deluxe city centre cinema and ballroom, originally built in 1927, but now showing signs of considerable disrepair, and relaunched it as the Glasgow Apollo in September 1973.

There are five main reasons why the Glasgow Apollo became a remarkable, if short-lived, success: local knowledge, timing, capacity, local rock fans' appetite for live music, and, probably most important of all, the boisterous nature of its audiences.

Following the acquisition of the building's lease, Lynch assembled a local management team, including Tobin and Simpson as bookers, who used their grasp of the local live music infrastructure to entice the rising tier of young London-based rock promoters such as Harvey Goldsmith, Jef Hanlon, Tony Smith, Paul Loasby, and Adrian Hopkins. They were impressed by the extensive local knowledge offered by the Apollo management team as well as by their willingness to help achieve sell out shows. In the words of Paul Loasby (2012), the Apollo was an attractive venue "because of the people who were running it; they were also incredibly helpful when it came to marketing, unbelievably helpful". Such good working relationships helped to attract a plethora of major artists, including David Bowie, the Who, Queen, The Clash, AC/DC, and the Rolling Stones, several of whom performed landmark concerts at the Apollo during their creative peaks.

Furthermore, the timing of the Apollo's opening was fortuitous. Its tattered persona befitted perfectly the rock aesthetic. As one spectator remarked, the venue had "nothing, but everything": nothing in the way of facilities, everything in the way of authentic atmosphere and ambience (Forbes 2012: 609).

At this time, the early 1970s, UK promoters who were keen to capitalise on the increasing appetite for live rock were frustrated by the limited capacities of UK venues: only 8–9 had a capacity of 2,500–3,000 (Frith *et al.* 2019: 51). The Apollo boasted a capacity of 3,336, which rose to 4,368 when its top balcony was reopened (Harkins 1995: 15). In the estimate of one promoter, the venue generated around 40% more revenue than a typical town hall and 25% more income than its nearest competitor, the Hammersmith Odeon (Hopkins 2012).

A key stakeholder in the success of the numerous rock concerts at the venue was the local audience, which was noted for its visceral display of boundless enthusiasm. The venue's infamous and somewhat precarious "bouncing balcony" was, in consequence, frequently activated, further heightening the occasion's liveness, as Yes keyboardist Rick Wakeman (2012) recalls:

Somehow [the Apollo} had that X factor that made it pure rock 'n' roll for band and audience alike. I can recall, as indeed many bands can, seeing the balcony bounce up and down and how it never collapsed was beyond me. The people in the balcony didn't care one iota and I think they would have gone on dancing in their seats had it collapsed.

As the Apollo audience's reputation grew among bands and their managers and agents it began to dictate touring schedule logistics. It was not unusual for major UK tours to be launched or concluded in Glasgow: the Apollo, as one key promoter put it, was the "jewel in the crown" of the British tour circuit (Hanlon 2011).

The venue's position as the UK's leading rock venue was relatively short-lived. Its declining appeal to the UK's biggest bands was first indicated by the Rolling Stones' 1976 UK tour, which served to make the Apollo's key attributes, its capacity and live music aesthetics, almost outmoded overnight. The Stones' tour highlighted a venue tier above and beyond what the Apollo could offer. The group launched the tour at the Apollo, performing four nights there, but their concluding dates were at the Earls Court Arena, to which they were able to attract 102,000 fans over 6 performances (*New Musical Express* 1976: 2). The Stones would have had to play in the region of 24 Apollo shows at full capacity to reach the same audience number. No matter that the London shows were regarded by sections of the music press as a "scandal", with an "atrocious" sound and poor sightline (Watts 1976: 3), it was now clear that the Glasgow Apollo, like other venues of its size, offered promoters limited scope to achieve similar economies of scale.

Facing a changing marketplace, Lynch relinquished the lease on the building in 1978 and a new leaseholder was sought. At one point it looked as if it would be taken over by a national bingo operator. This led to a large-scale local protest, which was eagerly supported by the Scottish media, which reinforced the fight to keep "our" venue open (Forbes 2015: 131). After a three-month closure, the venue's lease was taken over by the Manchester-based theatre group Maximus Investments, whose business was to refurbish dilapidated theatres, before relaunching them (ibid).

The venue's subsequent history, which assumed a downward trajectory, both culturally and economically, reflected market forces, most notably the burgeoning conglomeration of the live music sector (in which Maximus played a key role) and the rise of public-private initiatives. The combined result of these developments was the establishment of a UK network of large multi-purpose arenas.

In 1980 Maximus, now called Apollo Leisure, purchased the venue from the building's owners; Apollo Leisure, having expanded into ticketing and promotion, was then sold to the US company SFX which, in turn, was acquired by the global corporation Clear Channel/Live Nation. In 2002 the Apollo Leisure CEO, Paul Latham, became Chair of Live Nation UK (ibid: 31).

The venue's acquisition by Maximus meant that for the first time in over fifty years the Apollo was not under local control. Thereafter, local engagement with the venue soured. The venue's "foreign" ownership was commonly taken to explain locally why the venue had "lost its magic" (ibid:157). When concerts re-commenced after the 1978 takeover, albeit at a diminishing rate, the extent of the Apollo's disrepair was more prominently addressed by the once-supportive local media. The venue was now described the "Appalling Apollo" (McGurk 1983: 16–17), the "biggest pop slum in Europe" (Houston 1979: 10). Local audiences and promoters began to drift away and in June 1985 Apollo Leisure had no option but to close the venue. In short, the Apollo, celebrated for its down-at-heel local persona during the first half of its life became increasingly ostracised by its deteriorating condition and its increasingly fragile links to the locality in its later phase. Of course, in a not unusual scenario, a wave of local nostalgia for the venue quickly emerged within a short time of its closure, despite its tarnished latter period. Nonetheless, while Frith (2007: 9) may state that the trademark "filth and seediness" of a "legendary" live venue like the Apollo is one of the reasons why the Apollo is celebrated, it is also the reason why the venue closed.

Nostalgia for the Apollo experience' has, no doubt, been further spurred by the venue's re-placement. A few months after its closure in 1985, Scotland's first multi-purpose arena, the Scottish Exhibition and Conference Centre (SECC), opened in Glasgow. Contrary to claims that the SECC would greatly enhance the enjoyment of live music, the SECC was widely criti-cised by artists, promoters, and audiences for its lack of atmosphere and poor logistics (Forbes, 2015: 193). Nonetheless, the SECC's waterfront site has, over the years, facilitated a range of further developments, including the 3,000 seat Clyde Auditorium (which opened in 1997) and the 14,300 capacity Glasgow Hydro (which opened as a state-of-the-art modern arena in 2013).

T in the Park

If the opening of the SECC represented one of the first stages in the professionalisation of Scot-land's live music sector, then the launch and subsequent success of the *T In the Park* festival (1994–2016) signified the next phase.

T in the Park was launched by Glasgow-based promoter DF Concerts at the cusp of the rise of the UK festival environment in the mid-1990s and evolved over twenty years to assume a key position as one of the UK's major events. It attracted its largest crowd, 85,000, in 2015, having by then already hosted global stars such as Rihanna, Green Day, The Who, Oasis, Eminem, Lady Gaga, Kings of Leon, Coldplay, Beyoncé, Red Hot Chili Peppers, Jay-Z, Radiohead, and REM.

As the discussion to follow shows, achieving this status would have been impossible had DF Concerts remained a local concern. Instead, the promoters had to relinquish control to, and rely upon the joint resources of, an international partnership of major live sector operatives. And yet, even during this process, DF projected and maintained a local profile, a development that further underlines the complexities in the relationship between the local and global in the live music sector.

When *T in the Park* was initially launched DF was still 100% Scottish owned. The company was mindful that the previous attempt to establish a locally organised major music festival (the ill-fated *Loch Lomond Rock Festival*), over the course of two attempts in 1979 and 1980, had ended in insolvency. A risk-reduction offshoot of DF, Big Day Out Limited, was thus established to control the finances of the new event.

The first *T in the Park*, in 1994, was a relatively low-key affair, with an audience of 17,000. Taking place at Strathclyde Park in Lanarkshire, the festival headliners included Cypress Hill, Primal Scream, and Blur. The company lost money on the first festival, which left DF's Geoff Ellis to consider its prospects: "We wondered whether with that kind of line up, were we ever to be able to do more [audience] numbers" (quoted Leadbetter 2013).

Ellis's implicit question here is how to achieve economies of scale. As Holt (2010: 249) notes, the boom in the UK's live festival environment in the late 1990s, was stimulated by technical and logistical developments that enabled events to be much bigger. Attaining such economies of scale remained problematic for local live music promoters. In trying to meet increasing festival demands (by both performers and audiences) DF wasn't in a financial position to take on the high fixed costs that could otherwise be offset by increased purchasing power and an advanced level of resources. These were the market conditions which restricted the growth of local operators and benefitted global live music companies like Live Nation and AEG Live (Tschmuck 2017: 120).

DF Concerts had been established (as Dance Factory Concerts) in Dundee in 1982 by promoter Stuart Clumpas. In 1990 Clumpas opened Kings Tuts Wah Wah Hut as a club venue in Glasgow, subsequently making it DF's HQ. Clumpas launched *T in the Park* with Ellis in 1994; seven years later Clumpas sold all his shares to Irish-based MCD Concerts, which was part of Jersey-based Gaiety Investments (Cloonan and Frith 2010). In 2008 a joint venture with Live Nation to form LN-Gaiety Holdings led to its acquisition of Gaiety's holdings in DF, along with the stakes it owned in numerous other major festivals through its ownership of Festival Republic (ibid). By 2011 DF was 78% owned by LN-Gaiety Holdings, 19.5% by Manchester-based SJM Concerts, and 2.5% by Geoff Ellis (Frith *et al.* 2021: 30).

By being part of an international conglomerate, DF could engage with major artists within a minimum risk scenario and operate out with the realm of small profit margins (ibid: 34–38). These developments enabled *T in the Park* to grow, attracting major artists and massive crowds. But even if it was now controlled by a range of non-Scottish companies, in its promotion of *T in the Park* and other Scottish live music endeavours, DF were keen to convey its Scottish identity, in its marketing and media engagement, for example. Indeed, the strength of DF's links with the local music community at a grassroots level was part of its value to Live Nation, which was happy for DF to assume a substantial degree of independence in its day-to-day working relationships (Frith and Cloonan 2010).

In developing *T in the Park* DF had relied, for example, on the continued support of its main sponsor, Glasgow-based Tennents Caledonian Brewers (the 'T' moniker in the festival title).

Tennents fund numerous music events and initiatives in Scotland and have been regarded as a lifeline for local live music since the late 1980s (Williamson *et al.* 2003: 28). The brewers certainly became a vital benefactor of T in the Park, especially in its opening years. In 1997 *the* festival faced collapse when one of DF's ticketing agencies went into receivership, with the loss of £0.5 million in ticket sales; Tennents Should be provided DF with an interest free loan (Frith *et al.* 2021: 92). Correspondingly, Tennents' relationship with DF allowed the brewers to elevate their local identity, underplaying the fact that they were controlled by the multinational Anheuser-Busch InBev corporation until 2009, when they were acquired by the Irish-based C & C Group (Cloonan and Frith 2010).

As Anderton (2018: 76–78) notes, prominent involvement in festival sponsorship by brands like Tennents can help to define and characterise such events. This local brewer's name and logo being copiously exhibited and encapsulated in everything from the festival's title, tickets, publicity, stage names, on-site displays to the pouring rights, proved, for both sides of the deal, to be an almost perfect "Scottish" brand-fit, despite the non-Scottish ownership of both parties.

DF were also keen to localise the festival's success by extolling its specifically Scottish cultural and commercial dynamics, capitalising on the "collective effervescence" (Durkheim 2008) of the local audience and highlighting the immediate, local, economic benefits. Ellis regularly suggested, for example, that *T in the Park*'s accomplishments were due to the fact that Scottish live music audiences typically adopted a "more passionate" persona and were "less reserved" than their English counterparts (McClure 2003). Such claims carried added resonance locally, given that Ellis originates from Manchester. DF also commissioned annual economic impact reports, which quantified the festival's financial benefits to the local economy. The 2014 report, for example, reported that *T in the Park* had contributed £15.4 million to the Scottish economy (Miller 2014).

Eventually, however, *T in the Park* began to lose its identity, becoming a victim of the vast post-millennium growth in the UK festivals circuit, which compelled events to add extra days and additional stages (Anderton 2018: 35). As Robinson (2015: 47–48) relates, the resultant competition between the major events for both top and middle tier artists led to the creation of a headliner economy bound by exclusivity deals and shaped by the established relationships between the major live sector stakeholders. Artists were leveraged to appear on standardised line-ups across several festivals and there was an increasing commodification of the international festival environment, which further marginalised local input (Holt 2021: 229). These developments, which witnessed Calvin Harris appearing at *T in the Park* on eight separate occasions, acted to dilute notions of the festival's unique Scottishness (even if Harris was himself a Scot).

In 2015, *T in the Park* was forced to move from its second home, at Balado in Perth and Kinross where it had been resident since 1997, following a dispute with the local Health and Safety Executive about the potential risk of an under-site oil pipe. The festival moved to Strathallan Castle Estate in Perthshire, where it was staged in 2015 and 2016. Although it achieved its highest attendance of 85,000 in its first year at Strathallan, serious security and traffic problems led to the festival's capacity being reduced to 70,000 for the 2016 event, along with a host of new licensing conditions. Despite complying with all the stipulations, the 2016 festival attracted further controversy and indignation from the once-empathetic local media after experiencing three drug-related deaths, a rape and a series of violent incidents among the audience (Levine 2017).

To compound matters, a political dispute followed a Scottish Government decision to give DF a grant of £150,000 to cover the costs of moving from Balado to Strathallan (Hendicott 2015). Scrutiny in the Scottish Parliament exposed the flimsy basis of the grant application, which seemed to carry an implicit threat that the festival would have to "leave Scotland" if it was not awarded. In the resulting discussion, DF's ownership by a Live Nation dominated consortium was exposed (Brooks 2015), one of the few instances when DF's global ownership was highlighted in the media. Thus, in the festival's latter stages, DF's presumed Scottish persona, which had been underpinned and economically driven by its shared identity with the local audience, was damaged. DF suspended *T in the Park* in 2017, finally cancelling the festival in 2019.

Nonetheless, as Cloonan and Frith (2010) have highlighted, the key markers of DF's overall success had been their aptitude for playing the "Scottish card" and the way they had advanced perceptions of the "special" Glasgow or Scottish audience. Although incongruous in one sense, the strength of DF's relationship with local music communities and the degree of independence afforded by Live Nation and its other controlling partners, enables DF to maintain a local identity which is central to its role as Scotland's' leading live music promoter.

Conclusion

These case studies show that as the profile of the Scottish live music sector has risen over the decades, so its distinctly Scottish elements have been removed, which is inevitable given global trends within the live industry and Scotland's marginal economic base.

As the discussions of both case studies demonstrate, while the Scottish live music market has grown, the distinctly Scottish traits which shaped its foundations have diminished. However, it must also be underlined that this industry sector would not exist if it ceased to rely upon the local knowledge and expertise of Scottish-based promoters even it is also unsustainable without the global flow of capital and resources from entertainment conglomerates like Live Nation.

Within this scenario, the success of *T in the Park* clearly depended upon the local skillset of DF Concerts, which is to say that live music is as much a cultural expression as it is a commodity, that it relies upon the "fixity" of local traditions and roots, as well as upon the "fluidity" of hybridity and cultural alliances (Connell and Gibson 2003: 9–10). And it is equally apparent that the contemporary live music sector in Scotland assumes translocal dimensions which necessitate that "much of the promotion of locality is in fact done from above" (Robertson 1994: 35). What's involved here is "glocalisation", a term that encapsulates the complex and dynamic interrelationship of local music scenes and industries with the international marketplace (Shuker 1998: 132). As Angela Cresswell Jones and Rebecca Jane Bennett wrote in 2015,

> It is beginning to be clear that the dominant cultural force of the century ahead won't just be global and virtual, but a powerful interweaving of opposites—globalization and localization, virtual and real, with an advance guard constantly undermining what is packaged and drawing much of society along behind them.
>
> (Jones and Bennett 2015: 4)

In short, my two case studies highlight that local engagement with live music remains at the heart of cultural engagement in Scotland, irrespective of who ultimately controls the local live music sector, which, for the most part, is of no consequence to Scottish audiences.

As Frith (2018: 253) suggests, while Scotland's small economic base cannot be overlooked, the uniqueness of the local audience remains integral, as encapsulated by his observation that "what makes Scottish music culture distinctive is the remarkable importance here of playing and listening and dancing to music live'. Furthermore, it is apparent that the exuberance of this audience, who are keen to embrace what Frith (ibid: 255) refers to as the "buzz and rush and discovery of a Scottish Saturday night", retains significance throughout the recent history of live music in Scotland.

References

Anderton, C. (2018) *Music Festivals in the UK: Beyond the Carnivalesque*. New York: Routledge.

Brooks, L. (2015) 'Scottish culture secretary accused over T in the Park subsidy' *The Guardian* (Online) 29 Sept. Available at: https://www.theguardian.com/politics/2015/sep/29/fyona-hyslop-accused-t-in-the-park-subsidy (Accessed 22 August 2021).

Cloonan, M. (2020, October) 'Trying to have an impact: Some confessions of a live music researcher.' *International Journal of Music Business Research*, 9(2), pp. 58–79.

Cloonan, M. and Frith, S. (2010 August) Promoting business. In *14th Annual Conference of the European Business History Association*.

Connell, J. and Gibson, C. (2003) *Sound Tracks: Popular Music, Identity and Place*. London and New York: Routledge.

Durkheim, E. (2008) *The Elementary Forms of the Religious Life* [1912]. Oxford: Oxford University Press.

Forbes, K. (2012) 'Glasgow as a live-music city: An analysis of the "legendary" Apollo venue and its audience.' *Social Semiotics*, 22(5), pp.605–621.

Forbes, K. (2015) *You Had To Be There? Reflections on the 'Legendary' Status of the Glasgow Apollo Theatre (1973–85)*. Doctoral dissertation, University of Glasgow.

Frith, S. (2007) 'Live music matters.' *Scottish Music Review*, 1(1).1–17.

Frith, S. (2018) 'Afterword.' In: S. MacKerrell, and G. West (eds.) *Understanding Scotland Musically*. London and New York: Routledge.

Frith, S., Brennan, M., Cloonan, M. and Webster, E. (2013) *The History of Live Music in Britain, Volume 1, 1950–1967: From Dance Hall to the 100 Club*. New York: Routledge.

Frith, S., Brennan, M., Cloonan, M. and Webster, E. (2019) *The History of Live Music in Britain, Volume 2, 1968–1984: From Hyde Park to the Hacienda*. New York: Routledge.

Frith, S., Brennan, M., Cloonan, M. and Webster, E. (2021) *The History of Live Music in Britain, Volume 3, 1985–2015: From Live Aid to Live Nation*. New York: Routledge.

Hanlon, J. (2011) Personal interview, by telephone with Kenneth Forbes, 22 November.

Harkins, C.A. (1995) *We Want "U" In. The Story of a Glasgow Institution*. Erdington, West Midlands, Amber Valley Print Centre.

Hendicott, J. (2015) 'Culture secretary quizzed over T in the Park £150,000 'cronyism' accusation.' *NME* (Online) 29 September. Available at: https://www.nme.com/news/music/nme-422-1221374 (Accessed 26 July 2021).

Hogg, B. (1993) *The History of Scottish Rock and Pop: All That Ever Mattered*. London: Guinness.

Holt, F. (2010) 'The economy of live music in the digital age.' *European Journal of Cultural Studies*, 13(2), pp.243–261.

Holt, F. (2021) *Everyone Loves Live Music: A Theory of Performance Institutions*. Chicago, IL: University of Chicago Press.

Hopkins, A. (2012) Personal interview, by telephone with Kenneth Forbes, 31 August.

Houston, T. (1979) '(Fans Tell *The Record*) this pop palace is just a slum.' *Daily Record*, 31 May, pp. 10–11.

Jones, M.L. (2012) *The Music Industries from Conception to Consumption*. London: Palgrave MacMillan.

Jones, A. and Bennett, R.J. (2015) *The Digital Evolution of Live Music*. Oxford: Chandos Publishing.

Leadbetter, R. (2013) 'How T in the Park festival just grew and grew.' *The Herald* (Online) 2 January. Available at: https://www.heraldscotland.com/news/13086694.t-park-festival-just-grew-grew/ (Accessed 11 August 2021).

Levine, N. (2017) 'T in the Park ordered to pay back £50,000 to Scottish government.' *NME* (Online) 18 January. Available at: https://www.nme.com/news/music/t-in-the-park-ordered-to-pay-50000-back-to-scottish-government-1949434 (Accessed 26 July 2021).

Lewisohn, M. (2013) *The Beatles-All These Years: Volume One: Tune In*. London: Little, Brown.

Loasby, P. (2012) Personal interview, London with Kenneth Forbes, 11 September.

McClure, G. (2003) 'Geoff Ellis: Live music promoter (DF concerts).' *Music Business Journal* (Online) 16 June. Available at: http://web.archive.org/web/20030807045418/http://www.musicjournal.org/03geoffellis.htm (Accessed 20 July 2021).

McGurk, J. (1983) 'The appalling Apollo.' *Sunday Mail,* 6 November, pp. 16–17.

McNab, K. (2012) *The Beatles in Scotland*. Edinburgh: Birlinn.

Miller, P. (2014) 'T in the Park's impact on Scotland's economy increases by 60% to £15.4m.' *The Herald* (Online) 8 October. Available at: https://www.heraldscotland.com/news/13183798.t-parks-impact-scots-economy-increases-60-15-4m/ (Accessed 26 July 2021).

New Musical Express (1976) 'Stones add three more Earls Court dates.' 3 April, p. 2.

Robertson, R. (1994) 'Globalisation or glocalisation?' *Journal of International Communication*, 1(1), pp.33–52.

Robinson, R. (2015) *Music Festivals and the Politics of Participation*. Aldershot: Ashgate.

Shuker, R. (1998) 'The New Zealand sound recording industry: Cultural policy and New Zealand on air.' *Australian Journal of Communication*, 25(3), pp.129–139.

Tschmuck, P. (2017) *The Economics of Music*. Newcastle Upon Tyne: Agenda Publishing.

Wakeman, R. (2011) Personal interview, by email with Kenneth Forbes, 29 August.

Watts, M. (1976) 'Scandal of the stones.' *Melody Maker*, 29 May, p. 3.

Williamson, J., Cloonan, M., and Frith, S. (2003) *Mapping the Music Industry in Scotland: A Report*. Glasgow: Scottish Enterprise.

4

Fascinating Rhythm – The Life of Scottish Jazz

Alistair Braidwood

Alistair Braidwood in conversation with

Sophie Bancroft – Singer/Songwriter & Educator
Alison Eales – Academic & Writer
Haftor Medbøe – Founding Chair of the Scottish Jazz Archive
Stewart Smith – Music Historian and Writer
Rob Adams – Journalist, Promoter, and Agent
Graham Costello – Drummer, Composer, and Band Leader
Rebecca Vasmant – DJ/Producer, Curator, and Record Label Owner

Introduction

There have almost certainly been Scottish musicians playing jazz for as long as there has been jazz to play. To have a life in jazz, however, many Scottish musicians have had to leave the country. The jazz singer Annie Ross, for example, went from a Scottish showbiz family to a career in the USA; trombonist George Chisholm joined dance bands in London, saxophonist Joe Temperley jazz orchestras in New York and pianist Stan Greig various English trad bands. George McGowan and Harry Margolis were among the big band leaders who fashioned viable and lengthy careers in Scotland and beyond. The bassist Jack Bruce and guitarist Jim Mullen became global figures in blues and funk while, over the years, Scotland's brightest young jazz talents (Tommy Smith, Laura Macdonald, Alan Benzie …) have been awarded scholarships specifically to travel away, to study at Berklee College of Music in Boston MA. To stay in Scotland to play jazz has, it, seems been a limited musical ambition even if there have been estimable Scottish jazz musicians from The Clyde Valley Stompers through Carole Kidd to the players released on Tom Bancroft's Caber Music label between 1998 and 2006.[1]

In recent years, however, the local Scottish jazz situation has changed, something that has been recognised in the nomination of Fergus McCreadie's Forest Floor *for the 2022 Mercury Music Prize. Alongside him, there is an increasing feeling that the current group of young jazz musicians are forming a viable Scottish jazz community. Names such as Strata, Fat Suit, corto.alto. kitti, Marianne McGregor, Georgia Cécile, Nathan Somevi, Matt Carmichael, the Nimbus Quartet, Rebecca Vasmant, Mezcla, Aku!, Animal Society, James Lindsay and The Calum Gourlay Quartet*

DOI: 10.4324/9781003247470-6

make up as vibrant a scene as there is in Scottish music today, one that seems at ease crossing jazz with all kinds of other musical genres.

In this chapter I look at the circumstances that lead to this situation and to the emergence of a new breed of jazz artists. By talking to a number of people involved in Scottish jazz, both past and present, I explore the relationship between the country and the music. Why does jazz, often seen rightly or wrongly as a minority interest, continue to be important for the nation's often confusing cultural identity?

The Glasgow International Jazz Festival

For many casual and younger observers, jazz arrived in Scotland in 1987, with the first Glasgow International Jazz Festival, an event which was seen as integral to the city's successful bid to become the European City of Culture in 1990. Initially determined to concentrate on "international" jazz (so as to draw attention to Glasgow's would-be global cultural standing), that first year brought some of the biggest world names to Scotland, such as Sarah Vaughan, Chick Corea, Taj Mahal, and Benny Carter. The music had a higher profile among the wider populace than it had previously enjoyed, and this (despite some protestations) offered Scottish jazz musicians greater opportunities as well.[2]

Sophie Bancroft

The Glasgow International Jazz Festival really created a great platform for everyone working here, which in a way has been lost a bit because everything's been merged into one thing. So there was particular funding put into the Scottish section – branded funding, often from brewers[3] – and then it would use a lot of different venues all over Glasgow which was great. It was a full-on programme – there would be jazz from Scotland every day and night for ten days, and it was a varied programme. That was a great example of all the different varieties of jazz going on at that point in time.

Such a high-profile festival was seen as having a vital role, along with events such as Mayfest (1983) and the Glasgow Garden Festival (1988), in creating a new image for the country's largest city – a place which was still widely seen as one of industry, alcohol, poverty, and violence. Such events were supposed to bring the city together, however in many cases they caused yet more division in a city almost defined by such, and this applied to jazz as much as any other area of culture and society.

Alison Eales

Even with the Jazz Festival, for it to really have been any kind of success, it needed to have a trad presence of some sort. And there was a very definite tension between the kind of people financing it and running it, who I think wanted to attract the bigger names, and perhaps the artistic directors of the festival, who wanted to bring in Fred Frith and Gerry Mulligan.[4]

They wanted to bring in all these kinds of people, and actually the majority of the people of Glasgow wanted to do the Riverboat Shuffle. So, there's a definite tension there of how you position yourself as being a European City of Culture. Here's a cutting edge jazz festival when actually the local scene is predominantly, well, not just trad but also the kind of more mainstream big bands playing in pubs.

Although not the first Scottish jazz festival (Edinburgh's began in 1978), the Glasgow festival, which still exists today, left a legacy of similar festivals appearing annually all around Scotland.

The Schisms and Geographies of Scottish jazz

In fact Scotland had a long history of jazz music rooted in the dancehalls of the country's towns and cities, but it wasn't really until the 1970s and the rise in Scotland of Modern Jazz that real divisions appeared. Some saw this new wave as exclusive (restricted to art venues in Glasgow and Edinburgh), whereas jazz was increasingly seen by others as old fashioned, harking back to those fading dancehall days or to (still popular) pub sessions, and often there was little crossover over between the two worlds. How you view jazz in Scotland may depend on the time, place and the musical landscape in which you were brought up. This produced a schism in a country already awash with them.

Haftor Medbøe

I think Scottish jazz has always had a sense of an identity, but it's not always been an inclusive identity. [...] there's a musician's identity, there's a promoter's identity's and there is a press identity, and they don't really mesh. It's not one happy family.

This fractured identity has led to various factions forming, and it seems jazz almost encourages such division, it being a music "whaur extremes meet", to quote from Hugh MacDiarmid's Scots poem "A Drunk Man Looks at the Thistle".[5]

Alison Eales

There's a lot of factionalism in jazz. There was a major, frankly, snobbery between modern jazz towards trad jazzers, but I consider trad jazz, in terms of the social impact of music, is much more interesting in terms of what audiences want out of music. Glasgow, in particular – people love dancing. We know this. Glasgow is a dancing city and it's just easier to sell music that people can dance to.

Stewart Smith

I suppose the big thing with jazz in Scotland, maybe kind of interwar – post-war era, the era of the dance bands – there were lots of jazz bands around, and a lot of Scottish musicians did their apprenticeships in these bands. People like Alex Harvey (who would front the infamous and much loved rock band The Sensational Alex Harvey Band), for example, played trumpet in a dance band and they were kind of playing swing music, dance band music. And with the advent of rock and roll and the decline of the dance halls and the dance bands, that created new opportunities in certain respects, but I suppose jazz became more of a niche thing, and clubs playing modern jazz started to open up as well.

This clash of styles and genres was defined by not only by the music and venue, but often along social divisions as well. These battles were mostly played out inside the jazz world – but the definition of that world would depend not only on who you were but where you were as well.

Alison Eales

The way I would characterise it, in Glasgow, is you had pubs. And for years in Glasgow you couldn't charge entry for live music which could curtail things. And there was some consternation, going back into the sixties, that the police were coming down hard on anything like a jazz gig, I guess maybe there were connotations of drug use and stuff. Whereas if somebody was sneakily putting on something in a private venue for a classical gig, if there's a string quartet playing in a pub, they probably wouldn't have bothered. I did find some kinds of reports of, of that kind of thing. Musicians felt that it was a bit unfair, but you do tend to get, venue wise, trad jazz and the sort of mainstream big band stuff happening more in pubs and bars and even hotel function rooms and things like that, places where they could legally do it.

The Third Eye Centre is the obvious place in Glasgow where the more modern stuff happened.[6] And I think it's probably fair to say that that was a very, very hard sell in Glasgow. You'd expect in Edinburgh for it to have been an easier thing, but my understanding is that, from how Platform (the jazz organisation who put on events in both cities) were performing, they struggled there as well. The audience seems to have been best for jazz fusion. So people like Billy Cobham would sell really well. The Orchestra and John McLaughlin – that sort of thing – those artists had much more of an audience. In Glasgow, you're really talking about it being limited to the Third Eye Centre.

Foreshadowing the sort of arguments which would come to be made about the programming of the Glasgow Jazz Festival years later, this battle between Trad and Avant Garde jazz, and between supporting home-grown talent and bringing over the big names from elsewhere, would play out in other ways.

Despite claims to being a national music scene, there are notable schisms which go beyond those of the music itself. With some notable exceptions, Scottish jazz has been most visible in the Central Belt, and particularly Edinburgh and Glasgow.

Haftor Medbøe

It always switches between these two cities. I'm old enough to see the pattern. Edinburgh had a jazz festival which had been established in 1978, or 1979, depending on whose story you go by. So it had a jazz festival, which was becoming an international festival, and which was bringing in a lot of people who were inspiring the local musicians.

I remember in the eighties and nineties, I spent a lot of time going to Glasgow on the train. Edinburgh jazz musicians would go through to Glasgow and, similarly, Glasgow jazz musicians would come to Edinburgh. There's always been migrations one way and the other, but Edinburgh really was the epicentre at that point.

Sophie Bancroft

I became, a jazz singer on the Edinburgh scene back in the mid-eighties and I was working seven nights a week. There were enough gigs then – you could just gig all the time. I was lucky enough to get taken under the wing by Fionna Duncan, who was the major jazz singer at the time, and she acted as a sort of informal mentor to me in my early years as a singer.

While the importance of these two cities cannot and should not be understated, it's important to note that there was jazz being played and championed elsewhere.

Rob Adams

In Dundee there were places to put on gigs, but I think there were two places we used most – one was The Rep, which is still thriving as a theatre. It's a great space. And then there was a place around the corner called the Bonar Hall, which was good because it was adaptable.[7]

If the band had a piano player – great cause it had a Bösendorfer – that was that problem solved. But if the band didn't have a piano player they could come off the stage and set up on the floor and there were bleachers, so you could make it really intimate.

Apart from The Rep and the Bonar Hall, in Dundee you were struggling a bit, because it would have to be in hotel function suites or somewhere like that.

Haftor Medbøe

The rest of Scotland now forms part of a tour network[8], but it's very disorganised or haphazard ad hoc tour network. There are venues around Scotland – for example the Stirling Tollbooth – who'll put on jazz, or The Blue Lamp up in Aberdeen which has been there for many years now. There's also An Tobar on Mull. So there are venues dotted around that have some interest in jazz.

Education

Part of the brief for the GIJF from the start was educational work: among the performers in the first festival was the Strathclyde Youth Jazz Orchestra, which went on to take its place among other successful local authority youth jazz projects in Fife, Dumfries, Edinburgh and elsewhere and among other national training initiatives such as the National Youth Jazz Orchestra of Scotland (from 1996), the Tommy Smith Youth Jazz Orchestra (from 2002), Phil and Tom Bancroft's Apple Banana Carrot improvisation projects in primary classes and the jazz summer schools in Napier University. In most of the conversations for this chapter, however (and in the interview with Jill Rodger in the next section), when talk turned to the current state of jazz in Scotland, the most regularly mentioned driver of its success was the formal jazz education programme offered since 2009 by the Royal Conservatoire of Scotland.[9]

Haftor Medbøe

Jazz is all about education but, when I was growing up, it was kind of informal education. You'd learn from your elders at gigs that you'd go to – gigs with people twice your age, and they would shout at you throughout to tell you what you shouldn't be doing and what you should. It was much more aligned with the American experience of an apprenticeship model. Then, from the 1980s onwards, that's when jazz entered academia.

Sophie Bancroft

There's some amazing education going on in Scotland now, which is brilliant, and the frustration is that there's not enough places and spaces for everybody to go and do what they're learning. I can't imagine what would have happened if the education system hadn't developed the way it has with the lack of gigs, because that would have been a terrible shame. At least people are learning and playing and meeting each other at colleges and universities and workshops.

But I think there's a sense that it would be really brilliant to have a bit more understanding of what is going on in Scotland in jazz education. Over the years, there's been surveys done, but it's never quite been put together. It's such a great music for developing creativity, whatever your creativity is going to be. I was involved in an Education Scotland working group, a composition working group, and they brought people in from different genres to look at how composition and songwriting could be included, marked and assessed, in the school system. It's very difficult with anything creative, but it's great that there are people in the system who care enough to try and bring in people that are on the ground doing it.[10]

Haftor Medbøe

Now that Tommy Smith has started the jazz courses in the Conservatoire in Glasgow, there's a lot of amazing talent coming out which has to play somewhere.[11] And sadly, there aren't enough places for all of these people to play, or any of us for that matter. You know, gigs are pretty few and far between these days.

Scotland has National Jazz Orchestras such as Scottish National Jazz Orchestra, National Youth Jazz Orchestra, and The Tommy Smith Youth Jazz Orchestra, and regional youth jazz orchestras which are vital to Scottish jazz and intrinsically linked to the role education plays in the current popularity of the music.

Rob Adams

The youth jazz orchestras fuel the enthusiasm of young musicians. I think Fergus [McCreadie] was aged twelve when he started playing with the Fife Youth Jazz Orchestra, and Richard Michael of FYJO is a great guy for getting people interested.[12] So Fife Youth Jazz Orchestra is one of the sources of young players coming through, but there's many of them. Edinburgh Schools Jazz Orchestra, there's a big band in Dumfries where corto.alto's leader, Liam Shortall, comes from.[13] The youth big bands get the youth interested in getting through things like taking their first solo, which is a big rite of passage.

That's kind of brought about all these young players. They're the finishing schools where they come through the regional orchestras and then they play for a national orchestra. And if they play with Tommy's youth orchestra, they have a very good chance of getting into the Scottish National Jazz Orchestra. There are a lot of people who come through there and become top guys and girls.

Graham Costello

Tommy Smith started the RCS jazz course in 2009, so it's very new. When I joined in 2012 it was the first time there was a first year, second year, third year and a fourth year and I think you could chart a graph from when people graduated [to] new bands emerging.

One question I get asked a lot is, "How come you work with such brilliant musicians?" It just so happens that we went to a university where everyone was a beast musician. So your best mates are also beast musicians, and then you also meet other musicians who are not studying the same things you are.

For instance, with Cahill/Castello [Graeme's musical collaboration with guitarist Kevin Cahill] Kevin studied classical guitar which opens up a completely different world to what I was used to. I think the RCS is a really good melting pot, great for meeting folk from different disciplines with different backgrounds. And I think, especially from the Scottish jazz perspective, we're starting to see a lot of stuff blossoming and emerging from that course.

Rebecca Vasmant

I think we're in the tenth year of people graduating from RCS so it's exactly the right time, where everyone's left their courses, they've done their touring with the big bands and writing for other people, and now they're at the point where they're confident enough to go out on their own. The music that they're making is influenced by the music that they like, not just what they've been taught at uni. That's where it starts to get exciting.

Diversity

Scottish jazz has a reputation, or had one, for being the domain and interest of mostly white men. That may be changing, but possibly not as quickly as desired, and not without some fights still to be won.

Haftor Medbøe

What I'm still seeing is that women players are more likely to leave and make their career south of the border because there seems to be more opportunity for them there than there is in Scotland. We need to deal with that immediately so that doesn't keep happening. It's a sort of brain drain – the jazz drain. There's a lot of role modelling that needs to happen in Scotland. For example, in Scottish National Jazz Orchestra they now have two women in the orchestra, but that's taken a very long time. Too long, in my opinion, I'll go on record as saying that. As a nationally funded organisation to promote jazz, where are the women?

Sophie Bancroft

Around the time I started writing, it was an era in jazz in Scotland where the scene wasn't particularly welcoming to people writing original songs. It was still quite, "You must sing jazz standards and that's it". And I was a female musician, which was, and still is, a rare breed sadly. I ended up having to move into other worlds of music to be able to perform.

There are still not enough female instrumentalists which is a great sadness. There's great things that are happening and then there's some things that it's a shame they're not still here, for instance a crossover of the places where generations can meet and nurture each other.

An increased diversity in those playing the music leads to diversity in the music itself, with the current generation of players collaborating with musicians from other genres and playing different styles in the same groups.

Graham Costello

We tend to almost shy away from calling it jazz as calling yourself any genre, it does kind of restrict you whether it's a frame of mind, or literally in how you are booked or marketed.

The scene is up for working with anyone of any genre. Harry Weir for instance, he's really into hip hop and rap and he's going to be working with a new band called Blue Boar Brass Band to make music with singers and rappers, so collaborations are a big thing for our generation.[14] I think it's just a willingness to not always focus on the traditional, we just want to make new music. It just so happens to be that we studied jazz and the element of improvisation is in a lot of our music, and it is "jazz" but it's so much more.

I think the strong point is it is so different and varied, even with bands sharing members and everything. We're still a small community, but we all sound different to each other. And then you have someone like Rebecca Vasmant who comes from DJ'ing before she started playing jazz – playing in the Sub Club and around Europe, playing dance and other non-jazz stuff, and then introducing jazz to her audiences.[15] And that's how I got involved with playing drums for her.

Rebecca Vasmant

From the very beginning, when I discovered jazz, I always wanted and dreamed of being able to play jazz records mixed in with electronic music, but also sometimes playing straight up jazz.

It just works in clubs. People that are in clubs are used to hearing certain speeds or a certain energy level to the music. It's about matching that, rather than just focusing on, "Is it house music?" "Is it techno?" "Is it hip hop?" "Is it jazz?". It's using my knowledge that I've built up over the years take to hold of dance floors and for people to not just be like, "oh, this is a bit weird".

I feel like I've waited a long time for this moment. I wanted to do this ten years ago but there wasn't really anywhere to do it. The audience weren't open to it as much back then. So, It's really exciting and positive. I feel like we're at this historical moment in time that in twenty years we'll all look back on and go, "Oh, my God – that was amazing". I'm trying to appreciate that every day, because I know that at some point it will move on.

The Future

As for the future of Scottish jazz, it continues to be an exciting one, although with some lessons to be learned from history. It's a future of hope tempered with caution.

Haftor Medbøe

There are frictions within Scottish jazz and there are people who feel underrepresented. Some believe that there are areas of the sector which have too much power and too much control over who plays and what gets heard. I would say it's quite a sick sector at the moment and needs a lot of healing. And I think that's partly down to the fact that it's just so difficult now to be a jazz musician and it can bring out some of the sort of darker sides of the human condition.

It's a false economy, jazz. You get the pub gigs which don't pay enough to make a living from. And then you get the jazz festivals. I guess Scotland is quite lucky to have Aberdeen Jazz Festival Dundee Jazz Festival, Islay Jazz Festival, Edinburgh Jazz Festival, Glasgow Jazz Festival, but those festivals happen once a year. So, that would be five gigs that I've just counted up there and yes, they pay a better rate, but again, it's not really the rate that you can live on. Whereas if you go and play a festival in Norway you are getting paid a proper wage.

Graham Costello

It's still **SO** new, the new Scottish jazz scene. There's not tons of bands out there. Only a few bands and artists, and there's probably pros and cons to that. There's maybe not as much depth, but I think that will come with time, whether it's musicians from the RCS or musicians inspired by what's happening now, who think "I like this' and 'want to try that", but what I think is so good is to have the core strength of musicians that there are at the moment, who can rival anyone in the world. When people mention UK jazz it's not just London jazz they mention. Previously, it was rare that Scottish jazz got talked about, but that's changing.

I think maybe our generation are more focused on the newer music happening, whether it's the kind of hip hop jazz of corto.alto or the minimal jazz with Strata or Fergus [McCreadie's] Scottish folk with jazz. Scottish folk and jazz have always been present [together]but Fergus is doing his own thing with it. There's a Nordic element to the way he plays as well. So, a fusion of genres within the Scottish jazz scene has always existed, but it's really potent right now. We're just a bunch of young musicians who have got a lot of influences which we're putting into our music.

Sophie Bancroft

I think certainly the variety of jazz, or music that includes elements of jazz, has skyrocketed, which is really exciting. Certainly there is much wider vision in the jazz scene and that's a beautiful thing.

Conclusion

Scottish jazz has gone through many mutations since the 1950s but appears to have reached a piv-otal moment in the last few years, with so many musicians reaching audiences outside the genre. Fergus McCreadie's Mercury nomination is a very visible example. By dedicating his shortlisting to Scottish jazz, and Scottish musicians in general, he helps to engender the feeling that the cur-rent breed of Scottish jazz musicians are taking all that has gone before them, learning lessons, and making unique music of their own. Diverse yet together.

The schisms, which have undoubtedly left a mark on Scottish jazz, look to have been broken down or simply ignored by this new breed who embrace musical and cultural diversity, rather than squabble over it. There remain issues related to the diversity of musicians, the number of venues available to play, equality of opportunities, and getting paid, but Scotland's new jazz is making its mark, and what's most exciting is to see what happens next.

Notes

1 Formed in 1952, Clyde Valley Stompers were the first trad jazz band to appear on the Royal Variety Performance (in 1958) (see https://www.heraldscotland.com/opinion/18590985.days---clyde-valley-stompers-1957–1981/). For Carol Kidd see https://www.carolkidd.co.uk/. For Caber Music see Review of Caber Records published by the Scottish Arts Council in 2005.

2 For more on the Festival see Martin Cloonan's interview with the current Festival Director, Jill Rodger, in the second section.

3 For a more detailed discussion of the festival's origins and development see Alison Eales' PhD thesis, *Bunting and blues: A critical history of Glasgow International Jazz Festival, 1987–2015* (Glasgow University 2017).

4 Fred Frith is an English multi-instrumentalist, composer and improviser; Gerry Mulligan is an American jazz saxophonist, clarinetist, composer and arranger.

5 Published in 1926.

6 The Third Eye Centre was founded by Scottish writer Tom McGrath in 1975. It is now known as the Centre for Contemporary Arts (CCA).

7 Dundee Repertory Theatre, commonly known as the Dundee Rep, is a theatre and arts company. Bonar Hall opened in 1977 to serve the University of Dundee.

8 This is down in no small part to new venues in the Scottish Highlands and Islands and to the creation of the Highlands and Islands Touring Network (see https://thetouringnetwork.com/).

9 This includes a BMus (four years full-time), an MMus (two years full-time), and an MA (one year full-time).

10 Mention should be made here of the work that Sarah Raine, Haftor Medbøe, and others are undertaking in the Department of Music at Napier University with the Scottish Jazz Archive, the Jazz Summer School, research into contemporary jazz and blues, and more.

11 Tommy Smith is a Scottish jazz saxophonist, composer, and educator.

12 Richard Michael is a pianist, teacher and broadcaster. Fergus McCreadie leads a piano trio and is a recent grad-uate from the jazz degree at the Royal Conservatoire of Scotland.

13 Liam Shortall is a trombonist and another graduate of the RCS jazz course.

14 Harry Weir is a tenor saxophonist from Paisley.

15 The Sub Club is a legendary Glasgow club and music venue.

5

Place of Light

Carla J. Easton

You need a constant wall of examples… The record industry knows what sells, and 4 or 5 white guys sells, so that's what they keep pumping out.[1]

A teenage girl's bedroom. She's a music obsessive sound junkie, eclectic song collector and melomaniac. Crates of vinyl, boxes of mixtapes and old ticket stubs surround her. Every bedroom wall is covered in posters, gig flyers and scrawled out lyrics to favourite songs. A second hand guitar is lying against the wall; a beat-up mixer hooked up to an audio interface and SM58 mic are plugged into her laptop on her desk, ready for bedroom demos. There's an old keyboard in the corner she hasn't learnt to play yet – but will. Set lists from gigs, open journals full of half written songs, a school bag covered in band patches and badges.

She's lying on the bed in a sea of magazines with platinum selling girl bands on the front covers. Images look down from her walls of the fab four Lungleg, synth saviours Strawberry Switchblade, stadium sellouts The Mckinleys, post-punk pioneers The Ettes. She's listening to music on her headphones, eyes shut tight, dreaming she's on stage with her idols Twinsets, Sunset Gun and Pink Kross.

She forms a band with friends at school. They make noise, tour the world and tell journalists they were inspired by the bands they grew up listening to – the DIY pop of Sophisticated Boom Boom and the audacity of The Hedrons.

None of this is real.

I was a music obsessed girl. It was not until my late twenties I formed a 'girl band', releasing our debut record when I was 31.

This essay reveals my journey from growing up in a mining town, emigrating to the city pursuing a love of vinyl and making music, the confidence that grew with each new girl group or band unearthed in crates of vinyl, affirming my right to be on stage – on my terms – highlighting the importance and inspiration of my precursors in the shape of a parallel history of all girl bands in Scotland from 1960 to 2000.

****

On Long Leases, in.. the Thriving Village of Carluke, …, 18 miles from Glasgow, in a Country abounding with Coal, and the finest Quarries of Freestone, with considerable advantages to

DOI: 10.4324/9781003247470-7

Settlers…places of Public Worship, Schools, and Public Library, a Weekly Market, and Four Fairs annually. A Windmill has been erected for making Meal and Barley for the Inhabitants… There are Bakers, Butchers, and every other Trade requisite for an extensive population … Carluke, has considerable recommendations, being entirely lying to a south exposure, and reckoned one of the healthiest places in the West of Scotland.[2]

I grew up in the old mining town Carluke, which loosely translates as 'Place of Light' due to its elevated south facing position over the fruit growing Clyde Valley. Gaining the epithet "a town called courage" having had three of its sons awarded the Victoria Cross, more per head of population that any other community in Britain,[3] in 2006 Carluke was no longer the epicentre of mining and industry but one of continuously expanding new builds for city commuters around a collapsing, ageing high street and ruined mill. The youngest of three, with an age gap of ten years, the only 'light' for me was music.

I would raid my sibling's meticulously alphabetised CD collection, binge watch Top Of The Pops on Friday night and The Chart Show on Saturday morning. Steal copies of the NME or Melody Maker lying around the house. Bash on my upright piano, sing into my hairbrush and thrash out tennis racket electric guitars. Plaster my bedroom wall in posters and sign up to Fanclub subscriptions. Windowsills became stadium stages for my second-hand Sindy dolls. My brother would make endless mixtapes to listen to in the car. Windows down, shades on. Driving through the winding roads of the Clyde Valley, trying to get as far away as possible, listening to carefully curated playlists of singers I had never heard before, singing songs that seemed like I knew from before birth.

I would scrape together every penny, intentionally not eating school lunches to save the money to buy records, CDs and music magazines. Pilgrimages to Glasgow, a mecca for any small-town teenager seeking live music experiences and vinyl, only a half hour train journey away for a measly £3 Scotrail return ticket. HMV, Fopp, Missing Records and Oxfam Music beckoned me on Byres Road; King Tut's and the infamous Barrowland Ballroom – those flashing neon stars were all for me. The electric buzz from leaving venues late at night to catch the last train home to get to bed to wake up in time for school. My disaffected teenage peers spent pocket money drinking cheap alcohol down Jock's Burn or in front of the local chippy.

There were bands of pubescent boys thrashing out cover versions of Papa Roach, Alien Ant Farm or their own take on the American 'Emo' dominating MTV2 at the turn of the twenty-first century at local youth clubs and community centres. I'd stand in the audience and watch, accepting a position on the sidelines with the aspiring title of 'The Guitarists Girlfriend'.

I think there's definitely something to be said for seeing people who look like you picking up instruments that's very inspiring[4]

The first Girl Band I encountered was the fictional Hasbro funded, Sunbow produced animated Jem and The Holograms – a neon pastel band with guidance from Synergy: a 'holographic computer designed to be the ultimate audio-visual entertainment synthesizer'[5] that protagonist Jerrica Benton could access by way of red star-shaped earrings left to her after her father's death. Part superhero, part powerhouse, Jem and The Holograms were a racially diverse synth-pop phenomenon with their own record label – Starlight Music – and their own mansion – Starlight Mansion – for fostered orphaned Starlight Girls. Jerrica harnessed Synergy's holographic powers to project the alter ego of Jem onto herself, and visual effects around her, to dominate the pop charts and the world. Band member Kimber Benton, Jerrica's sister and youngest member of the band, was songwriter for all the poptastic hits.

And keyboard player.

Piano lessons ensued.

When I was 16, a girl in school knew I was 'into music' and loaned me a dog-eared copy of the Nirvana biography 'Heavier Than Heaven'. An avid reader, I completed it within three days. It did not make me want to delve into the fleeting back catalogue of Kurt Cobain. My interest was piqued by a band much closer to home – the band that had made a lasting impression on Cobain. I burst into my eldest brother's bedroom.

'Murray – do you know who The Vaselines are?'

'Yeah, I have their CD'

'Can I borrow it?'

Two decades later and it's never been returned. Track 1 of the Sub Pop released compilation *The Way of the Vaselines: A Complete History* is 'Son Of A Gun'. I listened via headphones plugged into my stereo system above my head, my personal heaven, eyes shut tight, and heard a girl called Frances sing the words *"the sun shines in my bedroom when you play..."*[6]

It was the first time I heard a voice, like mine, amidst a flurry of scratchy, raw guitar pop on record. I copied the CD to tape and took it to school the next day so my best friend Debs could hear it. We sat in the common room sharing headphones. One earbud each.

"Let's form a band"

We were called The Perfect Reason – it was me (keyboards), Debs (drums), Michelle (singer) and Lyndsey (bass). I dreamed of us being able to perform, like all the other bands, at the local youth club. I wrote some songs and we booked rehearsals at the community centre.

"Why can't I change the way you see, change the way I want those things to be"[7] Michelle sang over Debs Mo Tucker inspired beat and my string-soaked synth. It became my life.

I accidentally left lyrics to one of my songs in the rehearsal room when another band – a boy band – went in after us. Unable to handle the mocking and laughing that ensued at my fledgling writing and the idea of a girls making music together, The Perfect Reason disbanded and a gig never happened.

But the need to be in a band was still there.

It was my beckoning place of light.

Murray said "if you go to Art School you can make music. If you go to music school you can't make art", so three months after turning 18, I packed my records and stereo system and moved to Edinburgh to go to Art School. Creativity was my ticket out of Carluke.

In shoddy student accommodation I met fellow music obsessive Cecilia. We deeply bonded over scrawled notes detailing why each song had been selected to share on countless mixtapes that would wear thin with excessive play, tangling into an inaudible mess. When Cecilia told me I would like my Sculpture tutor Paul Carter I trusted her – she was right about me loving Luscious Jackson and The Breeders. Paul was a faded-denim-clad, skinny man, constantly smoking roll ups, with one of the greatest smiles I'd ever seen.

Paul made mix CDs for the students who became his friends. He came to the indie discos with us and would turn up at exhibition openings with the bag from boxed wine stored in his satchel. We'd thirstily raise our cups for wine while no one was looking. The Pied Piper for all the weird indie kids, thrown together at art school in a city they didn't know. Helming our new logical family where the blood running through our veins was a binding rhythm.

One day, Paul split us into groups to make a new piece of collaborative work. Using a Dymo Gun, he stuck the word "JOURNEY" on the Sculpture studio wall and told us to respond how we wanted to. I found myself back in Carluke dressed as a spaceman, wandering around filming a performance piece for some hastily hungover thrown-together concept that it felt alien to return home to the small towns where we had grown up. We had to soundtrack our short film so decided to write our own song in face of harsh criticism from previous projects using recordings by artists we loved.

The result was 'Lullaby', recorded in my then boyfriend, Harry's bedroom. I burned the track onto a CDR so Paul could hear it. He abandoned his class and we stood outside in the sunshine, Paul lighting up a rolled cigarette before pulling on my worn headphones and smiling that big brilliant smile. "This is great. You should form a band".

We were called Futuristic Retro Champions and were a concoction of fizzy happy-hardcore pop. A six piece consisting of me, Sita, Harry, Dan, Luke and Adam, we channelled the wist-ful pop of Belle & Sebastian super-charged by a processed-beats driven turbo dance thing ala Bis with song 'Jenna' telling the tale of that ubiquitous last girl on the dance floor to a skip-ping 'lectro jive; 'Oh My God' unrequited love at 200bpm; and chiming slowie 'Isn't It Lovely'.[8] A technicolour acid fuelled too-much-Disney Pastels, it was sheer elation to be in a place of light with these weird art school kids, finally making music together in a band.

We supported Kate Nash, Glasvegas, Ladyhawke, Friendly Fires, received Radio 1 play, extensive coverage and critical acclaim. "This boy/girl combo…', 'female fronted…', 'this boy-girl band…" were usually how reviews started.

I didn't notice.

Bedroom recordings evolved to the studio and a string of EPs resulted in a final album in 2011 to mark the end of a five-year career. Hand in hand with moving on in life, Futuristic Retro Champions had come to an end as a result of me falling in love with a poet which meant my relationship with Harry the guitarist had come to an end. Unlike Abba or Fleetwood Mac, we wouldn't be continuing on in a torturous post-partner situation that resulted in great pop music.

Paul never saw the band develop or how my career as a songwriter, and eventual singer, would progress. He died in a car crash in the Summer of 2006 shortly after Futuristic Retro Champions started. I have a picture of one of his artworks on my bedroom wall – his '1 Second Revolution'. Frozen for a brief moment in time, Paul stands on a cobbled street of Edinburgh with a burning banner saying 'You're Not Alone'.

Outside of making music and art, over the years I was still avidly collecting records, recently discovering Backbeat Records in Edinburgh's Southside, stumbled upon one afternoon down a side lane off Nicolson Street. A converted ground floor flat piled high floor-to-ceiling, you have to leave your bag at the door as you wind through teetering stacks of vinyl in, both, pristine and tattered sleeves.

"what are you looking for?" the owner asks.

"Northern Soul" I replied.

He leads me carefully through a minefield of vinyl skyscrapers that might collapse at any second, through to the back room – the Soul Kitchen – and suddenly I am surrounded by all the greats. Compilation after compilation of rare cuts. No alphabetisation. If you want a record from this shop you have to be prepared to work hard to uncover the gold.

My nose itched with dust and my arms ached from bountiful crate digging. I spotted a box shoved under a buckling table, slightly to the back, covered in a sheath of silver dust that must contain diamonds. "The Cookies" – three smiling girls on the front cover in a black and white photo on a pale rose pink background. Flipped over, the track listing revealed songs mostly written by Brill Building royalty Gerry Goffin and Carole King; creator of my favourite album "*Tapestry*". I quickly discarded the other records I was going to buy, deciding to spend the little money I had on this one LP despite not knowing how it would sound.

Rush home to turn on my old stereo system from Carluke that has been hauled from flat to flat in Edinburgh. Lift the lid and pull the jet black shiny disc from the tattered sleeve that promisingly glows like an inky full moon. Lower the needle and turn the speakers up full.

"*Don't say nothing bad about my baby*"[9] the words and melody soar. A unit of harmonies thick with sugar and sass, one voice made of three. "*So girl you better shut your mouth*"[10] lead singer Earl-Jean McCrea drips into the mic with a threat like an iron fist in a velvet glove.

An introduction to Girl Groups.

Back to Backbeat.

The shop owner starts keeping a crate, just for me, in the Soul Kitchen exclusively filled with Girl Groups from 1958 to 1963; the defining era of the 'Girl-Group', an explosion of vocal harmony groups dominated and led by predominantly young black women that flourished between the decline of Rock and Roll and The British Invasion. The American Girl Groups heralded the birth of the teenage girl, glorified messy hormones, expressed sexual desires in a world where 'accessible contraception' was a hushed word, and amplified the playground games centred around the skipping rope to new celestial heights.

The Sweet Inspirations, The Bobbettes, The Dixie Cups, The Shangri Las, The Shirelles, Martha Reeves and The Vandellas, The Goodies, The Marvelettes, The Sapphires, The Chiffons, The Blossoms, Honey Cone, The Fuzz. I started not eating again so I could bring these girls home. They sounded like gangs I wanted to be part of. I bought go-go boots to emulate The Shangri Las and vintage ballgown dresses to wear to the indie disco as though I was the missing member of The Supremes. I'd found this whole new wonderful world of music that made me feel like I belonged. Finger clicks that sound like bubblegum pops, shimmering tambourines and heartbeat drums. Dun dun-dun THWACK "*the night you left I knew I needed you so*".[11] Girls making music.

I hauled those records to flat parties across the city that I would DJ at with my new best friend, and fellow music obsessive, Jenna who I met selling shoes in a part time job. She reminded me of the girls that used to smoke round the back of the school that you were desperate to be friends with, except she exclusively smoked expensive imports from France, not cheap singles bought from the ice-cream van back home.

Christening ourselves The Sequin Sisters, we would DJ exclusively with vinyl, lugging boxes of LPs up stairwells of tenement flats wearing towering high heels, vintage dresses and bright red lips. We were paid with bottles of cheap vodka and pills. Jenna knew how to work the room.

"Heard this?"

"No what is it"

She pulled a seven inch from a sleeve with two polka dot princesses on it complete with magic-marker eyeliner reminiscent of Dusty Springfield and tangled hair full of flowing ribbons in all the colours of the rainbow. They looked like a Girl Group – but not from the era I had grown to love. From later.

"You'll love this. They're from Scotland"

I can't describe the feeling of first hearing the synth horns blast out of the homemade and hastily assembled PA in someone's kitchen. The polyphonic sparkling chimes that followed underneath, like shimmering fishes swimming in the sea under the waves of sugary sweet girly vocals and glorious harmonic "la la la la's".

This was my introduction to Strawberry Switchblade and girl groups from Scotland.

Charting at Number 5 in 1985, the year of my birth, 'Since Yesterday' is the only Top 10 single by a Girl Group/Band from Scotland. They released an album, toured the world, appeared on countless TV shows and graced the covers on many magazines. Rose McDowall and Jill Bryson were the ultimate new-wave pop stars. Originally starting out in Glasgow as a four piece with members Janice Goodlet and Carole McGowan, Strawberry Switchblade had catapulted ahead of other bands in the Glasgow Art scene – the much revered Orange Juice – to hit the Top Ten. I had never heard of them until now and I couldn't work out why they had been missing from my teenage bedroom wall.

If there was one girl group from Scotland then there had to be more of them for me to collect and bring home to my expanding collection of vinyl so I found myself trawling through record shops, finally finding a compilation titled 'Messthetics' featuring Scottish DIY post-punk bands in Avalanche Records on Cockburn Street. Included in the listing was a band called The Ettes. Could this be in reference to girl groups in my collection?

Skipped home and pulled my new find from the bag. The CD compilation came with an insert explaining all the bands contained within. The Ettes were three girls – Christine 'Teen' Baillie, Patricia 'Trash' Brown and Anne Morrison – who in the late seventies formed a band, played a couple of ramshackle gigs and wrote their own rules. Stories of ripping the silver linings from cigarette packets, scrawling their band name on them and attaching safety pins on the back to sell as badges at their gigs had me frothing at the mouth. The recording was a song called 'A Conversation', recorded in band member Teen's parents front room with cardboard boxes in place of a drum kit. It was rough and raw. A capital attitude from the capital city, barely audible above the home-recorded scuzz.

The Ettes operated on the fringes of Edinburgh's burgeoning post-punk scene, that would result in groups like Scars, Fire Engines and The Waterboys. I wished I had discovered them when I was sixteen, trying to form my first band at school. They normalised making noise with friends during teenage formative years. I wanted to know more and to hear more music, but was met with a deafening silence.

I was practically starving as my record collection grew with more obscure American Girl Groups and my desperate attempt to uncover and buy music by Scottish Girl Bands. The birth of the internet meant the rise of the fan forum and I quickly found myself trawling through blog posts, finally unearthing Sophisticated Boom Boom, a Girl Band from Glasgow considered part of the Postcard scene but only ever releasing one song on an obscure compilation secured from Discogs. Research revealed they recorded three sessions for John Peel on BBC Radio 1, toured the UK and recorded an unreleased album. Grainy pictures depicted lavish costumes and a flame haired Libby MacArthur dominating the stage backed by Trish Reid and Brown on guitars, Laura Mazzolini on bass and Jacqui Bradley on drums. I read how they morphed into the slickly studio produced His Latest Flame, Libby replaced by Moira Rankin, signed to a major and released one album before being dropped.

The eighties was an era of the girl band in Scotland – there was the LA soul from the Glasgow based Louise and Deirdre Rutkowski in the form of Sunset Gun and The Twinsets – two sisters from Edinburgh. Rachel and Gaye Bell were a post-punk rollercoaster ride of high heels, higher hair and whips on stage, playing long forgotten and shut down Edinburgh venues and a show for lifers at Saughton Prison. They had three John Peel sessions under their belts, 'handbag' roadies and a diehard fan base but nothing released. They became my Holy Grail. I couldn't find their music or elusive Peel sessions anywhere. A few contacts lead me to believe the girls were still living in Edinburgh but had abandoned music.

Wear the uniform, strike the pose, and what is left to distinguish viewer from performer?[12]

Armed with my consistent wall of examples, even if I couldn't hear their music, and notebooks bursting full of new songs, I formed a new band. A Girl Band, calling in Sita from the Champions, Debs (my childhood best friend and member of the ill-fated The Perfect Reason) and new kid on the block Emma who I met while working in a deli trying to scrape together enough money to keep buying records.

My new band was called TeenCanteen – named after a B Side song on a Showaddywaddy 7 inch that had made it into my record collection which I still maintain, to this day, I never bought. I removed the space between Teen and Canteen. There was no time for pauses.

After only five rehearsals, we were recording, soon to be followed by sold out shows purely via word of mouth and live sessions for Marc Riley on BBC 6Music. We played T in The Park, Kendall Calling, The Great Escape, Indietracks, Festival No. 6 and more – learning as we went and developing our sound. I barely stopped to think, writing and recording and gigging and rehearsing all the time. The critical acclaim was flying in for each new single before an eventual album, quickly followed by an EP, as our girl group harmonies soared, recontextualised with 'Hooky' bass lines and pulsing synths. We were nominated for awards and had songs in films and adverts. People would call me CarlaCanteen. People would ask for a photo with me. People started asking me to comment on being a woman making music.

No one had ever asked me that before.

We were always called an 'all girl band', never a band. Sound engineers would ignore us, looking around asking where the band was. I began to notice we were the only 'all girl band' on festival line ups or at gigs. I stood at the side of a stage and had a man-boy sway up to me with two warm sloshing pints in his hand. My synth was strapped to my back in its bag while I waited to go on and set up after the previous band had cleared the stage.

I can see you like a big instrument' he said.

He was referring to his dick.

"you can't set up your drums that way" a sound engineer once said to Debs as she set up her kit the way she had always set up her kit over years of rehearsing and gigging.

"your song doesn't work because the bassline is too high" another sound engineer said to me because he couldn't fathom that our bass acted in place of a lead electric guitar and that I was supplying the low end from the sub bass on my synth which was going through a DI which he patronisingly told me how to plug my jack lead into even although I had done that exact thing hundreds of times before.

"fire the rest of the girls in the band, record the album with session musicians and then we can audition new members for the band for the release and tour. But keep Debs – she can't play drums but she looks good" a male manager said.

"are all your songs about women's issues?" a journalist asked.

"what's it like to be in an all girl band?" another journalist asked.

Same as being in any band I imagine, only our menstrual cycles had synced up from spending so much time together in rehearsal rooms and recording studios, small hire vans and sharing beds on tour to keep costs down. Maybe that doesn't happen with every band.

"you should come out of behind your synth to perform" various men told me

"your record won't sell without the band on the front cover" a board member at the label who was releasing our record said.

My first solo performance was in New York having been flown over as part of a collective by a whisky brand. I was petrified and anxious, my stomach a mess prior to going on stage. After the show we all celebrated with a bit of too much of everything, ending up back at our rented apartment in Greenwich Village. A tag along included a local DJ who kept dancing too close causing me to spin away. I sat down at the kitchen table and he slid in behind me, his hands snaking up the insides of my legs. I froze. A songwriter on the other side of the table got up to leave, unaware of what was happening. I managed to mouth "don't leave" before everyone noticed what was going on and the DJ got thrown out.

I was told it was my fault.

At home, now in Glasgow, it was comforting to be surrounded by the bands in my notebooks or record collection. I wondered if they were asked similar questions or shared similar experiences to me and my journey. I kept digging for more Girl Bands, expanding my sonic sisterhood with more women that had gone before me. I rejoiced when I discovered the long lost girl group The McKinleys.

Coming out of Edinburgh around the same time as the original 'Girl Group' era of the early sixties, The McKinleys were sisters Jeanette & Sheila. Early recordings featured a teenage Jimmy Page, and they toured with both The Beatles and The Rolling Stones. By the end of decade, the sisters were either performing solo or with other acts earning Gold Discs and street-filled fan hysteria for public appearances. Semi-retiring to have families, they never stopped singing together, until Sheila's passing in 2012.

I discovered the nineties brought a new wave of guitar music to the charts, as indie and grunge went mainstream. Inspired by the Riot Grrrl movement, defiant Glasgow band Lung Leg mixed with stars-to-be Franz Ferdinand, Mogwai and Belle & Sebastian. Years later, Franz would cover a Lung Leg song, 'Made To Minx' for a BBC Live Session, highlighting the influence those girls had on Scotland's newest superstars. Jane "Egypt" McKeown, Annie Spandex, Maureen "Mo Mo" Quinn and Amanda "Jade Green" Doorbar – precursors to my TeenCanteen. Vic Blue, Jane Strain and Jude Fuzz of Pink Kross were cool girls in the school playground that you desperately wanted to be your friends but you knew if you approached them they would punch you in the face. They sucked me in with their sickly sweet sound backed by relentless pounding drums and ferocious vocals.

It took time and a lot of research to, partly, complete my rich heritage of women making music in Scotland. A logical family stretching back to Jeanette and Sheila McKinley in Edinburgh in the sixties, through to the post-punk of The Ettes in the seventies, the DIY pop of Sophisticated Boom Boom, The Twinsets, Strawberry Switchblade in the eighties, the slick studio productions from His Latest Flame and Sunset Gun, the empowering Riot Grrrl influence in Lungleg and Pink Kross in the nineties. This chain reaction of sonic sisterhood that, unknowingly, led to me, Sita, Debs and Emma in TeenCanteen.

Amazingly, in spite of this inaccessible archive of collectives of women making music together, there has been a post-millennium boom of Girl Bands from Scotland – The Hedrons, Streetside, Lemonescent, The Gussets, Zorras, The Van T's, Bratakus, Joyce Delaney, Agony Ant, Fallope and The Tubes, Tongue Trap, Sacred Paws, TeenCanteen, Honeyblood, Skinny Dipper, The Twistettes, Fisty Muffs, Honeyfarm, UNINVITED, Pretty Preachers Club, BDY PRTS, The Eves, SHE and more. But none of them have yet made their mark on the charts like Strawberry Switchblade over three decades ago – the only Girl Band from Scotland to ever reach the Top 30 never mind the Top 10.

This begs the question – what progress is being made and why are Girl Bands not supported by the industry in the same way Boy Bands are?

I've since tracked some of my precursors down. We've shared stories and experiences. They explained everything all in their own words. We all had to play harder and better than our male counterparts. We'd all been told how to dress or sound, shared similar stories of sexual assault, getting fired for becoming a parent, being told you're too old, too fat, too short, too tall, been told to lie about our age, how to dress, how to perform, sing and present ourselves; been told "the problem with girl bands is that you all get pregnant in the end…"

Throughout history, girls have been defending their right to be in the audience and, the often overlooked, women who armed themselves with instruments and microphones and took to the stage before now are being lost. We need to address the social impact of women making music in a male dominated industry and rightfully acknowledge their place within the history of popular music. It's time to 'normalise' women picking up instruments and forming bands with their friends and provide accessible historical context to women making music. I started with Scotland – my home country and the cities I made music in. I encourage everyone to do the same around them no matter where they are because there are girls in a garage making music and there always have been. All across the world are Places of Light and logical families. One big huge sonic sisterhood waiting to be unearthed.

Bibliography

Cyrus, Cynthia J. (2003) 'Selling an Image: Girl Groups of the 1960s' *Popular Music* 22 (2), 173–193.

Notes

1 *Since Yesterday: The Unsung Pioneers of Scottish Pop*, KT Tunstall (filmed interview), Directed by Carla J. Easton and Blair Young, Produced by Miranda Stern, Forest of Black, 2022.
2 P233. *Notices, Historical, Statistical and biographical, Relating to the Parish of Carluke, from 1288 till 1874*. Glasgow, Scot., W. Rankin, 1874.
3 Carluke. https://www.scottish-places.info/towns/townfirst423.html. Accessed 20/11/2021.
4 *Since Yesterday: The Unsung Pioneers of Scottish Pop*, Lisa Marie Ferle (filmed interview), Directed by Carla J. Easton and Blair Young, Produced by Miranda Stern, Forest of Black, 2022.
5 *Jem: Truly Outrageous!*, Animation, written by Christy Marx, 1985, USA, Sunbow Productions, Hasbro Inc., Multiple Sound Distributors Ltd., London, 1986.
6 'Son of A Gun', Recorded by The Vaselines. Kelly, Eugene; Mckee, *Frances: The Way of the Vaselines: A Complete History*. Glasgow: Sub Pop. 1992.
7 'Why'. Easton, Carla. Unpublished. 2001.
8 Malcolm Jack, *The List* magazine, 2006 retrieved 20/11/2021.
9 The Cookies 'Don't Say Nothing Bad About My Baby'
10 The Cookies 'Don't Say Nothing Bad About My Baby'
11 The Ronettes 'Be My Baby'
12 Cyrus (2003: 182).

Riverside Festival, Glasgow

An Interview with Dave Clarke and Mark McKechnie

John Williamson

Interviews by John Williamson, 4 November 2022.

Introduction

The tenth anniversary of the Riverside Festival in Glasgow – celebrated in 2023 – presents a useful lens through which to view a decade of political and economic upheaval that has impacted the independent festival sector generally but with some unique outcomes in the context of Glasgow and Scotland.

This chapter largely comprises an interview with the two club promoters who joined forces to establish Riverside in 2013. As they explain, Dave Clarke (one-third, along with Stuart McMillan and Orde Meikle, of both Slam Events and the long-running club night, Pressure) and Mark McKechnie (Electric Frog) set up the festival partly in response to these changes and opportunities, but here they predominantly focus on how the festival has survived and navigated subsequent travails (Brexit, COVID and the associated economic challenges). And while, at the time of writing, these remain omnipresent, Clarke and McKechnie also articulate some possible routes forward for independent festivals.

Setting the Scene: History, Geography and Economics

Before they do this, it is worth painting a thumbnail sketch of the historical precedents, the geographical issues and market conditions that surrounded the first Riverside Festival.

Outdoor music festivals in Scotland had until then followed a loosely similar trajectory to that in the rest of the UK, though with some additional climactic and logistic issues. The first outdoor festivals took place in the aftermath of Woodstock during 1970, but these were short-lived, amateur, money-losing efforts beset by logistical problems. Of these pioneering events only a very few (for example, the Loch Lomond Rock Festival in 1979/1980) made it as far as a second year.

If Woodstock was the first inspiration for such promoters, Live Aid was a second, with the likes of Fife Aid (1987/1988) and The Festival for A Nuclear Free Scotland at Murrayfield in Edinburgh (1988) following in its wake, while The Big Day, which was part of Glasgow's European City of Culture celebrations in 1990, included Scotland's largest ever outdoor (free) concert at Glasgow Green. The loosening of licensing restrictions in the city during the same year[1] was also an important moment for Scotland's electronic music scene, with Clarke and Slam at its core: their regular nights at the Sub Club being augmented by their Slam in the Park event.[2]

DOI: 10.4324/9781003247470-8

The latter acted as something of a precursor for T in the Park, which started at the same location in 1994 (see Kenny Forbes' chapter in this collection for a more detailed history), but it was with its arrival that Scotland had, for the first time, a large scale, well-attended festival that was able to attract the best festival acts of the time. The Slam Tent – a huge parallel world to the largely guitar-rock on the other stages – would go on to become a major component of T in the Park.[3] Headlined in its first year by Daft Punk, it would subsequently attract artists from around the world including Carl Cox, Nina Kraviz, Orbital, Sven Väth, Maya Jane Coles, Plastikman and Detroit techno pioneers like Jeff Mills, Carl Craig and Derrick May.

Over a decade or so, T in the Park disproved a few previously held conventional wisdoms about festivals in Scotland: that there was not a sufficiently large market in the country itself, that artists and audiences were reluctant to travel north to colder climates (or stay at home) at a time when low-cost air travel was making cheaper Mediterranean festivals increasingly accessible.

As Stuart Clumpas, the founder of DF Concerts and T in the Park told Radio 1's *The Rise and Fall of T in the Park* podcast:

> All the Europeans had started doing festivals and we started to visit them. All these promoters had their own festival that was their big flagship and I thought I could do this in Scotland. It was a little bit of people telling me "You can't do a festival in Scotland because of the weather", and I was like, "You think you can't? I'll show you".[4]

T in the Park – along with several other festivals of various sizes in Scotland[5]– proved that Scotland was increasingly receptive to and suited for not only large-scale pop and rock festivals but also a growing number of more specialist and genre specific ones.

By the time Riverside joined that market in 2013, the festival market more generally and in Scotland and Glasgow more specifically was in good health despite the slowdown caused by the crash of the global financial markets in 2008 and some specific issues related to the UK's hosting of the Olympics in 2012.[6]

Indeed, UK Music reported that "box office takings for live music events in the UK grew by 26% during 2013 to over £1.2bn" (2014: 22), with festivals being a major driver of this, and even claimed that "the pick-up in live music attendance last year might be regarded as a bellwether for general economic activity and consumer activity" (ibid: 1).

In Scotland, that year's *The List Guide to Scotland's Festivals* listed 125 music (or predominantly music) festivals taking place around the country from T in the Park down in scale to festivals on the Isles of Tiree and Gigha, and including genre specific festivals covering Americana, folk, jazz, dub, blues, and Pipe Band music.[7]

But Riverside Festival had a particularly local context as well in the shape of the development and regeneration of the areas along the River Clyde that had previously been occupied by shipbuilding, docks, and other industrial sites. This had been an ongoing process since the 1980s, with developments subsequently moving further west and two landmark buildings opening: The Riverside Museum in 2011[8] and the Hydro in 2013.[9]

It is here that Clarke and McKechnie pick up the story of the festival's origins, subsequent challenges and prospects.

Backstory and Origins

Dave Clarke

Slam had been running Pressure, a club night at the Arches,[10] for years. And Mark was involved in a daytime street party, which ended up in the street outside SWG3,[11] called Electric Frog.

Mark McKechnie

When Mutley[12] was starting to put SWG3 together, we'd have various parties down on Eastvale Street, outside the venue.

Dave Clarke

And probably about twelve or thirteen years ago, Pressure got involved in a stage at one of these, and then a day, and then we were pretty much co-promoting Electric Frog together. But then it just became too popular, but then also too noisy for the residents close to SWG3.

Mark McKechnie

Around same time, The Riverside Museum was opening, and the museum was in the middle of nowhere. And they were thinking about how do you reach kind of like an eighteen to thirty-year-old kind of audience? So, they asked us to go down initially and have a look at the space and see what we thought. And I was like, wow, we could do something cool here. And a lot of the things that were against them, like the location and the relative difficulty of getting there, were ideal for a party.

Dave Clarke

They must have had something in mind when they built the place because the space outside the museum is called Events Square, but I don't know if they were [thinking] of electronic music and clubbers coming down for an event.

Mark McKechnie

It just seemed that there was a really good story as to why it would be down there. You've got the Govan Dockyards and that was what Glasgow was built around, and then you've got this futuristic building which is in the absolute arse-end of nowhere with nothing around it, and that's basically just Glasgow.

Dave Clarke

Glasgow Life,[13] the people that run the space, we found them good to deal with and they were very supportive and helped make it happen. Previously, we had done different things in different Council venues, but it was always "you can't do that, or you can't do this". Or you need to pay this person to be there all night, and you need to pay for crew, but they can't pick anything up. And it just becomes impossible to finance, you know. Whereas there it was kind of a blank page so long as we did everything by the rules of events, things like no flyposting, health and safety certificates, insurance, neighbour notification, and all those things. You know, being part of the local community rather than being a problem to it, and as Mark said, yeah, they liked the idea of something for younger people to get involved in.

Mark McKechnie

For the museum, the festival would get people to go down and see where it is and what's going on around it. And then maybe they'll be more likely to take their friends and kids along to it during the day, some other time. They know what it is, where it is and how to get there. So, for them, we were opening that door for them. For us, we got an outstanding space to work with.

The First Year (2013)

The first iteration of the Riverside Festival – with a line-up that included Jamie XX, Josh Wink, Nina Kraviz and Underground Resistance as well as locals Optimo, Slam and Auntie Flo – was an artistic and programming success but beset by unforeseen logistic problems.

Mark McKechnie

A lot of things could have gone wrong, and some did.

Dave Clarke

I think in a way it we just saw it as something scaled up from what we'd done together in the street party outside SWG3. It was at least double the scale but in the first year we just did one day and yes, it was scary but manageable. I think it was more a case of learning how to do things the hard way. We had some problems with the bars and the site had some issues, but it was a learning curve.

Mark McKechnie

It's like anything new, I think when you take on something to begin with you don't realise how big it is until you until you get into it, and every year as we have grown, we have learnt something from it. Over the past six or seven years, there have been tweaks but the first year was the biggest learning curve.

The other thing is that when we started doing it there was no competition really for our type of event. So, it was easier to book DJs then than it is now and especially when you explained to them what it is and it's just new and everything, everybody kind of wanted to play at it.

Dave Clarke

Jamie XX was there, but his career was just beginning then. Though The XX were a big band, his solo career was kind of in its early days. But then on the old school side of things Underground Resistance coming over was a big thing. I think they were in Europe for the weekend from Detroit, so our timing was good.

Mark McKechnie

Really from the off we found that people – both the artists and audiences – really wanted to go to it, that was a big thing in our favour.

Dave Clarke

An accessible, easy to get to venue in the middle of Glasgow was a huge thing as well. Although it seemed a little bit out of the way, it isn't really, particularly with the transport hub at Partick, and being able to walk over to SWG3 afterwards.

Mark McKechnie

We sold out the first year.

Dave Clarke

In terms of tickets, it was a step up from about 1500–1600 to maybe about double that.

Mark McKechnie

It was 3500 capacity the first year, but the marketing was good, and it sold out in advance.

Dave Clarke

Because of the issues with the bar set-up and some of the infrastructure problems, it meant that instead of automatically going on to a bigger thing in year two, we had to fight a lot of negative publicity, just because we trusted the wrong person to get the bars set up. There's nothing worse than a Glasgow crowd that wants a drink and cannot get one, especially if they've got some drinks tokens in their pocket. But we did what we could. That was probably our first experience of customer service issues, because for months after I was sending out cheques to refund drinks tokens that people had ended up with and weren't able to use.

Dave Clarke

The evolution has been good. The team we've got working with us now do the bars at Glastonbury, you know, they're kind of top notch.

Mark McKechnie

But, aside from that, the artists really enjoyed it.

Dave Clarke

And, I mean, the dancefloors were full, people loved it. That side of it, we had no complaints whatsoever. But if people are queuing for a toilet or having to go and pee against the museum because they can't get into the toilet, or they cannot find it because we haven't even signposted it properly…

Mark McKechnie

There was a lot went wrong in the first year.

Dave Clarke

But Mark's now got a keen eye on where the toilets should go and how they should be signposted! I would say if we got to the end of an event, and no one's had to queue for either the toilet or the bar, that's of paramount importance.

Mark McKechnie

To give an idea of the first year, I think the marketing, the imagery, and everything was done very well. People were waiting for this event to happen, but the execution of it was poor. And so, in years to come, it was pulling things back from that angle.

Dave Clarke

But we were determined to go on. I guess our focus had been on the talent onstage, the vibe on the dance floor and how good the sound was, and stuff like that. But then you realise you must treat every aspect with that same care.

Years of Plenty (2014–2019)

In 2014, the festival became a two-day event and increased in size, with two stages and, over this and the subsequent iterations, it diversified musically, making both the line-ups and audiences less homogeneous. Nevertheless, it was still beset by some problems unique to the licensing regulations in Glasgow.

Dave Clarke

We went to two days in 2014, didn't we?

Mark McKechnie

Two days, two stages.

Dave Clarke

And it made sense, because what we realised was that if you want to put the proper infrastructure in, it doesn't work over one day. So, you need to programme two days, economies of scale and all that. A lot of it's just the transport costs for dumping the stuff there and taking it away again. So, whether you use it once or twice, the cost doesn't change.

Mark McKechnie

When it is over a couple of days, then you need to programme with a view to not have one day that's really strong and the other day that's playing catch up, that isn't quite there. That was quite difficult to do. But the good thing about it is that me and Dave have probably got slightly different music tastes and it's always worked well we complement each other's choices in the programming and our different musical tastes.

There's a kind of science to programming: what you've got to do is complement the more household names with giving the audience something extra to enjoy but where they are willing to say, "I have not heard them, sounds interesting, I'll check them out".

It's very easy to put together a line up that's just like wallpaper, you know, it's just travelling from gig to gig to gig, festival to festival and there is very little differential between any of them. What we try to do is to have something, a couple of things in there that folk look at and say, 'what is that'? Or 'oh, I don't DIDN'T expect to see them there'. Something that's a little bit different.

Dave Clarke

Festival line-ups can be very homogeneous, they just move from city to city, country to country over the summer these days.

Mark McKechnie

But even dating back to the early Electric Frog nights, and with Dave and his record label, there's always been a big focus on bringing through local talent. So that's always been a feature. And then, as well as the big ticket sellers that you've got to have in there, you start dropping in quite experimental stuff that's just coming through. When you get into that I suppose it's like making up a mixtape. Then you'll have something that hardly anybody's heard of but you know it's good. So, you add that into a festival and quite often it can be a big talking point. People are like "who was that? That was actually really good"!

Mark McKechnie

We've also been very aware of trying to make the festival much more diverse than it was at the start.

Dave Clarke

We have really genned up on it over the ten years – it was maybe something we didn't think about as much at the start.

Mark McKechnie

For one thing, there are now more and more female performers coming through. We always try and make sure that we've got a high percentage representation within the bill. You've got to look at it and take some form of responsibility for not having it just as a boys' club. Electronic music has been a boys' club for years. So last year (2022), we had a LGBTQ+ Day on which we worked with a promoter called Bonzai Bonner,[14] so you know that representation is a thing that we're keen to develop. I mean, Melting Pot and Pressure have always booked female DJs, but you never did it thinking about it as something that you needed to work on, you just programmed on the strength of the of the artist and it didn't really matter. But it is now something that we take responsibility for.

Dave Clarke

And I suppose that includes representing people from the trans community, the LGBTQ+ scene more widely, artists of colour both locally and touring. Just trying to have a broad outlook.

Mark McKechnie

There is also a lot of research points to the fact that people in the audience relate to the people that are performing at an event and if someone represents them, then they're more likely to turn up. And we've noticed, especially of late, the audience that we've been getting has changed slightly as well. I think we now get quite a mixed audience of all different kinds of walks of life.

Dave Clarke

And although there a lot more female artists now, for example, there might still be fewer female headliners around each year – artists at that level – but last year (2022) two out of the three headliners were women (Charlotte de Witte and Róisin Murphy).

Brexit, COVID and Recession

By 2019, Riverside had established itself as a regular fixture on the Glasgow events / festival circuit, taking place during the May bank holiday weekend, growing in scale and reputation. As with other events across the country, this came to an abrupt halt in 2020 with the lockdowns resulting from the COVID pandemic. The event did happen later in (September) 2021, being one of the first large scale festivals to return after that year's COVID restrictions before returning to a more familiar part of the calendar at the start of June 2022.

Although it could be argued that COVID impacted Riverside slightly less than some other festivals,[15] the challenges in the period between 2019 and 2022 cannot be underestimated. As well as the lost revenue and momentum caused by the 2020 cancellation and the tentative return in 2021, 2022 showed the full impact of the UK's withdrawal from the European Union agreements on people and equipment movement and the first signs of the (not entirely unconnected) economic downturn with its knock-on effect on consumer spending.

Mark McKechnie

When the first lockdown happened in 2020, we originally, just thought, 'no problem', we will move it from May into September and that will be fine. But then the closer it got, it seemed like things were still not going to open up, so we just moved everything until the following May (2021). But then it became clear the following May that it wasn't going to happen either.

All the time it was going on we were having to move artists about and reassure customers. To begin with, it was a case of bear with us for six weeks, but all the time you are refunding folk, moving bands, changing line-ups. We ended up working really hard over that period, we definitely couldn't sit with our feet up saying, oh this is the first time we have had nothing to do in however many years.

We also investigated support from Creative Scotland and various schemes, but there just seems to be very little interest in what we were doing.

Dave Clarke

Since COVID, it also seems like everything is focused away from Glasgow and Edinburgh. You can't really get any support from Event Scotland if you're doing an event in Glasgow or Edinburgh. We'd been speaking to them during COVID, but because of our company structure – we'd become a new company a year or two before COVID – we didn't qualify for any support for Riverside during the lockdown.

Mark McKechnie

I think there's also, within grant bodies, absolute snobbery around what has got a cultural value and what doesn't. So, you know, in New York and Lisbon, in Berlin, youth movement music is seen as something to be supported, and that brings value into the city, but that doesn't quite resonate in Scotland.

Dave Clarke

It can be a bit confusing. One of our other companies, Slam Events, was supported during the lockdown as a culturally significant organisation to ensure that we would still be here when things opened again. I thought that would be a door that would remain open, but… I think the fact is that they just don't have any money, or enough to go round. I think they view us differently now, and are aware of us and accept us, but that's about it.

Mark McKechnie

2021 was interesting. From the artists and agents' point of view, it was fine. Everyone was in the same boat.

Dave Clarke

If anything, COVID temporarily galvanised the music industry from people trying to get one over on you.

Mark McKechnie

I've never had so many phone conversations with big booking agents and realised that we've all got to be together and work our way through this because it's the only way that we were going to have anything to do out the back of it. But we're back to square one again!

Dave Clarke

Yes, but it is also different. It is not just one thing… costs are going up everywhere, for a lot of reasons. Yeah, I mean, the biggest current change has been ticket buying habits and possibly even 50% of your tickets go in the last seven days. It makes it hard because suppliers are trying to get the money off you up front and you don't have any, any cash flow happening. And then your mental health suffers because you're like, staring down the barrel of a gun the day before. You might be happy the next day, but…

Mark McKechnie

That's how it has played out with audiences, but with the agents and artists, it was just 2021 where everything became fairer. Now I've noticed that with the sheer volume of events on the calendar artist development has become much less important. They are usually looking to make as much money as possible from the off. I think social media is part of this as well, maybe the lifespan of an artist is not quite what it was.

  Because we are now looking at 10 plus percent inflation, what we're finding is when we say, "this is what we offer", they are going "no, give me 20–25% more". Why? For us, most of it comes back to the increase in fuel prices and how that affects everything else. The other thing we've seen is the market in Scotland get saturated. There were two new festivals in 2022, Otherlands[16] and Connect,[17] and loads of rescheduled gigs. There were so many gigs coming up that audiences were stretched financially, and I don't know many promoters that were making any money. But the competition meant agents were able to say "well, we can offer it to them, if you don't want to pay it".

Dave Clarke

Brexit has also made doing business much harder. We're having to spend way more people hours on admin for every single artist we get in from Europe, we're having to apply for permits for them to come and work. It's costing us to do the admin, but we are not able to pass on the costs.

Mark McKechnie

I think with Brexit though the issues are masked by everything else. Obviously, movement is far more difficult, and costs have gone up – everyone knows that – but we've had a pandemic since Brexit, and the invasion of Ukraine. The fallout of that has masked the real problems, so you've not been able to directly say, right these are the problems caused by Brexit – there's always room for an excuse.

The Future

Despite the obvious problems facing the independent festival sector, both Clarke and McKechnie are committed to continuing Riverside, though they are acutely aware of both the opportunities and challenges awaiting them: further development close to the site,[18] the cost of living crisis, and trying to make the event more sustainable.

Mark McKechnie

We are always looking for opportunities. We're looking at going through a period of development and then we'll see where we are with it, but I don't think we've ever really mapped out a five or ten year plan, maybe five or ten days!

Dave Clarke

We've been saying all along we are freezing the prices for next year.

Mark McKechnie

I just don't know how we can pass on those costs at the moment as folk just have less money for going out or whatever.

Mark McKechnie

A lot of our audience comes from Scotland, and nobody really drives to the festival, as shown by the bar sales. So, our carbon footprint is probably a lot less than most festivals, but it's far from perfect. The artists' travel, the majority are travelling by aeroplane.

Dave Clarke

And the environmental solutions for a festival our size are crazily expensive. We've got a plastic free site; we don't do paper tickets or anything like that anymore. Our marketing is now almost exclusively digital, but we don't have any substitutes for things like diesel generators, all the power on the site is from fossil fuel. And cells are still too expensive.

Mark McKechnie

I think the desire is still there from us, the energy is still here to develop new ideas and, put on new things that improve the festival, but it all needs to be done with a view to people having less money. And I don't know if that's going to change anytime soon. We must look at everything from payment schemes where folk can pay up over a period of time and other ways of keeping our costs down.

Dave Clarke

Something changes every year, and I'm sure that will continue. One thing we might look at is extending the use of the site beyond the main weekend, leaving the infrastructure up for a week and having a different type of festival the week after that we can share our costs with.

But yeah, I think we'll have to continue to be creative and adapt to whatever happens next. It's what we've always done…

Notes

1 During 1990, clubs in Glasgow were allowed to stay open until 5am.
2 A 4000-capacity tent in Strathclyde Park, just outside Glasgow, which was co-promoted by Slam and Scottish promoter, Regular Music, featured Jon Da Silva, Derrick May, Alex Patterson and 808 State.
3 It was part of the festival for twenty years, from 1997 to 2016.
4 https://www.bbc.co.uk/sounds/play/m0018rxg
5 Examples of these include Gig on The Green, The Fleadh, Download Scotland (all held at Glasgow Green), The Wickerman festival (in Kirkubright), Rockness (on the banks of Loch Ness) and the Belladrum Tartan Heart festival (near Inverness).
6 Notably, Glastonbury, the UK's biggest festival, did not take place in 2012.
7 The *List Guide* included both outdoor and indoor festivals.
8 The Riverside Museum is a custom-built space designed by Dame Zaha Hadid to house Glasgow's (former) Museum of Transport.
9 The Hydro – currently the OVO Hydro and before that the SSE Hydro – is a 14,308-capacity arena that is part of the Scottish Event Campus. Since opening it has become one of the world's biggest arenas in terms of ticket sales and gross box office income.
10 The Arches, a theatre, venue and club space in Glasgow closed in 2015. Its full story and significance is told by Innes and Bratchpiece (2021).
11 SWG3 is a converted warehouse that regularly hosts club nights, exhibitions and gigs in the west of Glasgow close to the site of the Riverside Museum and festival.
12 AKA Andrew Fleming-Brown, SWG3 director.
13 Glasgow Life is an arms-length external organisation (ALEO) spun off from the local authority (Glasgow City Council) as Culture and Sport Glasgow in 2006.
14 Bonner is a DJ and promoter who has run the club night, Shoot Your Shot at venues around Glasgow including The Berkeley Suite, The Poetry Club and Stereo.
15 Many of these had to cancel in both 2020 and 2021.
16 An electronic music festival held at Scone Palace in Perthshire. Staged for the first time in 2022.
17 A festival, promoted by DF Concerts, at Ingliston Showgrounds in Edinburgh. It originally took place in Inverary in 2007 and 2008 before being revived in 2022.
18 A new footbridge across the Clyde is being built, offering better connectivity, along with proposals for new housing and a water park.

Bibliography

Innes, K and Bratchpiece, D. 2021. *Brickwork: A Biography of the Arches*. Bristol: Salamander Street.

The List. 2013. *The Guide to Scotland's Festivals*. Edinburgh: The List. Available at: https://issuu.com/creativescotland/docs/scotland_s_festivals_guide_2013

UK Music. 2014. *Measuring Music*. London: UK Music. Available at: https://www.ukmusic.org/wp-content/uploads/2020/09/UK_MUSIC_Measuring_Music_September_2014.pdf

7

Performing in Gaelic
A Conversation with Joy Dunlop

John Williamson

Interviewed by John Williamson, 10 November 2022

Introduction

In her work as a Gaelic singer, teacher and BBC presenter, Joy Dunlop has become a high-profile figure within Scotland at the point where the country's music, languages, education and media intersect.[1]

Her story is revealing in several ways. As a Gaelic learner, she is unusual within the world of Gaelic music, where most participants are native speakers. Her musical career, which has seen her release two solo albums and several collaborations, illustrates some of the challenges of working in a minority language.[2]

While English is the main language spoken in Scotland, Gaelic is one of its four official languages,[3] and though some Gaelic language acts have gone on to receive wider international recognition (for example, Runrig, Capercaillie and Julie Fowlis), this has been the very rare exception rather than the rule. That Dunlop has a thriving portfolio career is, then, partly a result of the robust nature of the institutions and organisations that have historically worked to promote and protect Scotland's minority languages and cultures as well as of policy interventions by various governments in broadcasting and languages in the last two decades.

In respect of the latter, there are three significant acts of Parliament. The Communications Act (2003) formed MG Alba, the organisation tasked with the delivery of Gaelic language media. The Gaelic channel, BBC Alba, was launched five years later.[4] The Gaelic Language Act (2005) set up another public body, Bòrd na Gàidhlig, which is charged with "the preservation of Gaelic as an official language which enjoys the same respect as English in Scotland".[5] It develops a National Gaelic Plan every five years in which cultural activities including music play a significant part.[6] Finally, the right of parents to request a Gaelic education was included in the Education (Scotland) Act (2016).

These are some of the contributing factors in a reignition of interest in the language and involve something of a sea change in activities involving Gaelic, attitudes towards it and perceptions surrounding it. At the start of the century, Matheson & Matheson claimed that "the indigenous languages of Scotland [referring to Gaelic and Scots] are in a precarious position faced with the massive presence of English. Both have become marginalised in Scottish life and in the Scottish school" (2000:211), a statement in marked contrast to the optimistic tone of

DOI: 10.4324/9781003247470-9

Malcolm MacLean some twenty years later.[7] MacLean notes that the effect of "the [new] focus on Gaelic…has been to shift perception away from conservation towards development" and the question to "how can we move away from this abnormal, dysfunctional relationship with Gaelic that existed for more than 250 years" (cited in Campsie 2020).

Joy Dunlop shares some of this optimism in this interview, pointing to the educational and musical opportunities provided by long-established Gaelic organisations like the Fèisean Movement[8] and the Royal National Mòd,[9] the financial support for Gaelic recordings from Creative Scotland, and media visibility from BBC Alba and Radio Nan Gaidheal as integral to establishing herself in the years both before and after she won the Gold Medal at the Royal National Mòd in 2010. However, in a wide-ranging discussion, she also acknowledges the ongoing challenges that come with working in a minority language during the long tail of a global pandemic and in the midst of a global recession.

Learning to Sing in Gaelic at School, the Mòd and the Fèis

How did you get into singing in Gaelic? It seems like quite an unusual pathway, given that you are not from a Gaelic speaking family?

I'm from Connel, which is a wee village just outside of Oban. I've always sung around the house, and I would have sung in church and at community events, but my parents don't speak Gaelic, so we had no Gaelic in the home. We did a lot of music in primary school. I came from a very, very small primary school, which only had two classrooms, but we had a peripatetic music teacher who came around and taught us a lot of very basic musical knowledge. And coming from Argyll, with its very strong Gaelic and Highland heritage, you grow up knowing that you have that language and culture around you.

But it was when the Royal National Mòd came to Oban in 1992 that I started singing in Gaelic. They were really encouraging everybody in the area, especially schoolchildren, to take part in the Mòd. In Connel, we had a woman called Mary Pollock, who was a Gaelic speaker from Isla originally. She had said that she'd be willing to do a choir with the school, so for us that was the whole school. We fluctuated a bit in numbers, but it was around about twenty-four in my whole school when I was there, it maybe went up to about thirty. We were the choir. And then, I think she said if anybody was interested in doing solos, that she would teach us solos. A group of us used to go to her house on a Monday night after school, and she taught us all phonetically. We got the music, and we got the words, but we didn't understand the Gaelic. We did it by ear. She taught us to pronounce the words, so we learnt to sing. We did it together with our small group of singers.

And then around the same time the Fèis Latharna, the local Fèis, started up, and obviously the Fèis movement is about giving workshops to youngsters, and I think there was a tie-in with the Mòd coming to Oban as well.

I did get opportunities to learn instruments, but at the time, like a lot of rural schools, you bought in instrumental services. We got fiddles. I played fiddle because there was a teacher that went round. And, randomly, we did trumpet. It was very much for whatever you bought in, whatever the school choose chose to buy in.

So, between that and the Fèis, I had opportunities to play instruments, but I'm basically a very lazy instrumentalist, I can play a lot of them quite badly.

But from that first Mòd, I really enjoyed taking part, and I continued. I really enjoyed singing, and this gave me an opportunity to sing in Gaelic, and every year for your age group there was always a song that was prescribed. You learnt that song for the competition, and we just learnt them from CDs. We didn't have people that were passing it down, in the same way as other areas did. We went to ceilidhs, and you'd sometimes pick up choruses from that but every year I got a song, and by osmosis I learnt it to the point I could perform it. But really the only song you knew was the one that you learnt that year and maybe ones you had done before.

Through secondary school, there was a small group of us as well that went to the Fèis and competed in the Mòd. We also had a folk group, which was basically everybody nearby that was interested. Me, one of my brothers and our friend in the next village had a group that continued all through school, which sometimes performed at events, or ceilidhs, or even local hotels.

It was quite organic in that way, but I was only really learning Gaelic by ear, or from a CD, or by reciting the words, singing the words to Mrs. Pollock.

Learning the Language

If the Mòd and the Fèis were providing the musical education in Gaelic, how did you learn the language more formally?
I didn't start learning Gaelic as a language until I went to secondary school, and at Oban High, you all did French, and then you got a choice between Gaelic and German.

At school, I was quite academic, so I did well because I worked hard and could learn stuff for an exam or whatever.

But never was I thinking of doing either music or Gaelic professionally, that was just not seen as an option. It just wasn't there, and particularly if you were academic in school, they would tell you that you should be a doctor or do law. I was going to do medicine because I liked helping people, not because I was scientifically minded.

The biggest change for me was when I went up to *Sabhal Mòr Ostaig*,[10] which is the Gaelic college on the Isle of Skye, instead of doing my sixth year in school. I had the results I needed to go to university, so I decided to go to Skye for a year to do a year learning Gaelic, an immersion year. I was 100% planning that I was going to leave and do medicine after a year, but I absolutely fell in love with the place, the language, the learning. It was the right place at the right time for me, and I didn't leave there, they kept persuading me to stay for another year until I reached honours level.

After my first year, I was functionally fluent in the language. So, at the end of four years, I was capable of working. I'm not saying I was perfect or anything, but I was more than capable of doing everything through Gaelic.

Working in Gaelic

And you then went on to work in a Gaelic development role?
Yes. At the end of my degree, I got a job as a Gaelic Language and Culture Development officer with An Comunn Gàidhealach.[11]

I was covering Argyll and Bute and I was on my own. I was twenty-one. I had no budget, no job description, no directions. It was literally just that you have been employed to work with, promote and develop Gaelic in the area. I learnt an awful lot, because I had to do everything myself, so if, for example, I wanted to run a class, I not only taught the class, but I advertised it. I organised it. I did all the publicity. I did, all the marketing and everything to do with that.

So, it was just like being dropped in it, and if I didn't reach out to anybody, nobody reached out to me. It was sink or swim, and that wouldn't happen now. I think that nowadays there's an awful lot of information, a lot more support, a lot more jobs, particularly on the Gaelic side.

A Musical Career

That showed that you could work in Gaelic with elements of music, but when did you start thinking about a musical career of your own?
Initially, I never saw music as something I could do professionally. I didn't do a music degree, and I think that was the first thing: in folk music, at that point, everyone had come through the Academy.[12] I wasn't an Academy person, so I think I thought "I can never do that professionally". My brother is a classical pianist, so I thought, "oh, he's the musical one", because I never saw myself in that way, as it being a job.

Working for An Comunn Gàidhealach was making me do a lot more performing but I also started going back to competing at the Mòd as an adult, and as part of that you can compete in different competitions like the gold medal series.[13] And once you win that you don't compete again. When I started going back to do that, I realised that I really liked it, and it was something that gave me more opportunities.

Suddenly, people were offering to pay me to do a gig, whereas before I was used to singing for nothing. The more of it I did, the more I thought I'd quite like to give this a wee go, start trying to get funding, work with more people, play more and different shows.

But I did things in an odd order compared to a lot of people. I released my first album before I won the medal at the Mòd, which was quite controversial.[14] There was a bit of 'who does she think she is'? And that was also around the time I left my job which nobody could understand. Why I would be leaving a full-time job? But I thought I could do this – I wanted to be doing what would give something to me. And that's very unlike how I was brought up, where you were the last person in the line.

I had to explain to my parents what being a freelancer and self-employed was – they were going round telling everyone I was unemployed! Something with Gaelic seemed wild at the time, but it was less about the business side and mainly seeing if I could do more gigs and professional performing.

Was that when you moved to Glasgow?
Yes, I moved to Glasgow and have been based there since. Much as I love Argyll, I never wanted to be based there. None of my friends were in Argyll, we all went to university, and none of us came home. But it wasn't a case of go to the city all the opportunities were there, it was more that all my friends were there.

Making Records in Gaelic

How did making records fit in with the live performances? Your first solo album came out around the same time as all this was happening in 2010?
Yes. It's a big job to produce an album and I don't think I realised that when I started. My first album was totally self-funded, as at that time Creative Scotland weren't funding first albums, because they wanted you to prove you had a track record.

And that was part of the reason why I stayed in a full job time job longer to save up money, so I could do that. I don't think I had a clue what I was doing. I picked songs that I liked. I tried to find some musicians that I liked and that I could work with. I did a lot with my brother. I found a recording studio because it was an engineer that I knew, and we put it together.

My friend, she's a harpist, had already put out her own album and she was great, telling me things like "you know you need a barcode, an ISRC code" and things like that. I didn't know any of this language, or the PRS or MCPS side of it, none of that.[15] I don't think I had any of that when I started, I don't think I understood it at all. It was very much feeling my way around. I hadn't really thought of a concept, I hadn't really thought of anything other than I wanted to do some recording, and these were the songs that I liked. It all came together in the end and, in some ways the first album can sometimes be the easiest, even though you're totally in the dark.

You don't really know what to expect but I'm still very happy with my first album. Don't get me wrong, you listen back, and you're like oh, there's always bits you'd change or do differently, but as a process it was very enjoyable, and if I'm honest, it was a lot more so than some of the others I've done, where the pressure can start to kick in a wee bit.

You want the next one to be as good but trying to get attention for a second album is way harder than for the first.

I was just so thrilled to be doing it and so thrilled to be doing any gigs. I'd saved up all my money to spend on all this. The second one you're very much like, ok, I must make some money out of this. But I did get funding towards the second album which helped, but then you're looking at measuring success, and that is terrifying when you start doing that.

So, I think my second album was a lot harder than my first.[16] I know everybody now talks about like the difficult second album, but I wasn't aware of that. Ignorance is bliss. And you become busier, you have other responsibilities and I realised quite quickly I had to pay a mortgage. So, I had to do a lot of teaching, and I had to do a lot of other things as well to support what I was doing.

How much of an advantage – or obstacle – did you find it was to be recording in Gaelic?
I was also very naïve about the Gaelic language side when it came to performing more widely. I'd grown up with Gaelic music. My mum bought a lot of Gaelic CDs, and we heard it at ceilidhs and, although I wasn't a speaker, I didn't realise there would be a big language barrier. I just thought people would listen if they liked it. But then you are trying to book festivals and they turn round and say, 'we don't do Gaelic'.

And I was really shocked at that. I don't think you would hear we don't do Spanish, or we don't do Galician. I hadn't realised that, and I wasn't ready for the vitriol that some people would have. It didn't matter how good you were or who you were, they were just against it, just not interested if it wasn't in English.

There is also a lot of internal politics as well, and I'm a learner coming from the mainland, which meant I wasn't authentic enough for some. But I was too trad for others, so I fell in the middle, and that's not something you can change, unless you create some sort of persona, and I can't do that. It's not me.

Overall, it can sometimes work for you and sometimes against. I have got work because I am a Gaelic singer, but I've also not got work because I'm a Gaelic singer.

Touring

Did having the records out help with touring or has that always been difficult?
I think it is difficult across all genres, but I think, and it's a controversial opinion, that trad musicians do quite well. There is support and funding out there. But it is still hard to make touring financially viable. You have two choices. You either take the financial burden and the organisational burden yourself, and you organise everything, and pay your musicians. Which is what I've done a lot of the time, and it is terrifying, because if for some reason people don't come out to the shows, you can be staring at bankruptcy.

That's hard not just financially, but also mentally, and you need to find the time to do all that. The other alternative is effectively trying to bribe people to give you a gig, and I hate that. That is absolutely my worst part. I can sell you somebody else but trying to sell me is the most cringeworthy thing I've ever done, unless you also make me talk about money as well, and that's even worse.

It is hard either way. And it is a small world. I think I think our market is saturated now too. There are a few people that do exceptionally well because they're very talented, and because they timed it right, or there was something just worked in their favour.

But we have too many performers, musicians, singers, considering the amount of money and the number of opportunities out there. The quality of traditional musicians now is mind blowing. Unfortunately, the number of jobs, gigs and festivals is not going up at the same rate. People have less money than they ever had, and the opportunities are harder to come by.

The Small Matter of a Global Pandemic

Is this mainly down to the aftermath of the pandemic?
I don't know if it is just that, but I notice since places started to reopen there was like a tsunami of people trying to rearrange the work that been put off, which means that less new work is being commissioned and new tours aren't getting organised. There are no free slots at venues and festivals, and it is going to take a few years before it even starts to come back to normal. It's a good thing that promoters are honouring the commitments that they made two, three years ago, but if you are now needing to find gigs this year, then good luck. There are none!

And maybe in the past you would go, "I'll organise my own tour, it'll be fine". But are you going to do that? I'm not. I'm not paying for accommodation, travel, venue hire, advertising, marketing and so on, because I don't know if people going to walk through that door. I think a lot of people are not returning to gigs. They're out of the habit, and they potentially have less money, so you can't guarantee that the same numbers will turn up as before.

And you didn't exactly luck out with the timing of your last album either?
I'd been saying for a while that I wanted to do something with my brother, Andrew. We've been performing together since primary school, so we're like right, we're going to organise to do this album.[17] We got it together; we got it all recorded. Our launch date was the day that Scotland went into full lockdown.[18]

Funnily enough, if you're in a global pandemic no one cares that we have a wonderful new album out, everybody had far too much other stuff to deal with. Looking back, you have to laugh about it, it's the only way. All our gigs were cancelled, and we wasted money on things like paying a publicist to try and get reviews. Unsurprisingly, we got hardly any reviews and nearly no airplay because nobody was thinking about that. And then, six months later, when things start coming back, nobody wants to know about an album that was released six months ago.

We couldn't even do stuff from the house like some other people because we live in two different cities. Andrew lives in Leeds, and I am in Glasgow. So, it wasn't like even you could try and do anything. And even then, it didn't seem right. There was that sort of screen fatigue everyone had after a while and doing things to encourage people to download or stream the record just felt like it was in really bad taste, like "I know the world is burning, but, hey, have you heard our new album?"

Support for Gaelic Music

You said earlier though that you are a positive person and that you think traditional musicians in Scotland do quite well. Could you explain that a bit more based on your experience of the different organisations that support Gaelic and Gaelic music in Scotland?
I think there's a lot of organisations out there that help in different ways. Creative Scotland, for giving you funding and make it possible for you to realise projects, is so important. I genuinely feel that in that sense we're very lucky compared to what even a few other genres must go through and even compared to the English Arts Council and how their situation is. I do think that we do very well.

As I said, the Mòd was a huge deal for me, because anybody can take part in the Mòd. It doesn't matter who you are, whether you have got Gaelic, whether you come from the right family or whether you have had the right education. It is free for everyone to take part. I think now there is a small charge to participate, but that's it. And, as somebody who was an outsider to the Gaelic sphere, that was my way in. It gave me a focus every year. It provided me with repertoire and an insight to the culture. It was probably the most important one to me.

The Fèis movement was also very important, and I was lucky enough that my parents could pay for us, but they're now doing an awful lot to support those who are facing financial problems. But it was four children in our family, and if you are saying to parents, "you've got to pay for lessons for four people", it's a lot, and we were lucky to get that opportunity. They do a power of work throughout Scotland and the work they're doing is amazing. I can't praise them enough.

Having visibility is important when it comes to anything, be it language, culture or whatever, and that's what Hands up for Trad do so well.[19] They get traditional music and culture out there. When they have an idea, they're attitude is very much 'we'll make this happen'. Things like the Trad Awards[20] give a place, a respect to traditional music by saying, 'here's an award you can win'.

And, obviously, you work across the media, what role does it play for Gaelic language artists?
People also know that they can turn on BBC Alba or listen to Radio Nan Gaidheal, or even Travelling Folk on Radio Scotland and they can hear Scottish traditional music. You can hear Gaelic singing, and the Radio Scotland Young Traditional Musician of the Year award is very important because it gives a platform for these youngsters, and yes, only one person can win, but that's a competition. It's not about that necessarily, if you're in the final or the semi-finals even you're meeting eleven other people, you get a chance to work with accompanists, you're getting a chance to perform on television, on the radio, go on tour and so on.

I'm very much a fan of the more is more approach when it comes to getting music out there, getting Gaelic out there, supporting Scots, supporting all your indigenous languages and culture, so that it doesn't feel like It's something for the Highlands. Or that it's something for the islands. It's a thriving community, something that anybody can enjoy. You can be in Shetland. You can be in Aberdeen. You can be in the Borders just as well as you can be in Glasgow or Orkney or Stornoway or Benbecula, it's part and parcel of our language and our culture.

And I do think we're lucky, and it's maybe something we take for granted that we have BBC Alba. I remember things before BBC Alba and the opportunities that are involved with BBC Alba are huge.

We can always have more. We always want more money. We always want more opportunities. And if you compare Scotland to say Wales, who are so strong for the language and so strong for the culture, yeah, absolutely we can do more.

But the organisations are there, the courses now as well. You can go and do a full degree in Scottish music from a variety of institutions. There wasn't the case when I was going to university. I would love to have had the opportunity to do a course on Skye, for example, where I could do my Gaelic and my music, but that wasn't a possibility. At the time, everybody on the language course sang and everybody played an instrument, but we couldn't formally do it. We got no formal accreditation for that.

So, I think we are making huge steps in the all the right directions. But anything we can do to support all these organisations while not losing community support is vital.

That kind of community support – listening to singers, just people that get up and perform, going along to the accordion and fiddle society or performing at the local Mòd, things like that are so important, so good for youngsters to get your confidence up, to get your performing skills up.

My presenting skills came from ceilidhs, learning how to introduce a song, learning how to introduce other people, being comfortable talking and standing up there and doing all these things. I am inherently shy underneath it all, but I enjoy performing when I'm in a space that I feel comfortable with, and these community spaces give you that.

It has been all these opportunities all the way along that have given me the skills to do that. I just got so lucky. I think we can now see being a traditional musician, or being a Gaelic singer, as a career. For my mum and dad's generation that wouldn't have been conceivable.

There was Capercaillie and Runrig, these are the ones that you think of, but that wasn't a job opportunity. Whereas now, if you said, "I'm going to do music", it sounds quite pedestrian. There are loads of opportunities there, it's just accepted – and that's definitely progress.

Notes

1 As well as being a regular weather presenter on BBC Scotland, she has hosted The BBC Scotland Young Traditional Musician of the Year and a number of music programmes on the BBC's Gaelic channel, BBC Alba.
2 According to the 2011 census, there are just 57 375 Gaelic speakers in Scotland, the highest proportion of which are in the Western Isles.
3 These being English, Gaelic, Scots and British Sign Language.
4 MG Alba is also responsible for Film G and Learn Gaelic.
5 https://www.gaidhlig.scot/en/gaelic-language-plans/gaelic-language-scotland-act-2005/
6 Public bodies in Scotland also produce their own Gaelic language plans.
7 MacLean was former chair of UNESCO Scotland and past chief executive of Pròiseact Nan Ealan, the national Gaelic arts agency.
8 Fèisean Nan Gaidheal, the organisation that develops community-based Gaelic arts tuition / festivals around Scotland.
9 The Royal National Mòd (previously/often known as The Mòd) is a festival of Scottish Gaelic literature, music and culture that has been held annually since 1891. As well as the main event, which is in a different location each year, there are several local mòds around the country.
10 The National Centre for Gaelic Language and Culture: https://www.smo.uhi.ac.uk/?lang=en
11 The organisation that runs the Royal National Mòd. https://www.ancomunn.co.uk/
12 The Royal Academy of Music and Drama in Glasgow, which in 2011 changed its name to the Royal Conservatoire of Scotland.
13 Dunlop won the Gold Medal at the Royal National Mòd in 2010 and has won a number of awards at the Pan Celtic Festival and Scots New Music Award (https://www.joydunlop.com/joy/).
14 Dùsgadh was released earlier in 2010.
15 PRS is the UK's Performing Right Society. MCPS is the UK's Mechanical Copyright Protection Society.
16 Faileasan was released in 2013.
17 The album, Dithis, by Joy & Andrew was released on 20th March 2020.
18 Schools, cafes and pubs were told to close on 20th March 2020, the 'stay at home' order was issued the following Monday.
19 Organisation set up in 2002 to promote Scottish Traditional music – https://projects.handsupfortrad.scot/handsupfortrad/about-us/
20 MG Alba Scots Trad Music Awards is organised by Hands Up for Trad.

Bibliography

Campsie, A. (2020). 'Number of Gaelic Learners Outstrips Entire Population of Highlands and Islands', *The Scotsman*, 13 April. Available at: https://www.scotsman.com/heritage-and-retro/heritage/number-gaelic-learners-outstrips-entire-population-highlands-and-islands-2537435

Matheson, C. and Matheson, D. (2000). 'Languages of Scotland: Culture and the Classroom', *Comparative Education*, 36(2), 211–221.

PART II

Politics and Policies

Martin Cloonan

In David McCrone's famous formulation, Scotland is a stateless nation (McCrone 1992). Constitutionally it is a devolved part of a bigger entity – the United Kingdom. Recognising these two simple facts takes us a fair way down the road of the journey in understanding Scottish music politics and policies.

For our purposes we can see politics as related to power – the possession of it, the pursuit of it and the daily struggles around it. The politics of Scottish popular music can therefore be seen in its local power struggles. It can be discerned in the local intrigues of its scenes. In many ways the story here is not dissimilar to those in other small countries. Local musical artists, entrepreneurs and audiences interact with one another and with local and international products and meet in venues owned both locally and internationally and sometimes by a mixture of local and international capital. Scotland's local scenes contain the same power struggles as elsewhere. But they also take place within the bigger power struggles of the UK and its music industries.

Another important aspect of the politics of Scottish music is thus that power over key parts of it lie beyond the country's borders, being located in what is often colloquially known (in derogatory terms) as "Westminster". Under the UK's devolved arrangements the country's administrations in Northern Ireland, Scotland and Wales have been granted some powers while others – over defence, immigration, social security and foreign affairs, for example – are "reserved" to the UK Parliament and its executive, the UK Government. The full extent of such reserved powers varies across the three devolved areas, with the Scottish *Parliament* having more powers than the Welsh and Northern Irish *Assemblies* (the nomenclature is important). In the case of music, the powers of the Scottish Parliament include cultural and (most) economic policies, as well as the power (thus far unused) to vary income tax rates from those of the rest of the UK. But they do not include power over broadcasting, copyright or employment legislation – all matters vitally important for music. The regulation of live music in the UK has long been focussed on the local administration of central government policies but while such regulation remains for the most part resolutely local, some issues even in this sector, such as the ownership and the competition (or lack of it) between major promotion and venue-owning companies, are reserved to Westminster. It is not possible for the statutory Competition and Markets Authority, for example, to conduct an enquiry into the Scottish live music market; its remit is to regulate only UK-wide competition. As this example makes plain, the politics of Scottish music is therefore local, national and supranational.

It should be noted too that the agencies that collect royalties from the use of songs and recordings – PRS for Music (songwriters) and Phonographic Performance Limited (PPL); performers and recording rights holders – are also UK based, while the music industries' collective representative body, UK Music, concentrates its lobbying on Westminster. While there is a representative trade body in Scotland, the Scottish Music Industry Association (SMIA), its lobbying is understandably focussed on the more limited remit of the Scottish Parliament. More significantly, unlike UK Music, which is funded by UK-wide music industries organisations (and the UK-wide and global music companies which they represent), the SMIA relies on the support of public funds to supplement the limited income it gets from membership fees. At present it is therefore almost totally reliant on the grant it gets from Creative Scotland. Thus while the music industries at a UK level lobby as private/commercial interests, Scottish music industry lobbying is reliant on public money – and its lobbying activities are often for the receipt of more public money!

If politics can be seen as being about power, then policies can be conceived as the outcome of power struggles, as the implementation of ideas that have been variously campaigned for, argued about, implemented and accepted or resisted in various ways. In the Scottish case the policies that emerge are applied at various levels, both within Scotland and to Scotland within the over-arching political entity.

Even within Scotland one must distinguish between national and local policy areas. At the national level policy is determined by the Scottish Parliament. It allocates funding to two key bodies for popular music – Creative Scotland and Scottish Enterprise. Creative Scotland is the successor body to the Scottish Arts Council and funds artistic projects of various sorts, including the recording funds that have been so important for many Scottish acts. It also regularly reviews the state of Scottish music and assigns supportive funds accordingly. Scottish Enterprise (and the regional Highlands and Islands Enterprise) is the public economic development agency and has provided funds for artists who are operating as businesses as well as one off funding for events such as the MTV Music Awards in Edinburgh in 2003.

Scotland's local authorities have also provided support for music, over the years making a significant contribution, for example, to music education. As elsewhere in the UK, in recent years the general trend has been for local authorities to move away from supporting cultural activities in and for themselves to concentrating investment on those activities which also – and sometimes predominantly – have an economic impact. At the forefront of this policy direction has been Glasgow, which in 2007 set up Glasgow Life as an arms-length organisation to coordinate cultural activities across the city after two decades of investment in a number of high-capacity venues such as the Scottish Exhibition and Conference Centre (SECC, now the SEC Centre), the Glasgow Royal Concert Hall and the SSE Hydro.

In this section, then, we explore the politics and policies of Scottish music in a variety of contexts. We begin with Emil Thompson's discussion of rural music scenes, using the example of DD8 and the Bon Scott connection of the village of Kirriemuir in Angus. This is followed by a conversation with Jill Rodger, who has worked at the Glasgow International jazz Festival since 1990 and been its director since 2005. In a discussion of the institutionalisation of jazz in Scotland the issue of jazz education is raised – with reference to creation of the National Youth Jazz Orchestra of Scotland, for example, and in the next essay Sean McLoughlin and Graeme Smillie offer more general reflections on popular music education in Scotland, examining its range, history and controversies.

The question of national identity is addressed by Martin Cloonan, who explores Scottishness in (and beyond) the country's popular music in the context of broader debates around nationality and identity in an age of increasing migration, and by Dave Hook, who examines the place of hip hop in Scotland through his own practice as rapper Stanley Odd/Solareye. Finally, Adam Behr considers the place of music and the role of musicians in the campaigns for devolution and independence.

Overall these chapters explore a range of issues both born out of and impacting upon Scottish music. What is recurringly clear is that while, as a region of the UK, Scotland is integral to the Anglo-US dominance of popular music, as a nation it is peripheral and therefore has its own political story to tell.

Reference

McCrone, D. 1992. *Understanding Scotland: The Sociology of a Stateless Nation*. London: Routledge.

8

"Let There Be Rock" – How a Remote Scottish Village Reinvented Its Musical Heritage

Emil Thompson

Introduction

Academic research into rural music scenes and cultural micro-economies is currently an under-explored area. However, the study of geographically remote music networks and creative collectives can offer important insights into the mechanisms that aid social renewal and economic health in culturally underrepresented locations. In this chapter I aim to outline the functional trajectory of one such grassroots music collective based in rural north-east Scotland. It is an example that serves to illustrate how an initial seed idea driven by an immediately identifiable need, can, when given the chance, be grown into a well-established and culturally impactful resource, bringing beneficial economic and cultural opportunities to a region where such resources are scarce. This story also demonstrates how a small group of like-minded and determined individuals can leverage help from networks of associated actors from the local community and beyond to build and sustain a functional organisation that is ultimately greater than the sum of its parts. The story of DD8 Music and Bonfest is a case study that shows how creative collaborative processes that embrace a diverse range of mutually supportive individuals and skillsets can be harnessed through the vehicle of music. By drawing on existing, but underacknowledged cultural heritage, these grassroots organisations have successfully reframed their town's old-fashioned image within a contemporary context and subsequently had a measurable impact on the cultural and economic life of the community.

In recent years several studies have been instigated to address a perceived imbalance in what has been historically a metro-centric field of research. Lindsay Dunbar's *Forgotten Regions: Developing theatre through rural creative hubs* (2019), for example, looks at the importance of rural creative communities of practice. Dunbar notes that cultural policy has largely ignored rural areas, focusing instead upon urban regeneration facilitated by top-down civic arts strategies; she concludes that rural creative 'hubs' come in many different shades: serving to foster the growth of community networking spaces; acting as cultural ambassadors for local areas; and attracting outside interest that stimulates economic growth. Successful creative hubs can also help to stem the flow of young people out of remote locations and aid in the creation of culturally viable communities that attract incomers and fresh economic and cultural input (Dunbar 2019, p.5).

Another, closely related, study is currently being conducted by Dr Simon McKerrell into the importance of music in the creative rural economy of Scotland. The MuRCE Project (Music in the Rural Creative Economy) aims to engage with musical micro-enterprises in the Scottish

DOI: 10.4324/9781003247470-11

Highlands and Islands and to focus on how cultural policy can best support and nurture the activities of these enterprises.

Cultural policy research in recent decades has focused upon urban settings, both because of the growth of cities and the desire to conjoin the creative economy with urban regeneration. Micro-enterprises, despite being the most common business in the creative economy, rarely feature in research literature and the vast majority of the literature serves the urban, metropolitan creative economy (McKerrell, 2020).

The dearth of research carried out into the rural creative economy leads McKerell to call for contributions from a wide range of people with an interest in the rural creative economy of the Highlands and Islands of Scotland – musicians, promoters, festival and tour organisers, music teachers, instrument makers, policymakers, music publishers and stakeholders in the digital creative industries (McKerrell, 2020).

A different approach to 'remote' creative cultures is taken in a recent special edition of the academic journal, *Popular Music and Society*, which took a global perspective on rural music scenes. The contributors to *Researching Regional and Rural Music Scenes: Toward a Critical Understanding of an Under-Theorised Issue* (Bennett *et al.*, 2020) focus on the meaning of 'rural' and 'remote' in the digital age and consider how notions of remoteness can be dependent on factors like geographical scale and population density; what is remote in Scotland may not seem remote in Australia, for example. These studies demonstrate a growing awareness of the need to develop research into the functional elements at play in geographically isolated and rural creative economies and to define more precisely what is involved in the relationship between the rural and the regional.

The Story of DD8 Music and Bonfest

Kirriemuir is a small rural town of some 6000 inhabitants nestled in the foothills of the Angus glens and situated some 20 miles by road from the nearest city of Dundee. As a typical small post-industrial town, once dominated by weaving and farming industries, Kirriemuir has suffered in its more recent history from economic downturn and has seen increasing evidence of the social problems that result from this. From the early 1970s until the present time, the town has promoted itself to tourists as the 'Gateway to the Glens' and perhaps even more famously, as the birthplace of novelist and playwright J.M Barrie who in 1911 authored the globally revered *Peter Pan, or The Boy Who Wouldn't Grow Up*. A statue of Peter Pan currently stands in the town square and the childhood home of Barrie has been maintained as a tourist attraction by the National Trust for Scotland. Despite these attractions the town has suffered from economic isolation due, in part, to a lack of adequate signage from the main trunk road and an unsuitable local traffic system that prevents large tourist coaches from entering and parking in the town centre. Many potential visitors have therefore ended up visiting the nearby attraction of Glamis Castle and avoiding Kirriemuir altogether.

In more recent times though, the slightly staid image of Kirriemuir as a forgotten village stuck in the past has been challenged by another famous son. In 2004 some young local musicians found themselves desperate for places in which to play and rehearse. This difficult situation led them to visualise an opportunity to reinvigorate the town's musical heritage and to set in motion a series of events that would ultimately blow away the dusty image of Barrie's Kirriemuir, bringing the town once again to the attention of a contemporary global audience. The story of how DD8 Music reinvented the cultural significance of Kirriemuir involves two distinct but intertwining strands. The first was the inception of an officially constituted music collective by local guitarist Steve Gibbons and fellow musicians to support their bands' activities; the second was the simultaneous and completely serendipitous idea of two local music fans to put the town on the Scottish cultural heritage map for its connection with the Australian rock band AC/DC. These separate concerns were eventually fused together to the mutual benefit of both. The following study draws on personal interviews conducted during my four-year doctoral research project examining rural grassroots music collectives in Scotland. During this project I spoke with the progenitors of DD8 Music and many other key individuals who are cited below.

In 2004 a large disused primary school building became the subject of community interest; the building had been standing empty for some time and was beginning to fall into disrepair. A community consultation meeting was held where residents and councillors were invited to share ideas about possible future uses for the site. Around this time a group of young musicians from various local bands were also having discussions about the problems they were encountering trying to find rehearsal space and gig venues in the town. Many of the local halls were becoming excessively costly to hire for these impoverished young players, and other problems such as residential noise abatement and a lack of suitable venues willing to let them put on gigs were also seriously impinging upon their musical ambitions. In a proactive step driven by a growing frustration at the increasingly desperate situation, a small group of band members decided to attend the public meeting to discuss the future of the abandoned primary school. This single pivotal meeting proved to be the formative stage of what would later develop into DD8 Music – a highly effective and well-established music collective that would soon be bringing thousands of international rock fans to the town every year.

After Gibbons and his bandmates voiced their concerns at the community meeting, the young musicians became visible to the local council's Community Learning and Development (CLD) team, who approached the young musicians with the suggestion that the CLD could assist them in setting up a properly constituted group – this would significantly help to support their aims for obtaining accessible means to make music in the town. After an inaugural founding meeting in 2004 The Kirriemuir Band Association was officially formed. Several name changes later they finally settled on the snappier title DD8 Music, referring to the local Kirriemuir postcode. The group began to meet regularly to discuss how to move forward, explore possible funding strategies and to look at ways of facilitating new local music events.

As mentioned previously, the town had been well known on the tourist trail as the birthplace of the author and playwright J.M Barrie, creator of Peter Pan. What was less well known, and in fact almost totally overlooked, was that another of the town's sons had in some ways eclipsed the fame of Barrie yet was still completely unacknowledged in any of the official tourist information literature published by the local council. Ronald Belford "Bon" Scott was born in nearby Forfar in 1946 and crucially spent his childhood in Kirriemuir until the age of 6, when he and his family emigrated to Australia. Scott went on to front the globally acclaimed rock band AC/DC until his untimely death from alcohol poisoning in 1980.

In a local public house one evening, around the time of DD8 Music's formation in 2005, two rock fans, Dave Milne and Gordon Burke, were discussing the failure of the town council to acknowledge the legacy of Bon Scott and were wondering what they could do about it. They approached the newly formed DD8 Music with the idea of hosting a Bon Scott memorial concert: the concert would raise money towards the installation of a heritage plaque somewhere in the town. By 2006 both goals had been achieved, with a concert given by an AC/DC tribute band in the local town hall coinciding with the unveiling of a carved memorial paving stone in the town centre, displaying the opening bars of the song 'Let There Be Rock'. The memorial concert became an annual event (now known as Bonfest) and the activities of DD8 Music continued apace. The group began hosting local outdoors music events, such as Music in the Den, and weekly youth music sessions in the local community centre. Connections with the international

AC/DC fan club had also been formed and were raising awareness of Bonfest. Increasing numbers of rock fans began appeared at the annual event, many travelling from other parts of the UK and beyond. DD8 Music began to realise that they had some serious traction but would need to expand and find permanent premises, both as a base for operations and, additionally, to house their own bespoke rehearsal space and recording facilities (having outgrown the facilities offered by the CLD at the local council run community centre).

Luckily, Steve Gibbon's wife Victoria had become an employee of the local town council and, because of this connection, the local authorities were always kept up to date with the plans and activities of DD8 Music and were made aware of the group's intentions to find their own permanent premises.

> My wife Victoria ended up becoming a local town councillor's personal assistant at one point – which was another very useful link. It really helped us get the information to the people that could make a difference. A lot of it was about raising awareness, keeping people in the loop about what we were doing, and the council seeing that we were doing a good thing that was helpful for the town (S Gibbons 2017, personal communication, 30 March).

This connection, which demonstrates the crucial effectiveness of peripheral interactions within music scenes (Peterson and Bennett, 2004), eventually led to the group inheriting a vacant council building at a peppercorn rent in 2010. The community planning department's knowledge of possible funding streams helped DD8 Music to procure recording equipment and to pay for the refurbishment of the building they now inhabit. Although not involved musically, Victoria Gibbons was also instrumental in acquiring funding for the group – bringing her administrative talents to bear in this area, and eventually helping to locate an ex-local authority building as a hub for the collective's operations. The DD8 Music committee now includes local people who bring specific and vital skills to the table, including accounting, sound engineering, catering and design and marketing expertise. This effective involvement of non-musical partners, friends, family members and interested outsiders contributing to the success of DD8 Music clearly demonstrates the multi-faceted principles of cooperative working and delegation in an ever-widening network of creative engagement. Local traders have also fully embraced Bonfest by creating eye-catching AC/DC oriented window displays. The local music world that DD8 Music has created embodies what sociologist Howard Becker (2004) refers to, where unprecedented connections and skill sets combine to become integrative networks of collaboration that support the greater aims of the whole.

Realising the economic potential and cultural cache of the Bon Scott connection, in 2016 DD8 Music decided to commission from Ayrshire-based sculptor and AC/ DC fan, John McKenna, a life-size bronze statue of Bon Scott (to rival the existing monument to Peter Pan). Starting with a crowdfunding campaign supported by the local council and drawing on an enthusiastic network of ardent AC/DC fans around the world, DD8 Music succeeded in raising £55,000. Local surveys were then undertaken into the townsfolk's views on the statue's best location and later that year the permanently sited bronze was unveiled on the Bellie's Brae by former AC/DC bass player Mark Evans. The statue now attracts thousands of visitors per annum with passing fans making a pilgrimage to have their photograph taken next to it almost every day of the year. The presence of the statue has certainly helped the town economically, with many fans deciding to linger a while longer and investigate Kirriemuir a bit further, spending time and money in its shops and hostelries.

By 2007 DD8 Music had already achieved a significant amount in terms of realising their original ambitions, but they were about to move things onto an even higher level. Two years after DD8 Music's initial formation, Graham Galloway, a part-time gig promoter from Glasgow, was relocating with his family to the Dundee area due to his wife's new employment in the region. He was keen to get involved with a local music scene and entered the DD8 postcode into an online music search engine to see what might come up. His search returned both the Fence Collective of Fife's East Neuk region and DD8 Music in Kirriemuir. Ultimately it was the greater affordability of housing in Kirriemuir that determined his move to the town. Galloway enthusiastically joined the group and actively volunteered with them for several years until it became difficult to balance his family life and the need to earn a living against his increasingly demanding but still voluntary involvement with DD8 Music.

> To keep this place running was becoming more and more time consuming, I just couldn't do it on a voluntary basis and work at the same time. I was a stay-at-home dad, but I had to go back to work. The volunteers were doing a good job, but it was obvious that to reach full potential a paid post would be necessary. We applied in 2014 to the Young Start fund from the National Lottery and in 2015 the funding for this post started, but the real dream is to get the festivals and fundraisers to start paying for our salaries instead (G Galloway 2017, personal communication, 16 March).

By creating a full-time, paid position, the group could now push forward with its plans in a more effective way. Crucially, Galloway brought with him a new set of skills, ideas, and ambitions which shifted the dynamics within the organisation. His background in the Glasgow music scene and academic education in social sciences, together with his awareness of fundraising opportunities, helped to raise DD8 Music onto a new organisational level. Since assuming his position as chairman, Galloway has instigated Erasmus exchange programmes with young Estonian musicians, formed links with the local dementia group, set up a school's outreach project and entered DD8 Music into numerous national cultural competitions – its office walls are now bedecked with certificates and awards from various cultural bodies. As well as being a hub for the activities of local young musicians, DD8 Music have also become a conduit for the dissemination of funding opportunities, and the group's online webpage displays national opportunities for young people in the cultural sector, both voluntary and paid. The DD8 Music studios have also expanded into other media-related activities, offering short courses in photography, video editing and sound recording.

In 2016, given the year-on-year growth and popularity of Bonfest, DD8 Music decided to measure its economic impact. Here again Graham Galloway played a critical role by bringing his analytical expertise to the group.

> We survey attendees both during the event with face-to-face surveys and afterwards through an online survey monkey. This assesses their average daily spend, how far they've travelled and how long they stayed in the area for. These figures are then scaled up to the total attendance using an Event Impact Calculator, where the results are combined with our own figures for our direct spending within the local economy to get the overall direct economic impact (G Galloway 2017, personal communication, 16 March).

According to Galloway, the survey shows that the 2016 Bonfest attracted 3000 fans from 22 countries who spent almost half a million pounds over the three-day event (G Galloway 2017, personal communication, 16 March). The festival, which now has its own sub-committee and occupies a large site outside the town's perimeter, focuses upon a large marquee and main-stage area hosting headlining commercial acts and additionally provides a platform for the influx of regional traders and community groups, who set up stalls around the festival area. Artisan food companies and local micro-breweries are invited to populate the town's main car park, where a makeshift marketplace hosts a busker's stage for local musical talent with an AC/DC theme (this often means acoustic ensemble renditions of the band's classic hits). Every pub in Kirriemuir has a non-stop roster of local and regional performers, providing continuous live music for the entire duration of the three-day music festival.

DD8 Music, like so many small rural collectives, started life in a musical vacuum and was the result of a clear and present need for bands to be able to make music in what was then a restrictive and unsupportive environment. Its inception was entirely driven by the proactive efforts of a small group of enthusiastic local musicians, who knew each other through playing in one another's bands. The operations of DD8 Music aren't centred on the activities or popularity of a living music personality; rather, they draw on the intangible cultural heritage of an iconic persona, the late Bon Scott, who acts as a symbolic figurehead for the identity of the collective (and the town)- his statue is sited very close to the DD8 Music HQ. We can also see in this story how a critical mass of interested parties – musical, familial and from the local council services – collaborate and share resources, all of which helps to develop the stature of the group. An eclectic mix of enthusiastic and interested personalities has fed into DD8 Music's evolution, each bringing a unique skillset to the table and helping to foster the necessary 'collective effervescence' for it to successfully evolve (Crossley, 2015).

The arrival of Graham Galloway could be seen here as a crucial catalyst in the development of the DD8 Music story. He brought a vital new set of resources and 'know how' to the business of funding and networking. His background in television and gig promotion in Glasgow lent him the knowledge and tenacity needed to source and secure funds from many diverse sources, Galloway also brought an awareness of the bigger picture of Scotland's music industry and gave DD8 Music the confidence to apply for awards and seek recognition in a national cultural arena. Another factor which helped propel the group forward was the advent of online crowdfunding, a relatively new (at the time) means of funding specialist projects. The fact that DD8 Music were able to use this platform to commission and erect the Bon Scott bronze in the town car park facilitated major changes in the group's visibility.

Engagement with local authorities, although something often viewed as a necessary evil by DIY producers, is inevitable once the scope of a collective's activities begins to impact upon the wider community. Gaining permissions for events and having knowledge of legal procedures is of course an inescapable necessity for those who wish to stage public events. Local council policies involving risk assessments, Health and Safety regulations and noise abatement measures can present hurdles to the facilitation of DIY music activities, and indeed, there has been a historical tendency (especially visible in the 1970s punk scene) towards a healthy disregard for the demands of such legislations (Gosling, 2004 cited in Peterson and Bennett, 2004, p. 173). Fortunately for Bonfest and DD8 Music, the sympathetic and supportive views of local councillors like Iain Gaul (who was leader of Angus Council from 2012 to 2017) meant that many of these restrictive policies were waived. When I interviewed Gaul for my PhD thesis in 2018 he said he would also recommend the relaxing of licensing laws and the waiving of highways control fees during festivals and the provision of economic incentives during the early years of cultural projects, for example, cheaper rates on buildings and the offering of peppercorn rents to help small collectives afford premises.

Iain Gaul had been involved with the growth of DD8 Music since its earliest days but was very keen to stress his 'hands off' approach. He stressed that it was the key players like Steve Gibbons and Graham Galloway who drove the group's ascendency.

> Graham Galloway has spread it out because he's one of these guys who can sit for hours reading rules on how you apply for something, other people would go nuts, but Graham is able to

find out how to get funding and which hoops to jump through to get it. He will jump through the hoops and jump through the hoops until he gets what he needs, and that has expanded what they've been able to do because he has been able to get funding for them. They've expanded into so many things now, they've got craft groups, dementia groups, schools' outreach, the Erasmus exchange, photography, video classes and more (I Gaul 2018, personal communication, 16 May).

Gaul also suggested that council policy on funding and economic development has significantly changed over the last ten years. The old policy provided money from a centralised fund but it came with an attached set of caveats that had to be satisfied before it could be released. In the new policy model the local council is a funding enabler rather than a funding provider. It advises groups on how to apply for external funds or to set up of crowdfunding campaigns.

> [….] what we do now is help organisations to source their own money, for example, we help with crowdfunding, it's an ethos of – it's you that's doing it not us. For example, if you want to learn to ride a bicycle, we can show you where to get a bike and we can steady it until you learn to ride it, that sort of stuff – it's your bike and not the council's bike (I Gaul 2018, personal communication, 16 May).

For Gaul, councils should play a supportive but strictly non-invasive role in the activities of grassroots organisations; he repeatedly asserted that councils should expect nothing in return for their help, giving examples of how top-down council involvement had 'killed off' the activities of local youth arts and music initiatives. Groups should feel 'ownership' of their domain and not to be answerable for any conditional assistance granted. It is worth noting that Iain Gaul himself used his connections with local businesses and departments within the local council to source and provide cheaply (and sometimes for free) the resources that DD8 Music needed to become established. None of this assistance was attributed to the local council, not even the expensive refurbishment and sound proofing of their central hub premises, the former Kirriemuir Aviation Museum.

> In lots of other groups, you've got specialist interest, money from the council, you've got policies from the council, rules, regs and everything else but you've got nothing growing underneath because there's too much fertiliser being put on from the council on top and it just kills everything else. Just let them grow and let them come on by themselves (I Gaul 2018, personal communication, 16 May).

DD8 Music was obviously lucky to have made contact with a councillor with such a farsighted and non-invasive understanding of grassroots organisations, but Gaul himself is keen to point out that DD8 Music's success had far more to do with the group's networking activities and hardworking tenacity than with anything that the council may or may not have done to help them.

> It's like a root system. DD8 Music is like a mushroom with extensive roots spreading through Kirriemuir, that's what makes it successful, and I think it will be there for a long time. As for economic benefits, that's going to expand as well, you've got people going up there every day of the year taking selfies by the Bon Scott statue. And during the festival when the health and safety people come with clipboards, they are told to keep out of it because it's not a council event. If anything happens it can be reported in the normal way, just leave them alone to get on with it, and that is the message that's always been there (I Gaul 2018, personal communication, 16 May).

In summary, the success of Bonfest and DD8 Music's live events has hinged on several key factors. Firstly, the pro-active but 'light touch' approach of the local council, which gently supported DD8 Music with the provision of cheap repurposed premises and the waiving of restrictive bylaws and prohibitive access costs at music events. The council also pointed the way towards funding sources and involved itself in crowdfunding efforts alongside the group. Secondly, the arrival and enthusiastic involvement of Graham Galloway, who brought an entirely new outlook to the scope of what DD8 Music could achieve. Galloway's tireless efforts to procure funding, win national cultural awards and form links with community partners has transformed DD8's efficacy as a force for change in the town. Galloway also cleverly created a full-time paid position within the organisation, which meant that he could dedicate more time to the task of administering Bonfest and the other DD8 Music projects. Thirdly, the sustained efforts of a dedicated committee of volunteers and other connected friends and family members who have brought specialist skills and support to the everyday running of the DD8 Music hub and the annual organisation of Bonfest. There does seem to be a community-wide belief that DD8 Music is good for Kirriemuir and many local people are only too happy to lend a hand at events. This is an invaluable benefit that the collective has fostered over the years by demonstrating a consistently good-natured willingness to take positive action for the greater good of the community.

Conclusion

The story of DD8 Music and Bonfest illustrates how a small rural community can reinvent its identity by leveraging existing cultural heritage and reframing it in a contemporary context. In this story, many strands come together to turn an idea into a reality. Beginning with a group of young musicians looking for somewhere to play and two music fans fantasising about a rock superstar's unsung local links, DD8 Music successfully drew on the help of friends, families, the local council and a global network of AC/DC fans to build a world class music festival and to create opportunities for economic upturn and cultural enrichment in a geographically isolated community. Currently, almost twenty years after their initial meetings, DD8 Music are actively pushing forward with plans to create yet further cultural attractions for rock fans in Kirriemuir and from around the world, this time a 'museum of rock', situated in unused commercial buildings on the high street. The group show no signs of relaxing in their mission to celebrate contemporary rock music culture in the remote Scottish glens. As Bon Scott once proudly exclaimed, "Let There Be Rock!"

References

Becker, H., 2004. 'Jazz Places'. In A. Bennett and R. Peterson, eds., *Music Scenes: Local, Translocal, and Virtual*. Nashville: Vanderbilt University Press, pp.17–30.

Bennett, A., Green, B., Cashman, D. and Lewandowski, N., 2020. 'Researching Regional and Rural Music Scenes: Toward a Critical Understanding of an Under-Theorized Issue'. *Popular Music and Society*, 43(4), pp.367–377.

Crossley, N., 2015. *Networks of Sound, Style and Subversion: The Punk and Post-punk Worlds of Manchester, London, Liverpool and Sheffield, 1975–80*. Manchester: Manchester University Press.

Dunbar, L., 2019. *Forgotten Regions: Developing Theatre through Rural Creative Hubs*. Available at: <https://issuu.com/lindsaydunbar2/docs/forgotten_regions__developing_theat> [Accessed 9th March 2020].

McKerrell, S., 2020. *Music in the Rural Creative Economy Project*. Available at: <https://simonmckerrell.com/research/music-in-the-rural-creative-economy-project/> [Accessed 20 November 2020].

Peterson, R. and Bennett, A., 2004. *Music Scenes: Local, Translocal, and Virtual*. Nashville: Vanderbilt University Press.

9

Interview with Jill Rodger, Director, Glasgow Jazz Festival

Martin Cloonan

Jill Rodger has worked for the Glasgow Jazz Festival for over thirty years, primarily as its Director.[1] She has been a member of various boards and committees including the Scottish Jazz Federation, Scottish Music Industry Association and the Jazz Services National Touring Panel. She has been a judge for the Parliamentary Jazz Awards and the Scottish Album of the Year Award and a mentor on the Music+ scheme for fourteen to nineteen-year-olds.

Interviewed by Martin Cloonan on 24 February 2022.

Could you tell me how you got involved in the festival and describe the various roles you've had over the years?
I did a Business Studies degree back in the 80s and worked in the whisky trade for five and a half years and I was disillusioned with that.

I'd always run events at college or at school, always been interested in events and always attended music gigs from when I was fifteen at the Apollo,[2] coming into Glasgow and buying records. From the age of twelve onwards that was all I wanted to spend my money on. So I think it was a happy accident that a friend said that there was an admin job going at Glasgow Jazz Festival and I applied for it and got down to the final two and got it on the strength of my typing speed. An electric typewriter it was. This was 1989.

So I started as admin assistant in January 1990 which was obviously full on because it was the lead up to, it was the beginning of the City of Culture year. That was quite a festival for my first one: Miles Davis, BB King, Dizzy Gillespie. You name it. It was *huge*, absolutely huge.

In those days we didn't even have a computer, we didn't have a fax machine. It was all very old school. But I sort of loved it and it was really exciting.

I didn't know much about jazz. I had a copy of *Tutu* [1986 Miles Davis album]. That was the only thing really that I had. But I obviously knew the names. I knew that this was pretty big.

We were also working on the Frank Sinatra at Ibrox gig when I started. That was going to be part of the Jazz Festival but then there were various contractual and financial things that happened. We were working with [the promoters] Regular Music at the start but then they took over and the date changed. So I remember typing up the article for *The List* [magazine] for the Sinatra gig and going to it a few weeks after the first Jazz Festival that I worked on. So that was the fourth year of the festival, which was my first year. And then over the years staffing changed.

DOI: 10.4324/9781003247470-12

1990 was lots of private sector sponsorship. There was lots of money floating about the city at that point.

And then I became administrator and then in 1990.... I can't quite remember the dates now I became General Manager on an equal footing with Olive Millen who was Artistic Director. So we were running the company as such and she did all the artistic side.

After a few years Olive decided that it wasn't for her anymore and the Board asked me if I could programme because we were a bit tight for time before we had to announce it. And I said "That's not me. I'm behind the scenes. I'm definitely not programming. I don't know enough". They said "Could you just do this for one year" and, yeah, ever since!

So it was a steep learning curve I suppose. I mean I knew who played what, what roughly they would sell, what the audience would be for them. So I came at it from a business side of things rather than fabulously artistic. There's obviously got to be a bit of that as well, but it was hard finding that balance.

In the years you've been at the festival how has the role of the festival itself changed and what have been the important factors in those changes

I think sponsorship mainly. Obviously we've had varying amounts of large cash sponsorship over the years. Royal Bank [of Scotland] has been one, Glenmorangie whisky. I think in the early days spirits weren't allowed to advertise on television for a while, so there was quite a lot of cash sponsorship going around for things like... a sailing on the Waverley was [sponsored by] Black Bottle. Glenmorangie were title sponsors for three years. But then once TV advertising changed those rules and they were allowed to advertise and put their budget in to that again I think for us that cash definitely tailed off.

We got Royal Bank money, I mean like six figure sums for four years in a row, but it cost six figures to put on what they wanted. So, a big stage in George Square, Tony Bennett for a fiver in George Square. Really *huge* – but very expensive.

And that coincided with the Fruitmarket being closed for renovation [just] at the time we'd opened and discovered it (in 1993).[3] So it was seen as the home of the Jazz Festival although people don't really remember that, that we were the ones to open it.

So we sort of lost our main venue, we moved to the Square, most of the events were free. But when that money was pulled it was hard to then get people to start paying for tickets again, to build up your paying audience. So that was a real challenge over the years I think.

The festival has been everything from fourteen days to three and everything in between, just depending on funding and sponsorship. This year will be four days I think. We've been five days for the last few years but I think with the loss of funding... and obviously the last two years has been virtual only. So, hopefully, touch wood, we'll be back to an in-person festival.

What role do you think that the festival plays on the wider Scottish music community?

I think in the early years it was bringing people like Al Green, Tony Bennett, who now I would say a lot of the bigger promoters, who are promoting all year round, have maybe taken on that role. We've lost that. But we were the ones who were bringing them over first and then I think the bigger promoters were looking and thinking "Oh, that works. That sold out the Concert Hall for them". So then we couldn't compete in that marketplace anymore because we didn't have that year round stability of funding or anything to book artists early. And I think gradually we've just lost that ability to programme big names.

I mean when you look at who we *have* brought to the city over the years, in the first twenty years it's pretty incredible really. We just don't have that money anymore. The entire artists' fees budget this year is less than what it would cost, half of what it would cost, to bring *one* of these people in. So (laughs...).

But it's good, I see… there's a lot of … bands like Sons of Kemet[4] who sold out Òran Mór[5] last week. Everybody's raving about it now. But we put them on in the Rio Club six years ago, nobody knew them. And people will say "Oh, why don't you book them? Have you heard of them?". "Yeah we did and nobody came".

So there is quite a lot of that when I see all these new people raving about them. We got there early, but then we lost them to the bigger promoters. So I do feel there's a bit of that going on.

From what you say, it was bringing big names over but promoting local people as well?
Yeah. We've definitely become… Obviously with the virtual stuff for the last two years I wanted to get as much money out to the Scottish players as possible because obviously everybody was in a bit of a nightmare situation. So it tended to be Glasgow again. There were even restrictions about travelling from Edinburgh to Glasgow at one point when we were filming. So it was very much Glasgow-based players that we were filming for the virtual festivals.

It's obviously been a weird time for everyone. But we did something. We were one of the first festivals to go virtual and actually have something up there. I was really proud of the 2020 festival that we put on, to get there and do it. We had a mixture of films and DJ sets and everything just to get more of a festival-type flavour. And we tied in with Radio Scotland for the last night and did mix-tape-type things, history of the festival-type programme as well.

Fingers crossed for this June, we can actually have it.

I think that it's remarkable that you've survived over the last couple of years. The festival is now thirty-five years old. Will it be going in another thirty-five years?
I don't know. I don't know.

I hope so. I've definitely put most of my life into it, so it would be sad [if it ended]. And I do keep saying "Yeah, I'm gonna move on, I'm gonna move on" and then suddenly "Well, the funding application needs to be in then". Because it's a three-month decision process and then we get the funding. So it would be a hard task to pass it on to someone at the moment. But, yeah, I keep saying … (laughs).

The title of the book we're doing is called *Made in Scotland* and I wondered if you thought that the festival itself was kind of made in Scotland. In other words to what extent is it a particularly *Scottish* jazz festival?
I think it's become more so. As funding has been depleted it's been more of a homegrown-type event which I think is a great thing.

And obviously coinciding with the Jazz course at RCS[6] and the scene in Glasgow with the younger players becoming much much bigger. There's some amazing talent to choose from here now that is going to sell as well. I think that's changed over the years. I think when I started the Edinburgh scene was much bigger in jazz than the Glasgow one possibly. I got the feeling that that's shifted now and I think that's the RCS that definitely caused that to happen.

But there's some really great stuff happening. I feel I'm too old. I'm not going to go out and go to the clubs and everything every night. I'm way too old for that now. But I try and follow it on social media and find out what's happening.

It's hard to keep relevant. Obviously I've had other people helping me with that, with programming as well. Young people! (laughs)

I was wondering how much your perceptions of Scottish audiences has influenced your programming. How much do you think "Oh, they'll like this, they won't like that"?
That's a hard one.

People have such high expectations I think because of the history of us and because of hugely successful festivals like Celtic Connections, [7] it's sort of expected that we'll be the same. But we're not. We were before, we were bigger than them at one point. And it's great, their programming is brilliant and they're now programming, Donald's[8] programming, a lot of jazz and a lot of Scottish jazz as well which is brilliant.

I think, yeah, that's a hard one. I get a lot of satisfaction… I was just looking at the Love Supreme festival, just outside Brighton, down at Lewes[9]. They've got a great Scottish jazz programme this year. Ciro (Romano), their Director, is Scottish, he's from Glasgow. It's just the pride I feel, seeing the gang getting these gigs is just brilliant. They still call me "Jazz Mum" a lot of them!

But yeah, Georgia Cecile, [10] she's doing brilliant things. She got a gig as part of the London Jazz festival opening Jazz Voice concert. And just seeing her perform on BBC4 I was totally crying … [and] messaged her. We always have Georgia on. You know she played for us in Silverburn shopping centre just about three years ago and from there [to see] her at the Royal Albert Hall is just about …

And Fergus McCreadie[11] has got the only UK showcase at Jazz Ahead in Bremen[12] this year. So it's just so great. I'm just so proud of them all (laughs). You know I message them going "Oh it's brilliant you've got this". They're all really decent guys and they're working hard.

And sometimes… For instance programming this year's festival, the ones that are doing really well, it's great but it's hard to just replicate that and programme them all again and I've only so few slots [in which] to programme them. But then it feels strange not to programme them either.

Yes I was wondering how you keep all the Jazz Festival's different constituencies happy. The audiences and the musicians – how do you balance all that stuff?
I mean already this year there's a couple of umbrella gigs that we're looking at with one of the bigger promoters just to do with venue clashes. Because we only found out about our funding a couple of weeks ago we couldn't commit to booking any of the venues or paying any deposits. So we lost our first few nights. But they are Americana/Blues/Soul gigs so they've agreed that we can put them in the programme. But I already know that I'm going to get grief for that because obviously musicians who haven't got a gig, Scottish musicians who haven't got a gig, will say "Well why [have] they got a gig and I haven't? You've paid them". But we're not [paying them], it's all smoke and mirrors really. Not all of it, but some of it is.

Plus we are funded in a way to be an international festival. We've got international in our name so I have to spend some of that limited budget on bringing a couple of visiting acts. Because that's part of our remit, especially for Glasgow. We're not funded by them anymore, but that was always [our remit] bringing people to the city, it was always for the citizens of Greater Glasgow. 65% still, roughly, of [our audience] is Greater Glasgow based. We've never had a huge international audience. So if you're just programming Glasgow bands who are also playing other venues all year round it doesn't become so much of a festival.

You have to develop a bit of a thick skin too and to disappoint them and to let them down (laughs).

I was wondering how you _do_ keep that balance. Obviously the press expect bigger names and with all due respect to local artists… So how do you maintain that balance?
It's hard.

I used to always do my jazz wall in the office which if there was somebody I was thinking of booking I would print out a photo of them, stick it up on the wall and have it as a visual image of what the final programme would look like and [on] that wall the blu tack was all over the place.

Now we don't have the office any more as such. Because you know we've got a store and working from home it's not as easy to do it. I miss that and I think that worked, because I could see, especially as it was obvious from the photos the instrumentation of the lead player, you know, "God I've got ten drummers that night".

So I'm trying to do a virtual jazz wall (laughs)

Maybe there is some app you can get!
I think there should be – a Jazz Wall App!

You've already mentioned collaborators and sponsors and I wondered how you keep people like the City Council, Creative Scotland, the BBC, the venues, etc., happy?
Obviously now it's just Creative Scotland that are our funders, so that's going to be easier. As I said, with the Council it was very much about bringing international names in. We were set up by ostensibly the City Council back in 1986 and it was always sort of ownership almost. The Lord Provost was patron, we had two elected members who were sat on our board. We don't have that anymore.

This will be the first live event we've done without funding or input from Glasgow City Council. As I say, I'm still programming just now. I've just started really because I now know how much money and which venues we've got.

It's just getting that balance. It's getting the balance that you'll get the audience out. We've struggled over the years to [organize] selling something like the Counterflows festival, where you can get a weekend ticket.[13] People will say "Why don't you have a weekend ticket". But there's so many different styles that are having to fit in to the programme that when we've done it in the past we've sold about nine or ten and [it has not been worth] the actual administration it takes to set these things up with all the different venues and umbrella gigs that are in the programme and all that.

So keeping the trad jazz, early jazz, all the different styles… As I say the two Blues/American gigs that are on the first two nights I know are going to cause comments but yeah… (laughs) ultimately what's going to happen?

I'm sure your skin has got thicker over the years!
It certainly has. And sometimes it does still really affect me because I do get emails, I get really sometimes pretty nasty things. I've sort of come off social media quite a bit. I'm on it for the Jazz Festival and things but not personally anymore. It's hard. Sometimes if I was scrolling through Facebook of an evening and suddenly people know that you're on, there's all these pop ups "Can you give me a gig? Can you give me a gig? Can you give me a gig?". "Well, it's nine o'clock in the evening, I can't", you know?

Plus there was also… I suppose over the years if I *did* go a gig, I went to one gig over another one that was a local, Scottish, band there would be some sort of sniping a wee bit "Oh why did she go to that gig and not ours". I've been in bars before sometimes and just about to leave when the band's arrived and if it's a jazz band and I leave…. (laughs)

So as a result I've probably not gone to that much local stuff. Even like if I shared something on social media and didn't share another one … so I stopped all that as well. And I find that really hard as well because I want to support the younger ones as well. But I can't do it all.

And if I go to conferences, bands will get in touch, Scottish bands will get in touch and say "Could you introduce me to this festival Director because if you introduce me then that's like a kite mark almost". That's really hard to do one over the other because of the grief it brings and it's just really difficult (laughs).

I wondered how much your own taste in music influences your decisions about programming
Um, probably to a certain extent. There's a lot that I programme that's not my taste in music at all. But as I say I probably come to it from a business side of things, definitely more than maybe an artistic or a personal choice side of things.

As you know yourself there are so many different types of jazz that I don't think anybody could possibly love them all equally (laughs)

As I say my Jazz Wall gave me a sort of rough idea of how that would work for an audience.

It tended to be always that Edinburgh Jazz Festival was more the trad side of things and Glasgow slightly more contemporary jazz. That's blurred over the years as well with when they've had different programmers and things. But they're now a much, much, bigger event than we are. They're part of Edinburgh's festivals and the Expo fund[14] and all that and so we can't possibly compete. But we're clinging on (laughs).

You mentioned different types of jazz and I wondered whether you thought that there is such a thing as Scottish jazz?
There are threads of Scottish jazz coming through with players like Fergus McCreadie and Matt Carmichael,[15] there's that sort of Scottish folk element coming into their playing definitely. And I think that's great because that gives it something special, something different.

I think I've had this discussion as well with Ireland, to see if they had similar ideas about that sort of trad/folk element coming through traditional music rather than trad jazz. But we were speaking about going to Jazz Ahead in Bremen and having a Scottish presence there as well, that's something we've been discussing with Creative Scotland recently about all that.

Yeah I do think there are a few players that are bringing that element in, the younger ones.

How important is Glasgow, the city, as a location for the festival? The spaces that you use, etc.
I think the city… I mean I *love* Glasgow and I'm always going to love it.

The spaces are good. Possibly they'll always be a slight lack of a 200 capacity, cabaret style, place which is what we really need now. The Fruitmarket, as our budget has got smaller it's been harder and harder to fill. Although the last festival we did in 2019, the last in-person festival, was probably our best audience for a long, long, time. And like three sell outs in a row at the Fruitmarket over three nights. The ticker sales were incredible and we though "Yeah we're back. We'll build on this" and then the pandemic set in so…

There've always been nightmares with booking venues, City Council venues, in Glasgow. St Lukes[16] is fantastic for us but there were so many rescheduled gigs and weddings and things (obviously in June we're up against wedding season as well), so many rescheduled events that it's been a struggle to get a four-day run in a venue. We can get a date here and there but then moving the sound equipment and everything from one venue to the next the cost is … It's just not doable.

But yeah I think Glasgow and UNESCO City of Music[17] badge is great. I think it needs to be shouted about a bit more. It's maybe not been mentioned, well it has been mentioned but (needs) more funding behind that. I had a meeting recently with the UNESCO guys from Tallinn and they'd just been awarded UNESCO City of Music heritage status and they were all sort of enthusiastic and I sort of remember when we were like that. But (laughs…)

It's just like what does it really mean to anyone? And it's great. I see there's various initiatives going on for Glasgow Music City-type things and it's brilliant. Maybe too much choice so maybe the audiences are divided. And especially now, I hope people are starting to feel brave enough to go back into the live setting.

We may do a couple of gigs hybrid and onstreaming. But it's so expensive to do it and I mean last year we did the virtual festival. The first year we did it free and we got great figures and then last year we it was behind paywall and it was a real struggle to sell passes. Plus then there were different rights issues as well with PRS behind a paywall.[18] I wish we'd just gone free, with free access. But we didn't (laughs)

If you look back over the years, if the festival stopped tomorrow, what do you think the festival's legacy would be? What's been its main impact over the years?
I would like to hope that, maybe in tandem with some of the education work – and again that's been funding dependent – it has helped grow audiences. A lot of the education work that we have done over the past few years has been in primary schools. So maybe it sinks in somewhere that that was the event.

We've been quite good with our branding I think. We've spent a wee bit of money on that and it's been fairly attractive I would have hoped.

Yeah, I would like to hope that, maybe in tandem with the degree course at RCS and other music colleges as well, that we have helped keep that going and keep the scene going. But it's hard when you're only once a year as well.

With the virtual stuff we did do some year-round events. So we did Winter Wednesdays and Spring Sessions. Every Wednesday there was a half hour concert that we put on which gave the guys work. We went in for a couple of days, filmed it in a venue over two days, and put it out over six to eight weeks and then it disappeared. And so we got some great footage as well to do some more re-edits I think.

But obviously people were trying to make a living from filming things so the cost of these things went really high as well if you wanted decent quality and we don't have a huge amount of money to do it.

I hope we've got a legacy. I would like to think so. A lot of the players like Paul Towndrow and Laura MacDonald[19] are still talking about gigs they went to in the Glasgow Jazz Festivals back in the 90s when they were part of the [Jazz] Youth Orchestras … it was seeing those international players in Glasgow that made them want to continue. That was a brilliant influence on them and if we hadn't brought those people over their careers would be different because they could have decided to take another [career] route

I think that's really important, that you give musicians inspirations to keep going is really important.
Yes

What's been your favourite moment of the festival over the years? Do you have one stand out moment?
That's a tough one.

Obviously Tony Bennett in George Square for a fiver, that was pretty good.

And especially we had put him in a day room at the hotel on George Square. But the stage door was almost at the door of the hotel. But we needed to get a car, a limo, to get him from the hotel right round the Square to the stage door. But after the gig he said "Ah, I don't need the car. I'll just cross the road at the lights there". So I pressed the button waited for the green man, with Tony Bennett. You know it was waiting for the light to go to red so the green man came on and thought "this is surreal!"

There are, lots, lots of moments. Taking Jimmy Smith shopping for clothes because the airline had lost all his luggage. Yeah, there are a lot of stories that are my favourite moments, a lot of them musicians being really grumpy, swearing at me and things like that. They are no longer with us but you know.

I can't imagine who you mean!
I know. Some people say "You should write all these down" and I probably should.

I think you should – and do your book
Except I hate writing!

That's been great. Thank you.
No, thank you. Hope it's been all right.

Notes

1 For a history of the festival see Eales (2017).
2 For a history of the Glasgow Apollo see Forbes (2015) and Chapter 3.
3 A Glasgow venue capable of holding around 1500 people. See https://www.glasgowconcerthalls.com/old-fruitmarket/Pages/default.aspx
4 Sons of Kemet is a London-based jazz band formed in 2011. See https://en.wikipedia.org/wiki/Sons_of_Kemet
5 A Glasgow venue with various performance spaces. See https://oran-mor.co.uk/
6 The Royal Conservatoire of Scotland. For details of its jazz provision see https://www.rcs.ac.uk/courses/bmus-jazz/.
7 Scotland's biggest winter festival. See https://www.celticconnections.com/.
8 The Director of Celtic Connections, Donald Shaw, is a former member of the band Capercaillie. See https://en.wikipedia.org/wiki/Donald_Shaw_(musician)
9 https://lovesupremefestival.com/
10 For singer Georgia Cecile, who did the BA Hons Popular Music course at Napier University, see http://www.georgiacecile.com/
11 For pianist Fergus McCreadie, who graduated from the jazz programme at the RCS, see https://www.fergusmccreadie.co.uk/
12 https://jazzahead.de/en/
13 Counterflows is a well-established Glasgow-based contemporary/experimental music festival. See https://counterflows.com/
14 A Scottish government scheme to support the country's festivals. See https://www.gov.scot/news/support-for-scotlands-international-festivals/
15 Saxophonist Matt Carmichael is another graduate of the RCS jazz programme – see https://www.mattcarmichaelmusic.com/
16 A former church which is now a venue. See http://www.stlukesglasgow.com/
17 See https://www.glasgowlife.org.uk/glasgow-unesco-city-of-music/who-we-are
18 PRS for Music collects fees on behalf songwriters and composers whose music is used in public performances, generally based on a percentage of the ticket price.
19 Paul Towndrow and Laura Macdonald are Scottish saxophonists, composers and educators. For Towndrow see http://www.paultowndrow.co.uk/; for Macdonald see https://en.wikipedia.org/wiki/Laura_Macdonald.

Bibliography

Eales, A. 2017. *Bunting and blues: A critical history of Glasgow International Jazz Festival, 1987–2015*. Glasgow: University of Glasgow, unpublished PhD, https://theses.gla.ac.uk/8026/.
Forbes, K. 2015. *You had to be there? Reflections on the 'legendary' status of the Glasgow Apollo theatre (1973–85)*. Glasgow: University of Glasgow, unpublished PhD, https://theses.gla.ac.uk/6794/.

10

The Place of Popular Music Education in Scotland – Institutions, Access, and Responsibilities

Seán McLaughlin and Graeme Smillie

Introduction

This chapter outlines the place of Popular Music Education (PME) in Scotland by providing an overview of the educational landscape as it exists in the early 2020s. This overview takes place at what feels like a transitional point in Scottish music education. Large-scale reform of awarding bodies and instrumental tuition services, coupled with an existential uncertainty surrounding the arts' place in Further and Higher Education institutions, make this work all the more pertinent. In addition, the Music Education Partnership Group (MEPG, 2021) are in the process of devising and implementing a coherent national vision for music education in Scotland, and at this point, it is vital to have a frank and open discussion about PME's role in this moving forward. This discussion naturally touches on some of the more general problems associated with the institutionalisation of popular music in a Scottish context, but these problems are perhaps indicative of those facing popular music education on an international level. The essential questions for any study of this nature are: What does popular music currently look like in formal educational contexts? What could it be? And what should it be? Although we do not seek to provide definitive answers to any of these questions, this chapter focuses its analysis on two key areas as examples of necessary points of discussion – *instrumentalism* in pre-tertiary PME and *vocationalism* in Higher Education Institutions (HEIs). We focus on these case studies because of the tangible links between the issues. A focus on instrumentalism is often indicative of not only the dominance of Western European Art Music (WEAM) value systems, but also of neoliberal and outdated vocationalism in PME (see Bennett, 2017; Parkinson and Smith, 2015).

We begin by looking at the current structure of music education in Scotland, from compulsory primary schooling through to UG study. We suggest that the prevailing approaches to PME in formal pre-tertiary education are neither sufficiently inclusive nor adequately economically supported (see also Broad et al., 2019). While local authority instrumental services have improved access to formal music education since Williamson, Cloonan and Frith (2003) found provision to be lacking, the last two decades have seen enough variation in local authority instrumental tuition fees and priorities to create a two-tiered system (Improvement Service, 2020; Wilson, Hunter and Moscardini, 2020) – meaning those who have the means to pay for additional or private tuition are more likely to excel or continue into tertiary education (Broad et al., 2019). While extra-curricular widening access initiatives and non-formal interventions have worked to redress inequalities seen in formal music education, such undervalued and fragile schemes rarely connect with the expectations of HE institutions.

DOI: 10.4324/9781003247470-13

We then discuss Scottish tertiary PME, which has largely developed in colleges and other institutions that were granted university status following the Further and Higher Education Act (Scotland) 1992. These institutions include Edinburgh Napier University, The University of the Highlands and Islands, and The University of West Scotland. More recently, PME courses are also now offered by private FE and HE institutions. One of the consequences of practical PME being housed in these post-92 settings is that popular music degrees in Scotland tend to focus far more overtly on employability than music degrees in chartered and ancient universities, which are more likely to deliver courses centred on wider *Popular Music Studies* (PMS) (see Dylan Smith et al., 2017). In short, despite some sporadic efforts in traditional HE and the conservatoire sector, 'music education' in the established Scottish universities remains a semantically loaded term, effectively synonymous with the WEAM tradition (Cloonan and Hulstedt, 2012), thus limiting institutional choice for Scottish popular musicians (Reay, David and Ball, 2005).

Post-graduate programmes in popular music practice in Scotland are also notably scarce and are resultantly limited in the attention they receive here. The University of the West of Scotland's MA in Songwriting is the only notable focussed, practice-based example. Other PG programmes avoid this level of specificity and instead include popular music as a branch of musicology or music industries studies.

The Structure of Music Education in Scotland

Learners enter compulsory education between ages four and six and complete seven years of primary education. Between ages eleven and thirteen learners then begin six potential years of secondary education (S1–S6). Up until S4, all learning is delivered as part of a Broad General Education (BGE), then at age fifteen to sixteen, S4 students enter their Senior Phase, and work towards qualifications that are regulated by the Scottish Qualifications Authority (SQA).[1]

Scottish colleges most commonly teach SCQF Level 6 (NC/NQ), level 7 (HNC) and level 8 (HND) qualifications, which are also regulated by the SQA.[2] University programmes span three-years for an ordinary or bachelor's degree (SCQF Level 9), which are awarded outwith the SQA by HE institutions, while full Honours degrees (SCQF Level 10) require four years of study. Scottish postgraduate (PG) certificates, diplomas, and master's degrees are SCQF Level 11, while doctoral qualifications are Level 12.

Stepping in and out of this framework, we look first at pre-tertiary PME, including school and community based informal and non-formal delivery. The discussion then moves into tertiary PME, focusing on FE colleges delivering HNC and HND programmes before, finally, addressing HE institutions which offer UG and PG degrees.

The Place of PME in Schools

Most of the Scottish school system is state funded (Smith, 2018) and controlled by Scotland's thirty-two local authorities; since 2010 it has been delivering the Curriculum for Excellence (CfE) (see OECD, 2021). Many elements of popular music are firmly embedded in the formal music curriculum – there are well-established pathways towards SQA qualifications in music at National (SCQF 5), Higher (SCQF 6) and Advanced Higher (SCQF 7) levels. The curriculum, in theory, allows learners to engage with popular music practices by including relatively open stylistic compositional aims, analysis of music in its socio-cultural contexts and the use of Digital Audio Workstations (DAWs) in their module descriptors. Assessment matrices, however, remain rooted in WEAM terminology and values, and performance exams often simply replace canonised WEAM repertoire with its popular music counterparts. Pragmatism and teacher expertise means that classroom delivery of instrumental tuition in guitar, bass, drums, keyboards, and vocals remains the dominant way in which PME is delivered in Scottish schools. A socialised, autonomous, contextualised and interdisciplinary approach that would reflect how popular music *actually* works (Toynbee, 2000) is inconsistently found, and is frequently the result of particularly pro-active instrumental or teaching staff moving beyond the curriculum.

While using popular music repertoire and instrumentation as the focus of practical classes in schools can serve to widen access to SQA qualifications, Broad et al. (2019) found considerable teacher scepticism over the suitability of these qualifications in preparing students for tertiary study. Additionally, Wilson, Hunter and Moscardini (2020) found that middle-class parents were more likely to organise external activities or private music tuition while those from less-affluent areas relied entirely upon their schools for any form of music provision, contributing to a stratification of HE articulation (Broad et al., 2019).

Scotland's most effective institutional countermeasure to this inequality is provided by schools' Instrumental Music Services, which augment classroom provision with peripatetic instrumental specialists. However, pupil demand to learn popular music instruments drastically outweighs the supply of specialist popular music instrument teachers (Improvement Service, 2020, p24).

The Place of PME in Instrumental Services

Scotland's instrumental music services provided lessons to between 56,198 and 61,615 primary and secondary pupils per year between 2012/2013 and 2019/2020 (Improvement Service, 2021, p20).[3] These services were discretionary; fees, resources, approaches, and values, especially in relation to PME, varied according to the differing priorities of each of Scotland's thirty-two local authorities. The last decade has also seen a sustained period of increasing fees, funding cuts, and shrinking local authority workforces. While both the Scottish Government and the Convention of Scottish Local Authorities (COSLA) have committed to removing all instrumental tuition fees following a manifesto pledge in the 2021 Scottish Parliamentary elections (Scottish Government, 2021), it remains unclear if this will result in either the growth of pupil capacity or a more consistent delivery of instrumental lesson across Scotland. Among service providers there are fears that, with the removal of external income generation, "music service capacity and provision will have to be cut back and access to services will be reduced, rather than improved" (Improvement Service, 2021, p10).

Prior to this pledge, only six Scottish local authorities were able to provide lessons for all pupils who wanted them (Improvement Service, 2020, p24), and this was a particularly acute problem in PME. In one school survey, Wilson, Hunter and Moscardini (2020) found that guitar was the most attainable instrument for the majority of first year pupils, and that demand for instrumental lessons was around three to four times capacity (p482). In this case, extra-curricular rock clubs were established within the school, which in effect created a 'two-tier' system. Those who could afford instrumental tuition excelled in areas of instrumental specialism, while others, although participating authentically in non-formal music-making, were engaged in a practice unlikely to be recognised by any WEAM-informed HE institution.

Burnard and Bennett's (2016) recognition of multiple creativities suggests that a meta-literacy *across the 'continuum'* of formal instrumental study and non-formal/informal, student-led, and collaborative learning would be beneficial for both tiers (Vasil, Wiess and Powell, 2019, p92). This should be the approach taken towards PME on a national level but, as Wilson, Hunter and Moscardini (2020) reiterate, approaches to PME in schools are commonly informed more by pragmatism than educational philosophy: in guiding such large numbers towards SQA performance exams, the most pragmatic approach for educators is to revert to the simplicity provided by graded music syllabuses that have characterised WEAM. York (2021) has recently celebrated the use of the RockSchool (RSL) and Trinity Rock and Pop graded syllabuses in the UK, but while these courses have proven to be invaluable in introducing canonised popular music repertoire in formal educational contexts, such learning alone cannot be hailed as the successful inclusion of PME in Scottish education.

PME's Place beyond Formal Pathways

In addition to school provision, there are numerous opportunities for non-formal engagement with PME at the pre-tertiary stage, facilitated by industry partnerships and community music organisations. Since the implementation of the Scottish Government and Creative Scotland's Youth Music Initiative (YMI) in 2003, there has been a concerted drive to facilitate universal access to music education from a young age (Broad, Duffy and Price, 2003). Due to the targeted nature of funding, these programmes and interventions have increased in prevalence in lower ranking areas of the Scottish Index of Multiple Deprivation (SIMD). Unburdened by formal assessment and institutional conventions, YMI-funded programmes and other charitable or lottery funded community projects are able to widen participation and foreground authentic PME practices and pedagogies. These range from well-established participatory initiatives (SoundLab, New Rhythms for Glasgow, Tinderbox Orchestra, Gardyne YMI, Music Broth, Girls Rock Glasgow, Girls Rock School Edinburgh, Reeltime Music, Erskine Arts and Beatroute Arts to name but a few) to targeted programmes funded by government, public or research council money, such as Vox Liminis' numerous songwriting projects, Articulate Cultural Trust's 'Track' programme, or Wheatley Care's Ensemble project. Mentoring and links to the music industries are actively facilitated in many of these programmes (as recommended by Brennan et al., 2017), especially evident in the Scottish Music Centre's Musicplus+ programme for fourteen to nineteen year-olds.[4] The creation of the Scottish Music Industry Association (SMIA) in 2008 (Brennan and Behr, 2013) also increased access to Continuing Professional Development (CPD) opportunities and industry workshops with practitioners active in the field. However, increased SMIA engagement with the pre-tertiary stage would be welcomed.

It is perhaps here, outside of school settings, where PME's authentic practices are best reflected. Non-formal activities are frequently facilitated by practising artists (McBay, 2017) – thanks to the casual, flexible and mutually beneficial nature of employment (Smillie, 2011). However, as Broad et al. (2019) highlight, there are limited synergies between the non-formal sector and the transition into FE and HE institutions.

PME Transitions into FE/HE

A study by Moir and Stillie (2018) illustrates how unprepared students can often feel for undergraduate study in popular music. In recognition of the protracted journey into tertiary music education, the limitations of SQA qualifications, the over-subscription to local authority instrumental services and the pressures participatory music initiatives are placed under (Reeve, 2020), Scottish HE and FE institutions have occasionally themselves taken on the responsibility of facilitating pre-tertiary to HE transitions.

Despite having no undergraduate PME provision, The Royal Conservatoire of Scotland, distinct from its interdisciplinary widening participation Transitions programme,[5] has since 2015 been running a Popular Music summer school for a small cohort of twelve to seventeen year-olds working towards a live performance or recorded piece of original collaborative work. Although Napier University has enjoyed considerable recognition for its popular music UG programme, it has had limited success with its similar, pre-tertiary 'juniors' models. More recently, other (primarily private) institutions that specialise in popular music, music business and sound production have also begun providing vocational pre-tertiary programmes. The Academy of Music and Sound (AMS), for example, has recently offered free short courses for students aged 14+ in Women's Employability in the Music Industry, Employability in the Music Industry, Sound production, Digital Synthesis and Sampling, and Live Music. Riverside Music College also has a full range of private instrumental tuition and band workshops that focus on getting students "industry ready" (RMC, 2021).

However, the problem with these transitional models (with the exception of the AMS) is that although bursaries may be available, the fees charged are considerable. Many also adopt instrumentalist or vocationalist approaches in alignment with the post-92 or private HE institutions. Few embed popular music teaching in a broader interdisciplinary educational experience, the kind of experience that may also open pathways into the chartered and ancient universities. The unspoken rules and dispositions, particularly in relation to the student selection practices (Bourdieu and Passeron, 1990) of WEAM-informed HE can still implicitly exclude those from marginalised backgrounds (Smillie, 2021). It remains the case that the professional, university-educated quotient of the music industries is disproportionately populated by those with significant economic capital (and a private school education) (Brook, O'Brien and Taylor, 2018).

Tertiary Popular Music Education in Scotland

Cloonan and Hulstedt's (2012) study found forty-seven Higher Education providers across the UK offering degrees in Popular Music. These authors used the broad umbrella of Popular Music Studies (PMS) as a catch-all term for courses that deal with Popular Music in its various guises – Popular Music, Commercial Music, Music Industry/Business and so on. Yet, as Dylan Smith et al. (2017) argue, it may now be more useful to distinguish between UG programmes that are interested in practical music making and performance (an area now widely recognised as Popular Music Education – PME) and those that do not require active creative practice and/or musicianship. That said (as outlined in Moir and Stillie, 2018) there is still no clear inter-institutional consensus on what PME should prioritise. Consequently, the skills developed for Higher/Advanced Higher Music in schools often have little-to-no alignment with tertiary level study. This tension is caused, on the one hand, by HEIs' aspirations for PME (and the relative flexibility they are afforded in designing and amending courses and programmes) and, on the other, by the pragmatism already noted in the overstretched pre-tertiary system (whose curriculum is largely dictated by the SQA). Sitting across these worlds are the SQA-validated post-compulsory music programmes in Scotland's colleges.

Tertiary SQA Programmes

The SQA currently validates four tertiary music qualifications at three SCQF levels for FE and HE colleges in Scotland. These include the NC Music (SCQF Level 6), NPA Music Performance (SCQF Level 6), HNC Music (SCQF Level 7) and HND Music (SCQF Level 8). These programmes are delivered by twelve of Scotland's twenty-seven publicly funded FE/HE institutions – from Ayrshire College in the South, to Shetland College in the North.

In recent years there has been a decrease in the number of distinct institutions presenting candidates for these qualifications, in large part due to the merging of twenty-five local colleges into ten regional colleges between 2012 and 2014,[6] and a resultant reduction in the number of student presentations for the HNC music qualification.[7] In addition to the merging and regionalisation of Scotland's colleges, some institutions have ceased delivery altogether, with Dundee and Angus College no longer offering an HNC in Music, despite its former popularity.

The SQA music qualifications currently delivered by colleges in Scotland are centred on music as technical performance practice; any contextual material taught tends to focus on WEAM discourse (often crudely applied to popular music – see Tagg, 2013), vocationally focussed learning about the business of popular music, and histories of genres/record labels. Although a composition pathway is occasionally offered in HNC/HND Music, the programme design encourages little student-led creative practice.

An emerging issue among lecturers at FE/HE institutions is that capturing evidence of student learning given the large number of individual units that populate SQA Music qualifications) is so labour intensive (for staff and students alike) that there is little time for authentic music creation in teaching and learning. Tertiary SQA music education in Scotland's colleges suffers from much the same pragmatism as pre-tertiary SQA delivery in secondary schools. HNC Music, for example, is composed of five core modules (focused on repertoire, technical proficiency, music theory, and music business) and five additional modules, selected by the institution to make up the total credit value. Each of these contain three or more learning outcomes, meaning that students may have more than thirty examination points over two seventeen-week semesters! This intensive assessment programme, coupled with course structure and ethos, means that it is highly unlikely that students on HNC and HND programmes in Scotland will develop strong creative musical identities and collaborative music-making skills. Most 'new music' created on these programmes is likely to be the result of extra-curricular activity. The overall aims of the HNC Music, for example, are very vague on musicianship, collaborative practice and creativity, yet specifically reference "career aims", "business application", and "music industry protocol" (SQA, 2018, p13).

Undergraduate Programmes in Popular Music

There are currently twenty-one practical music performance and creative practice undergraduate music degree programmes delivered at the seven Scottish universities,[8] with three further programmes delivered by Scottish FE Colleges, two of which are validated by English Universities: Edinburgh College (by Kings College London) and The Academy of Music and Sound (by the University of West London). Very few deliver curricula that could be described as PME, tending to conflate 'music' with WEAM in their course offerings. The exceptions to this rule are, arguably, Edinburgh Napier University's BA (Hons) in Music & Popular Music, The University of the Highlands and Islands BA (Hons) Applied Music and BA (Hons) Popular Music, The University of West Scotland's Commercial Music BA (Hons)[9] and the aforementioned English undergraduate degrees – Edinburgh College's BA (Hons) in Music and the AMS BA (Hons) in Music and Sound. The remaining HE programmes either focus on studying the music industries (The University of the Highlands and Islands' BA (Hons) in Music Business, for example), or prioritise practice-based music performance in the WEAM tradition. Alongside the aforementioned contraction of the college sector, Edinburgh Napier University is currently phasing out one of only two remaining undergraduate programmes in 'Popular Music' (the other one being delivered by the UHI)[10] and the loss of the BA Applied Music at the University of Strathclyde in 2011 is still deeply felt.

Private Tertiary Music Education

Scottish students in Scottish universities do not need to pay tuition fees for undergraduate study; these are ordinarily funded by the Student Awards Agency Scotland (SAAS) – an Executive Agency of the Scottish Government, who have remained committed to fully funded HE study for all citizens. This said, there are also nineteen private colleges and training providers in Scotland with varying funding models. Three of these institutions offer programmes in music:

The Academy of Music and Sound (AMS), Riverside Music College (RMC) and Lossiemouth Entertainment Academy (LEA).[11] Though SAAS commits a fixed annual tuition fee of £1205 to students at these centres, the total cost to the student varies quite dramatically. LEA publish their tuition fee top-up as £3,545 per year – with the student's contribution totalling £7,090 for a two-year HND Music programme (LEA, 2021); RMC's HND Music Performance programme costs the student £2,195 per year – £4390 in total (RMC, 2021). AMS programmes in Edinburgh and Glasgow do not publish their additional tuition fees, stating that the HNC/D programmes are 'partially funded by SAAS', but their one-year top-up BA (Hons) in Music and Sound costs the student £7495 if studying in Edinburgh, and £6495 if studying in Glasgow (AMS, 2021). The two smaller institutions, unsurprisingly, serve some of the least deprived areas of Scotland – in Lossiemouth (LEA) and East Renfrewshire (RMC) (see SIMD, 2020).

The existence of these intuitions reflects two major characteristics of the post-compulsory popular music education landscape in Scotland. Firstly, it reflects the fact that there is demand for tertiary popular music education beyond that which Scottish universities and colleges currently provide. This argument is also supported by the expansion of FE/HE colleges (Edinburgh College and New College Lanarkshire, for example) into BA (Hons) PME, and the recent expansion of the UHI's BA (Hons) in Popular Music to RMC. Secondly (though the comparative value of the overall learning experience in private institutions in relation to public institutions can be contested) given the individual financial investment required, the two-tiered system of access to individual support on a principal instrument seen in Wilson, Hunter and Moscardini's (2020) research, is clearly also evident in tertiary education. Perhaps the unique selling point of private institutions is the level of individual support provided, particularly in instrumental studies. RMC, for example, offers one-to-one weekly support of thirty to forty-five minutes on a student's principal instrument, whereas Perth College UHI's model is based on groups of eight to eighteen. Collaborative learning / group music-making is a central tenet of authentic popular music pedagogy (Boespflug, 1999), but publicly funded tertiary education providers will always struggle to provide the individual support that students receive in private institutions or conservatoires- echoing the issues of delivering the subject at primary and secondary levels of Scottish education outlined earlier in this chapter.

Conclusions

So what is the place of PME in Scottish Education at this time of transition? The Curriculum for Excellence and Youth Music Initiative have been philosophically inclusive of PME, but its full potential can only be realised across sectors when national and regional priorities, institutional structures and resources allow. In the absence of formal legitimacy (in the case of some YMI and community music activity) and capacity (in the case of CfE and Instrumental Services), a reversion to type, centred around the WEAM tradition is prevalent- reproducing old inequalities and mis-recognising the authentic practices of popular music creation. The MEPG's forthcoming strategic vision for music education and a paradigm shift already evident in increasingly progressive and reflective BEd, BMus (Education) and PGDE programmes in Scotland provide optimism that formal structures can work to deliver a responsive and responsible PME pedagogy at the pre-tertiary level.[12] In tertiary education, however, there is trepidation that the restriction of degrees and FE qualifications in popular music to post-1992 and private institutions means that PME may be caught somewhere between a neo-liberal hinterland (Dylan Smith, 2021) and a peripheral and illegitimate position in the HE field. More broadly, there is a lack of inter-institutional dialogue (particularly between the SQA and HEIs) regarding PME as a concept, resulting in a disconnected landscape of pedagogical practices. We hope that in highlighting these ideological (and socio-economic) issues we are contributing to the continuing discussion shaping the national vision for Scottish music education.

Notes

1 At the time of writing. Large-scale reform was announced by the Scottish Government in August 2021.
2 SCQF: Scottish Credit and Qualifications and Credits Framework
3 The COVID-19 pandemic led to a considerable decrease in engagement: only 41,594 were provided in 2020/21.
4 https://www.musicplus.org.uk/
5 https://www.rcs.ac.uk/fair_access/transitions/
6 As an example, West College Scotland was founded in 2013 as an amalgamation of Reid Kerr College, Clydebank College, James Watt College, and Greenock College, centralising the administration of NC, HNC and HND programmes in Music.
7 FOI request from SQA 21/22 114, received 17 December 2021.
8 The University of Aberdeen, Edinburgh Napier University, The University of Edinburgh, the University of Glasgow, The University of the Highlands and Islands (UHI), The Royal Conservatoire of Scotland (RCS) and The University of West Scotland (UWS). The Open University also offers a BA (Hons) in Music.
9 UWS also validates New College Lanarkshire's new BA in Music Performance.
10 The Edinburgh Napier prospectus states that they have '…launched a new BA (Hons) Music course… [combining the existing]…BMus (Hons) Music and BA (Hons) Popular Music courses' (Napier.ac.uk, 2021; see also UHI, 2021).
11 The School of Audio Engineering (SAE) also offers courses in Music Business and Audio Production at its Glasgow premises, but these are outside the definition of PME for the purposes of this chapter.
12 The Royal Conservatoire of Scotland offers a BEd at UG level to train secondary music teachers; the University of Aberdeen offers both a BMus (Education) for the formal schools sector and BMus (Music and Communities) for the non-formal sector; PG teaching qualification for music graduates are offered at the Royal Conservatoire of Scotland, the University of Aberdeen and the University of Edinburgh at the time of writing.

References

AMS, (2021) *academyofmusic.ac.uk*. [online] Available at: https://www.academyofmusic.ac.uk/course/ba-hons-music-and-sound/ [Accessed 1 December 2021].

Bennett, J. (2017) 'Towards a framework for creativity in popular music degrees', in G. Smith et al. ed., *The Routledge Research Companion to Popular Music Education*. London: Routledge, pp. 285–298.

Boespflug, G. (1999) 'Popular music and the instrumental ensemble: Music educators can make use of student-composed music in popular styles to teach musicianship and skill in the use of recording technology', *Music Educators Journal*, 85(6), pp. 33–37. https://doi.org/10.2307/3399519.

Bourdieu, P. and Passeron, J.C. (1990) *Reproduction in Education, Society and Culture*. London: Sage.

Brennan, M. and Behr, A. (2013) *Scotland on Tour: Strategies for Promoting the Scottish Music Industry*. [online] Available at: https://www.pure.ed.ac.uk/ws/portalfiles/portal/19449723/Scotland_on_Tour_Cultural_Engagement_Project_Report.pdf [Accessed 4 December 2021].

Brennan, M., Bhachu, D., Collinson Scott, J. and Smillie, G. (2017) *A Manifesto for Music Education in Scotland*. [online] Edinburgh: University of Edinburgh. Available at: https://www.pure.ed.ac.uk/ws/portalfiles/portal/36267082/Manifesto_for_Music_Education_in_Scotland_May_2017_FINAL.pdf [Accessed 2 December 2021].

Broad, S., Duffy, C. and Price, D. (2003) *What's Going on?*. [online] Glasgow. Available at: https://pure.rcs.ac.uk/portal/files/11342739/2003_with_Celia_Duffy_and_David_Price_W_2_.pdf [Accessed 2 December 2021].

Broad, S., Hunter, K., Moscardini, L., Rae, A., Smillie, G. and Wilson, A. (2019) *What's Going on Now?*. [online] Glasgow. Available at: https://www.rcs.ac.uk/wp-content/uploads/2019/02/Whats-Going-On-Now-report.pdf [Accessed 2 December 2021].

Brook, O., O'Brien, D. and Taylor, M. (2018) *Panic! Social Class, Taste and Inequalities in the Creative Industries*. [online] Edinburgh/Sheffield: Arts and Humanities Research Council. Available at: http://createlondon.org/wp-content/uploads/2018/04/Panic-Social-Class-Taste-and-Inequalities-in-the-Creative-Industries1.pdf [Accessed 1 December 2021].

Burnard, P. and Bennett, D. (2016) 'Human capital career creativities for creative industries work: Lessons underpinned by Bourdieu's tools for thinking', in R. Comunian and A. Gilmore, eds., *Higher Education and The Creative Economy: Beyond the Campus*. London: Routledge. https://doi.org/10.4324/9781315688305.

Cloonan, M. and Hulstedt, L. (2012) *Taking Notes: Mapping and Teaching Popular Music in Higher Education*. York: Higher Education Academy.

Dylan Smith, G. (2021) 'Doublespeak in higher music education in England: Culture, marketisation, and democracy', in R. Wright, G. Johansen, P. Kanellopoulos, P. Schmidt, eds., *The Routledge Handbook to Sociology of Music Education*. London: Routledge, pp. 219–231.

Dylan Smith, G., Kirkman, P., Moir, Z., Rambarran, S. and Brennan, M. (2017) *The Routledge Research Companion to Popular Music Education*. London: Routledge.

Improvement Service (2020) *Instrumental Music Services: Results from the IMS Survey 2020*. Available at: https://www.improvementservice.org.uk/__data/assets/pdf_file/0009/22050/IMS-Survey-Report-2020.pdf [Accessed 25 November 2021].

Improvement Service (2021) *Instrumental Music Services: Results from the IMS Survey 2021*. Available at: https://www.improvementservice.org.uk/__data/assets/pdf_file/0020/29216/IMS-Survey-Report-2021.pdf [Accessed 25 November 2021].

LEA (2021) *lossieentertainmentacademy.co.uk*. [online] Available at: https://lossieentertainmentacademy.co.uk/courses/ [Accessed 22 November 2021].

Legislation.gov.uk (2021) *FHE Act 1992*. [online] Available at: https://www.legislation.gov.uk/ukpga/1992/37/contents [Accessed 5 December 2021].

McBay, N. (2017) 'Music: Teenage femme club – behind the scenes of the Girls Rock Glasgow summer school'. *The National*, [online] Available at: https://www.thenational.scot/news/15449859.music-teenage-femme-club-behind-the-scenes-of-the-girls-rock-glasgow-summer-school/ [Accessed 3 December 2021].

MEPG (2021) *Home*. Available: https://wemakemusicscotland.org/. [Last Accessed 6 January 2022].

Moir, Z. and Stillie, B. (2018) 'Haphazard pathways: Students' perceptions of their routes to music study in higher education in the United Kingdom', *Journal of Popular Music Education*, 2(3), pp. 199–216.

Napier (2021) *napier.ac.uk*. [online] Available at: https://www.napier.ac.uk/courses/ba-hons-music-popular-undergraduate-fulltime [Accessed 24 November 2021].

OECD (2021) *Oecd-ilibrary.org* [online] Available at: https://www.oecd-ilibrary.org/sites/bf624417-en/index.html?itemId=/content/publication/bf624417-en [Accessed 2 December 2021].

Parkinson, T. and Smith, G. (2015) 'Towards an epistemology of authenticity in higher popular music education', *Action, Criticism and Theory for Music Education*, 14(1), pp. 93–127.

Reay, D., David, M.E. and Ball, S. (2005) *Degrees of Choice: Social class, race and gender in higher education*. London: Institute of Education Press.

Reeve, J. (2020) 'How Glasgow's Beatroute arts has stayed at heart of the community during Covid'. *The Scotsman*, [online] Available at: https://www.scotsman.com/news/people/how-glasgows-beatroute-arts-has-stayed-heart-community-during-covid-2931513 [Accessed 5 December 2021].

RMC (2021) *riversidemusiccollege.ac.uk*. [online] Available at: https://www.riversidemusiccollege.ac.uk/fees-funding/ [Accessed 14 November 2021].

Scottish Government (2021) *Music Tuition and Core Curriculum Fees Removed* [online] Available at: https://www.gov.scot/news/music-tuition-and-core-curriculum-fees-removed/ [Accessed 2 December 2021].

SIMD (2020) Scottish Index of Multiple Deprivation [online] Available at: https://simd.scot/ [Accessed 29 November 2021].

Smillie, G. (2011) *The Realistic Balancing Act of Independent Musicians in Glasgow: A Social and Cultural Study of Producing New Music and 'making a living'*. Unpublished M. Litt thesis. Glasgow: Glasgow University.

Smillie, G. (2021) *Pre-tertiary Transitions in the Performing Arts: A Qualitative Study of the Tensions and Hierarchies in Widening Access to a Conservatoire's Cultural Systems,* Unpublished PhD thesis, Glasgow: Royal Conservatoire of Scotland: Glasgow [Accessed 29 November 2021] http://hdl.handle.net/10023/23438.

Smith, I. (2018) 'Educational provision: An overview', in T.G.K. Bryce, W.M. Humes, D. Gillies, and A. Kennedy, eds., *Scottish Education: Fifth Edition*. pp. 20–34. Edinburgh University Press.

SQA (2018) *Group Award Specification for HNC Music at SCQF Level 7*. [online] Available at: https://www.sqa.org.uk/sqa/files_ccc/GP1215_GP1516.pdf [Accessed 25 April 2022]

Tagg, P. (2013) *Music's Meanings*. Huddersfield: Mass Media Music Scholar's Press.

Toynbee, J. (2000) *Making Popular Music*. London: Arnold.

Uhi.ac.uk. (2021) *Uhi.ac.uk*. [online] Available at: https://www.uhi.ac.uk/en/courses/ba-hons-popular-music/ [Accessed 5 December 2021].

Vasil, M., Weiss, L., and Powell, B. (2019) 'Popular music pedagogies: An approach to teaching 21st-century skills', *Journal of Music Teacher Education*, 28(3), pp. 85–95.

Williamson, J., Cloonan, M. and Frith, S. (2003) *Mapping the Music Industry in Scotland*. [online] Glasgow: Scottish Enterprise. Available at: http://livemusicexchange.org/wp-content/uploads/Williamson-Cloonan-Frith-Mapping-the-music-industry-in-Scotland-2003.pdf [Accessed 4 December 2021].

Wilson, A., Hunter, K. and Moscardini, L. (2020) 'Widening the gap? The challenges for equitable music education in Scotland', *Support for Learning*, 35(4), pp. 473–492.

York, N. (2021) *Pop Music Education in the UK – 1960–2020*. Teddington: RSL.

11

Jock Rock?

Putting Scotland into Scottish Popular Music

Martin Cloonan

Introduction

Like many chapters in this collection, this one could easily form a book. Many of the concepts invoked here – 'popular music', 'national identity' and 'Scottishness', for example – are topics about which much more could be said. This chapter, then, might best be read as the start of a conversation. In it I wish to explore whether it is actually possible to talk about 'Scottish popular music'. Does such a label even make sense? I will argue that it *does not*, but that is only the beginning of the story.

There is obviously a great deal of popular music in Scotland and many of the country's musicians make what might be broadly termed popular music. However, if one was to ask whether they make *Scottish* popular music, then a series of questions would arise. Does Scottishness here relate to the nationality of the artist? To the type of music performed? To the characteristics of its audiences? From this perspective it is clear that there is no such thing as Scottish popular music *per se*. As Motti Regev (2013) has argued, pop-rock and its derivatives are forms of music which span the globe. While the particular origins of examples of such music can be traced, the form is global:

> the cultural uniqueness of each nation or ethnicity cannot but be understood as a unit within one complex entity, one variant in a set of quite similar – although never identical – cases (Regev 2013: 7).

From the kilt-wearing early rock 'n' roller Jackie Dennis onwards what is on display is not Scottish popular music but Scottish attempts (more of less successful) to react to, interact with and shape global sounds. What we have is Scottish artists making and performing global music, sometimes trying to articulate and establish versions of Scottishness within that music and sometimes having such characteristics attributed to them.

The rest of the chapter falls into four parts. The first discusses the links between popular music and identity, with a focus on Scottishness. The second looks at the ways in which Scottish-made popular music has been written about and notions of nationality alluded to historically. The third examines attempts to define Scottishness and the search for national distinctiveness, while the final part considers attempts that have been made to articulate Scottishness within and around popular music.

DOI: 10.4324/9781003247470-14

Popular Music, Identity and Scottishness

Simon Frith once wrote that:

> The first reason… we enjoy popular music is because of its use in answering questions of identity: we use pop songs to create for ourselves a particular sort of self-definition, a particular place in society. The pleasure that pop music produces is a pleasure of identification – with the music we like, with the performers of that music, with other people who like it (Frith 1987: 140).

Frith thus locates questions of identity at the core of popular music and Scottishness is clearly one form of identity. The construction of identity involves processes of exclusion and inclusion, empowering those who oversee such processes. People may identify as "Scottish" and/or have that identity assigned to them in various ways in various arenas.

Attempts to define distinctive Scottish music in terms of identity can be dated back to at least the early eighteenth century and the work of poet and publisher Allan Ramsay (c1684–1758). In an insightful article, Matthew Gelbart argues that "it would be difficult to overestimate his role in creating the idea of 'Scottish song' in the first place and…. the idea of 'Scottish music' in a broader sense" (2012: 81). He shows how Ramsay forged "a link between popular song and national identity" (ibid: 83) and concludes that: "Ramsay and the networks around him are… a powerful example, in a country that was culturally divided and politically subordinated, of the working practice of inventing and embedding 'national' musical culture" (ibid: 108). What emerges from this account is the *construction* of a national music in ways which are *not* mirrored within popular music, wherein any Scottish contribution is always within a hybrid, cross-national artform: not Scottish music but Scottish rock or Scottish jazz.

It is also important here to emphasize how fluid such identities are. They are constantly being made and remade. Further the nature of Scottishness is fundamentally ambiguous. McCrone's definition of Scotland as a "stateless nation" (McCrone 1992) *within* the UK continues to have resonance even post-devolution and it is easy enough to see Scotland as still a marginalized country politically. However, as part of the UK, Scotland is also an integral part of a major international music industry just as historically at least part of its population was significantly involved in British industrialization and imperialism.[1]

One problem here, as Peter Symon noted twenty-five years ago, is that "no adequate history of recent popular music in Scotland exists from which to draw conclusions about the role of music in people's lives" Symon (1997: 205). More recently Janne Mäkelä lamented that "Relatively little has been written on modern Scottish popular music and its relationship with national identity" (2005: 110) while Nichola Wood noted the lack of work on the performance of Scottishness even though "a small number of commentators have argued that there are certain traits that can make a piece of music 'Scottish'" (Wood 2012: 197). But no-one has done what Cloonan did twenty-five years ago with Englishness (Cloonan 1997) and developed a typology of pop Scottishness. And no one has done in Scotland what has been done in Finland (a country with a comparable population size) and examined arguments about 'authenticity' among its popular musicians (Anttonen 2017).

In his essay Symon called for "further study of the specific historical processes of change which have helped to transform the production of music in Scotland and its reception locally, nationally and internationally" (Symon 1997: 214) and this work remains to be done. It is also striking that Scotland lacks a critical public space in which notions of 'Scottish' popular music might be played out and debated. The spaces that exist – such as *Is This Music* magazine, the allied Jockrock website (https://www.jockrock.org/) and https://jocknroll.wordpress.com/ – are there to celebrate and provide information, rather than to debate and critique.

Scottish Pop History

While there are journalistic survey histories of Scottish pop,[2] in this section I will provide some snippets from more specialist academic studies, which offer a better insight into the difficulties of its definition.

John Williamson, for example, suggests that in the 1950s the most significant 'Scottish' contribution to popular music culture were kilt-wearing television singers Williamson (2021) and while young musicians in Scotland as in the rest of Europe were already aping American styles it was only in the mid to late 60s that they started writing original material. Bob Anderson (2013) thus notes that in the 1960s Glasgow bands trying to make it would invariably record material written by others – "in general Glasgow bands were dependent on trends elsewhere" (ibid: 200). Although there were bands such as The Poets and the Beatstalkers who wrote their own material, Scotland's first successful singer songwriters (Bert Jansch, for example) came from the folk scene.

The 1970s produced perhaps the biggest Scottish pop act ever: The Bay City Rollers. Mäkelä (2005: 112) describes them as "the first Scottish pop group to make their identity and cultural background a fundamental part of their fame". But this was on the level of image, rather than the use of recognizably Scottish instruments, tunes or singing voice. By the time of punk more Scottish acts were writing original material and local labels were being formed, of which Postcard was perhaps the most important (see Chapter 2).

In the 1980s Scottish rock did begin to be heard (at least by Scottish historians) as an assertion of national identity. In his *The Scottish Nation* Tom Devine, for instance, writes: "Rock bands like Deacon Blue, the Proclaimers and Runrig were emphatically Scottish in style… Runrig celebrated Gaelic culture in particular and Scottishness in general to a younger generation of Scots increasingly confident in their own national identity" (2000: 608). Jeremy Tranmer (2016: 134) also notes Cairns Craig's argument that following the failure of the 1979 devolution, energies which had been put into the politics of independence were instead put into culture, resulting in a new self-confidence among Scottish artists and a new sense of national self-consciousness among Scottish bands. Tranmer contrasts the Scottish cultural turn towards politics with what happened in England, where musicians seemed to turn away from politics following the Conservatives' third successive general election victory in 1987. He concludes that "the reaction of many Scottish musicians was clearly rooted in a sense of Scottishness" (2016: 134) and that "the close relationship between popular music and politics in the very late 1980s and early 1990s is a singularly Scottish phenomenon" (ibid: 134).

This may be true but it is certainly not the case that such political self-consciousness was a necessary characteristic of most Scottish bands in the 1980s. Janne Mäkelä, reflecting on the success of Simple Minds, Orange Juice, Aztec Camera and Josef K (2005: 116), notes a different kind of local identity: "Glasgow became a hugely fashionable pop city in the mid-1980s"; and Mark Percival suggests that by the time of Britpop in the mid-1990s it was the "ordinariness" and un-flashiness attributed to a number of Scottish (and Welsh) bands that led to their being celebrated in the music press as a reproof to flashier (English) Britpop bands (ibid: 124).

The success of Travis and Stereophonics was often framed by the bands themselves and by journalists in terms of their Welshness or Scottishness, and associated national stereotypes of self-deprecation, Celtic passion/sentimentality and an authenticist appeal to their regional and class origins' (ibid: 126)

The arguments here about cities (rather than countries) being the basis of 'ordinary' musical identities continue to resonate. In 1998 The *Guardian*'s Tom Cox called Glasgow "undisputably the UK's second music city" (cited Percival 2010a: 134) and by 2004 it was being cited by *Time* as being as important as musical cities such as Detroit and Liverpool in their heydays (Porter 2004). Glasgow has gone on to garner a formidable international reputation as a music city (Homan *et al.* 2016: 94–102) while the fact that the multiracial, award winning, band Young Fathers comes from Edinburgh has enabled Scotland's so-called First City too to claim to a distinctive local musical identity.

Definitions and Distinctiveness

Artists located in Scotland are, not surprisingly, referred to as "Scottish". But it is surely pertinent to ask in what sense are, for example, Belle and Sebastian, Emile Sandé, Snow Patrol, Franz Ferdinand, Young Fathers, Sharleen Spiteri and Amy MacDonald *Scottish*. In what ways does their Scottishness affect their music making and in what ways is it reflected in that music?

To search for national characteristics, whether in music or anywhere else, is to search for *distinctiveness*. Asserting an identity means deciding what not to assert and historically the search for Scotland's distinctiveness has involved attempts to be different from the English (see McCrone 1992) although, in an interesting case study, Peter Symon notes that for more folk inclined Scottish musicians in the 1970s, the problem was to distinguish their music from Irish music – at that time Irish tunes were better-known by Scottish musicians than Scottish ones. Symon writes that: "The search for non-Irish vernacular Scottish sound took two main forms: searching out and learning 'authentic' Scottish tunes and songs; and learning to adopt agreed performance styles' (Symon 1997: 207). One solution was the use of the bagpipes and the Scottish snap rhythm (1999: 207 and 210). Symon quotes Cedric Thorpe: "To multitudes of people the world over, the Scottish nation is symbolized by the sound of the great Highland bagpipe" (cited ibid: 211) but the important point here was not that Scottish musicians 'naturally' played the pipes (or the fiddle or the accordion) but that they used them to *construct* a form of Scottishness.

> By taking part in the musical world of Scottish folk and traditional music these young men were negotiating their Scottishness in ways which could be recognized by other players, audiences, journalists, girlfriends, mothers and fathers. It was their way of *becoming* Scottish
> (Symon 1997: 214, my emphasis)

From another perspective – for record companies or tourist boards, for example – the pursuit of a distinctive sound is in order to create a Unique Selling Proposition. Acts are marketed to have a distinctive place in the global music economy. Musical Scottishness becomes a commodity whose distinctive characteristics, like its commercial value, fluctuate.

Scottish Articulations

This section examines ways in which Scottishness has been articulated and discerned in in popular music in five areas: voice, clothing, image, performance and through the lens of migration.

Voice

The importance of voice in popular music has, of course, been noted in numerous places.[3] Importantly, it has also been seen as a key marker of Scottishness – or not. Wood suggests that

"Language and accent can play a significant role in the formation of national cultures and identities. This is because they can reify the notion that a nation has a form of communication that is culturally distinctive" (2012: 204). Scott Hames notes that: "Voice and its giving and joining have been key motifs in Scottish literary and political discourse of the past few decades" (2013: 202). In their post-devolution research, Kiely *et al.* found that many of those born and raised in Scotland denied that those who were not born in the country could be really Scottish and "drew attention to the way that migrants' accents contradicted and undermined their Scottish claim" (2005: 167).

The question of the Scottish voice in pop first came to prominence in the 1980s with the rise of The Proclaimers. They sing in audibly Scottish accents and Tranmer suggests that this is "highly unusual as most Scottish performers (and British artists in general) tend to adopt a mid-Atlantic accent" (2016: 138). While this is contestable, there is no doubt that The Proclaimers' vocal style caused debate – was it authentic or a gimmick – perhaps used in an attempt to stand out?

Today the Proclaimers are much revered in Scotland, as the popularity of the jukebox musical (and subsequent hit film) *Sunshine on Leith* indicates. To sing in a resolutely Scottish voice was, though, to bemuse English listeners. As recently as 2018 the local paper review of a Proclaimers appearance in York suggested that "Their trademark spectacles and strong brogue have led to the pair being unfairly labelled as a novelty act".[4] As Tranmer suggests, if the Proclaimers' refusal to abandon their vocal identity came to be celebrated in Scotland in other parts of the UK "it was simply a novel feature differentiating them from their contemporaries" (Tranmer 2016: 138). How we hear voices is shaped by our location – what is normal in Scotland is odd or a "novelty" elsewhere, which is to draw attention to the need to differentiate between cultural perceptions inside and outside the country (Percival 2010b: 197) but also between what we expect to hear in immediate and mediated settings. I can still recall my amazement at hearing Aidan Moffat's spoken word introduction to Arab Strap's debut single, 'The First Weekend', on the John Peel Show. To hear a Falkirk accent on a UK-wide BBC UK services was not a regular occurrence in 1996.

A voice, in other words, is both a signifier of authenticity – a genuinely Scottish sound – and a novelty – something outside the mid-Atlantic and/or BBC English norm. As ever, artistic intent may not square with audience reception.

Clothing

Gelbart (2012: 91) notes that clothes began to be national symbols in the eighteenth century. In Scotland the kilt and tartan became the key signifiers, as they continue to be within popular music (Percival 2010b, Williamson 2021). Scotland's 1950s TV-pop stars Jimmie Shand, Kenneth McKellar and Andy Stewart always "appeared in kilts and Highland dress, lest there be any doubt about their nationality" (Williamson 2021: 6) and twenty years later the Bay City Rollers' use of tartan was so pronounced that "For fans of the band, tartan meant "Bay City Rollers" and not in any direct sense 'Scotland'" (Percival 2010b: 201). Percival also suggests that the Rollers' use of tartan foreshadowed its use in punk and postpunk. Whereas serious Scottish rock musicians in the 1970s disowned tartan, by the 1980s, Alan Horne, owner of famous Glasgow label Postcard, was happy for it to feature in the company image.

It was in part a statement that the seriousness of the bands and movements before Postcard had been supplanted by an affectionately ironic Scottish understanding of tartan. It signified a lightness of touch that situated the bands on Postcard as modern pop rather than the rock of the previous decade. It was also an unironic signifier of national identity for the first genuinely innovative and successful independent label in Scotland' (ibid: 204)

Tartan was also used by one of the 1980s' mainstream Scottish rock acts, Big Country, a band also noted by Tranmer (2016) for signaling their Scottishness with their clothing. For Percival the band's early work was characterized by "innovation, risk taking and often-spectacular statements of national identity" (2010b: 206). "The music's Scottish themes were reflected in the tartan shirts frequently worn on stage in the breakthrough year of 1983 by Adamson, second guitarist Bruce Watson and bass player Tony Butler" (ibid: 205). Describing Big Country's New Year's Eve show of at Glasgow's Barrowlands in 1983/1984 Percival writes:

> The whole show is an unambiguous celebration of Scottish traditional and contemporary culture in a context that would have been almost unthinkable for early generations of Scots rock performers. Tartan is deployed as a symbol of mainstream Scottish culture of the people, not the aristocracy or subcultural punk (ibid: 206)[5]

Percival also documents a more recent usage: "A deeply intelligent independent Scottish band like Arab Strap, audibly defiantly Scottish, [has] used traditional Scottish formal kilt outfits in press photographs taken in the Highlands in the early 2000s". Arab Strap's fans, it seems, recognized this as "an affectionate swipe …. directed at earlier generations of artists … This deployment of tartan and traditional Highland imagery captures the essence of something peculiarly Scottish, which might be described as critical patriotism" (208).

Tartan is both a symbol of Scottish distinctiveness and kitsch, both authentic and inauthentic. It "continues to signify not just Scotland, but many Scotlands" (ibid: 196, 210).

Image: The Dour Scot

The word "dour" has been used to describe a certain sort of downbeat, pessimistic, Scottishness linked to the country's Calvinist heritage (Schwartz 2009) and a certain understatedness can be discerned in the attitude of 1980s' bands such as The Proclaimers and Runrig, something which marked them out in an era of excess (Tranmer 2016: 140–141). Writing of a set of bands on Glasgow's Chemikal Underground label, John O'Reilly said:

> It's not nationality or record label that binds together Mogwai, Arab Strap and the Delgados. What marks out their sound is a musical honesty that is also utterly self-effacing. It is the same dry existentialism that is often disguised in a writer like Irvine Welsh by his tales of chemical excess. But Mogwai's *Come On Die Young* has taken self-effacement to the point of disappearance (cited Percival 2010a: 136).

Early in the 2000's bands such as Travis enjoyed great commercial success and used the media promote their work, but still avoided rock star excess. In 2003 the band's singer, Fran Healy, said: "Being Scottish, we're very reticent about being famous pop stars: it's encoded into our DNA that we can't be brassy or show off" (cited Percival 2010a: 130). As Percival notes:

> Healy emphasizes the notion that one key characteristic that distinguishes Scots from the English is a modest self-awareness that is at odds with the requirement of being famous, and is reflective of the essentialism that tends to dominate popular discourse on national identity (ibid: 130/131)

A number of writers, following Tranmer (2016), invoke Michael Billig's (1995) concept of banal nationalism to explain Scottish bands' Scottishness. Justin Williams, for example, suggests that within Scottish hip hop the use of Scottish slang and references to historic battles is also a form of banal nationalism (2020: 104), something which Nichola Wood identified in her interviews with Scottish folk musicians (2012: 207).

Performance

Wood also argues that nations are produced by performances on and off stage: "national identity is equally (re)produced through the popular culture of everyday life such as music, film, television, novels and newspapers" (ibid: 196–197). The most commonly acknowledged Scottish musical traits are linked to particular uses of instrumentation, language, and melodic and rhythmic styles. Noting that other work has shown "music not only *reflects* ideas of identity and place…. But… also provide(s) a medium through which notions of identity and place can be *created* and *lived*" (ibid: 200, emphasis in original), Wood goes on to examine perceptions of audiences and musicians at two Scottish festivals, the folk-inclined Celtic Connections and the more rock-orientated T in the Park.

Wood concludes that two things mattered here "First, people experienced 'Scottishness' through a perceived bond between audience members and performers that was based on a shared national identity. Second people recognize the music as being 'Scottish'" (ibid: 201). At Celtic Connections particular sounds, especially those of the bagpipe and fiddle, were held to be Scottish. Musicians spoke of producing Scottish music, in terms of methods, rhythmic style, instrumentation or as being sung in Gaelic, Scots or Scottish accented English (ibid: 203). People spoke of the *feel* of the music, thus emphasizing the importance of performance: "It is the *performance* of them that gives them their national distinctiveness" (ibid: 204, emphasis in original). Elaborations of Scottishness came from the ways in which musicians played with sounds, in their response to audience demands and via their creative performances (ibid: 207). Wood concludes that "Scottishness" is usually found in those symbolic expressions that are understood to have links to "authentic" and/or "traditional" ideas of the Scots although "Ideas of 'Scottishness' are not fixed but are both dynamic and heterogenous" (ibid: 210).

Migration

Complicating any simplistic notion of Scottishness is the importance in Scotland's cultural history of various forms of migration. For example, as Bob Anderson notes, between 1871 and 1914 Glasgow had the fastest growing population in Europe (2103: 194), something not irrelevant to its development as a "Music City", and if for many people birthplace is still taken to be *the* definer of Scottish identity (see the data in Keily *et al.* 2005), then it is remarkable how many prominent Scottish musicians were *not* born in the country.

Take Big Country. Earlier I quoted Mark Percival's description of the band's 1983 New Year's Eve performance at Glasgow's Barrowlands as "an unambiguous celebration of Scottish traditional and contemporary culture" (2010b: 206). However, as Mäkelä (2005: 115) points out, the band's prime mover, Stuart Adamson, was not born in Scotland but in Manchester, albeit to Scottish parents who moved back to Scotland when Adamson was four. Of the rest of the band's classic line up at the Barrowlands show, drummer Mark Brzezicki, is English-born of Polish descent, bassist Tony Butler, was born in White City, London, to Dominican parents and guitarist Bruce Watson was born in Canada before moving to Scotland as a young child.

Or, to give an example of a more recent Scottish band, take Franz Ferdinand. The group was formed in Glasgow in 2002 and the four founding members were Glaswegian in the sense of being located there. However, while the band has always had a Glasgow base, singer Alex Kapranos was born in Gloucestershire, to a Greek father and English mother, bassist Bob Hardy hails from Yorkshire and original guitarist Nick McCarthy was born and raised in Munich. Only Glaswegian drummer Paul Thomson, is a born Scot.

The point here is not to make essentialist claims as to who is or is not "Scottish", but to highlight that bands routinely referred to as Scottish may actually contain musicians from diverse backgrounds whose Scottishness is a matter of civic identity rather than of blood or birthplace. This raises the question of how musicians qualify as Scottish – which brings us to Sir Rod Stewart. Born and brought up in the London suburb of Highgate but with a Scots father, Stewart can claim to be *partly* Scottish and has sometimes played this up with his tartan scarves and very public support of the Scottish men's football team. Outside Britain he is, indeed, widely considered to be Scottish. For example, Janne Mäkelä writes that when he told Finnish colleagues that he was going to write about Scottish pop, they said not to forget Rod (2005: 114). Mäkelä continues that:

> When I was young, I always thought that Rod Stewart was a Scot and (Dunfermline's) Nazareth a band from somewhere in southern England. Nazareth did not talk about their background and cultural identity whereas Rod Stewart appeared to me as an ambassador of all things Scottish (ibid: 115).

In his article Mäkelä concludes that Stewart should be regarded as "a wannabe Scot" (ibid: 113) and ten years later Scotland's largest-selling newspaper, the *Daily Record*, told its readers that "Tartan-daft Rod Stewart doesn't consider himself Scottish, saying links are just 'spiritual'" (Taylor 2015). That said, it is hard to think of his music as particularly Scottish, even if only in spirit. He has by now made five albums of the *American Song Book* but no album of Scottish music.

Conclusion

I began by noting that this chapter could have been a book and this means that there are serious omissions here. I have not touched on gender, ethnicity or sexuality. Mea culpa. I've scraped the surface. But I hope I have done enough to show that while there is no such thing as Scottish popular music, there are Scottish popular music makers, some of whom at certain times represent Scottishness in particular ways, while at other times some attributes of such musicians have been designated as being "Scottish". I think it can also be said that articulations of Scottishness in popular music more often than not relate to *extra*-musical elements such as attire and performance and exude a form of *civic* Scottishness. My final point is that musicians' reasons for articulating Scottishness matter less than their reception. And that is something that lies beyond the scope of this chapter.

Notes

1 See, for example, Newman and Mullen 2018, a report on the role of Glasgow University in the slave trade.
2 See, for example, Galloway (2018), Hogg (1993), Kielty (2011) and Wilkie (1991).
3 An excellent non-academic account can be found in Thorn (2016).
4 www.yorkpress.co.uk/news/17009657.review-proclaimers-york-barbican-october-17/
5 See https://www.youtube.com/watch?v=l90asFOSxF8&t=2750s

Bibliography

Anderson, B. 2013. 'Clan Balls, luvvers and incredible strings: Popular music in 1960s Glasgow', in E. Bell and L. Gunn (ed.) *The Scottish Sixties: Reading, Rebellion, Revolution?*, Amsterdam: Rodopi, pp. 193–208.

Anttonen, S. 2017. *A Feel for the Real: Discourse of Authenticity in Popular Music Cultures through three Case Studies.* Joensuu: University of Eastern Finland, PhD.

Billig, M. 1995. *Banal Nationalism.* London: Sage.

Cloonan, M. 1997. 'State of the nation: "Englishness," pop, and politics in the mid-1990s', *Popular Music and Society*, 21:2, pp.47–70.

Cloonan, M. 2007. *Popular Music and the State.* Aldershot: Ashgate.

Devine, T. 2000. *The Scottish Nation.* London: Penguin.

Finlay, R. 1997. 'The rise and fall of popular imperialism in Scotland, 1850–1950', *Scottish Geographical Magazine*, 113:1, pp.113–121.

Frith, S. 1987. 'Towards an aesthetic of popular music', in R. Leppert and S. McClary (eds.) *Music and Society: The Politics of Composition, Performance and Reception*, Cambridge: Cambridge University Press, pp.133–149.

Galloway, V. 2018. *Rip It Up: The Story of Scottish pop.* Edinburgh. NMSE.

Gelbart, M. 2012. 'Allan Ramsay, the idea of "Scottish Music" and the beginnings of "national music" in Europe', *Eighteenth Century Music*, 9:1, pp.81–108.

Hames, S. 2013. 'On vernacular scottishness and its limits: Devolution and the spectacle of "Voice"', *Studies in Scottish Literature*, 39:1, pp.201–222.

Hogg, B. 1993. *All That Ever Mattered: The History of Scottish Rock and Pop.* London: Gullane.

Homan, S., Cloonan, M. and Cattermole, J. 2016. *Popular Music Industries and the State. Policy Notes.* London: Routledge.

Kiely, R., Bechhofer, F. and McCrone, D. 2005. 'Birth, blood and belonging: identity claims in post-devolution Scotland', *The Sociological Review*, 53:1, pp.150–171.

Kielty, M. 2011. *Big Noise from a Wee Country.* Lulu.com.

McCrone. D. 1992. *Understanding Scotland: The Sociology of a Stateless Nation.* London: Routledge.

Mäkelä, J. 2005. 'Tartan Boys – Scottish popular music in the 1970s', *Studia Celtica Fennica*, 2, pp.110–177.

Newman, S. and Mullen, S. 2018. *Slavery, Abolition and the University of Glasgow.* Glasgow: University of Glasgow.

Percival, J. 2010a. 'Britpop or Eng-pop?' in A. Bennett and J. Stratton (eds.) *Britpop and the English Music Tradition*, Aldershot: Ashgate, pp.123–143.

Percival, J. 2010b. 'Rock, pop and tartan', in I. Brown (ed.) *From Tartan to Tartanry: Scottish Culture, History and Myth*, Edinburgh: University of Edinburgh Press, pp.195–211.

Regev, M. 2013. *Pop-Rock Music.* London: Polity.

Schwartz, B. 2009. 'Cloudbusting: Is the dour Scot stereotype an accurate one?', *The Scotsman*, 12 June, https://www.scotsman.com/arts-and-culture/cloudbusting-dour-scot-stereotype-accurate-one-2443716.

Symon, P. 1997. 'Music and national identity in Scotland: A study of Jock Tamson's Bairns', *Popular Music*, 16:2, pp.203–216.

Taylor, D. 2015. 'Tartan-daft Rod Stewart doesn't consider himself Scottish saying links are just "spiritual"', *Daily Record*, 4 January 2015.

Tranmer, J. 2016. 'Popular music and Left-Wing Scottishness', *Études Écossaises*, 18, pp.133–149.

Wilkie, J. 1991. *Blue Suede Brogans: Scenes from the Secret Life of Scottish Rock Music.* Edinburgh: Mainstream.

Williams, J. 2020. *Brithop: The Politics of UK Rap in the New Century.* Oxford: Oxford University Press.

Williamson, J. 2021. 'The kilt is my delight? Popular music on early television from Scotland', *Journal of Popular Television*, 9:1, 105–122.

Wood, N. 2012. 'Playing with "Scottishness": Musical performance, non-representational thinking and the "doings" of national identity', *Cultural Geographies*, 19:2, pp.195–215.

12

Hip-Hop in Scotland

A Footnote in the History of Popular Music?

Dave Hook

Introduction

Hip-hop exists in the margins of the central narrative around popular music in Scotland. In a recent national exhibition about the history of Scottish pop music, hip-hop artists appear as passing comments in the accompanying book – the first scholarly history to mention them at all (National Museum of Scotland 2018). This highlights the minimal degree to which hip-hop made in Scotland has entered wider Scottish consciousness. On a national level, Scottish hip-hop could be considered little more than a footnote in the history of Scottish pop music: a brief, bare acknowledgement of its existence, outside of the central text. Despite support from new-music sources, the general narrative over the last twenty years appears to be stuck in a cycle of 'could this be the time Scottish hip-hop goes overground?' (Boyle 2015, Rimmer 2018, Hawthorne 2021). Simultaneously global and local, hip-hop is paradox. It is a mass, world-wide culture, that demands, as a core element, local representation. A global commercial force, associated with protest and amplifying marginal voices. Yet in Scotland the idea of local artists making hip-hop is still often met with ridicule and derision (Rimmer 2016). Misconceptions remain around perceived conflicts between the 'authentic' expression of Scottish culture and that of hip-hop culture. These conflicts involve issues of national identity, accent, dialect, vernacular, post-colonialism and spaces for local voices. This is a story of trying to unpack some of that. A conversational opportunity to look at Scottish hip-hop in relation to these ideas and have a blether about what it might all mean.

Focusing on rap lyrics, poetic and music analysis will be used to unpack their cultural value, creative power and societal substance, revealing something brand new, intertwined with tradition. First, I will place hip-hop in Scotland within the wider context of Scottish popular music. Second, I will outline a conceptual framework of local/global relations, duality and post-colonialism, followed by a brief history of hip-hop in Scotland. Finally, I will provide analyses of three artists' works, evidencing the ways that hip-hop is being employed to chronicle, create and reflect contemporary Scottish culture.

Dusty Feet, Double Consciousness and Dualities

Pennycook and Mitchell (2009) discuss Somali-Canadian hip-hop artist K'Naan's album *The Dusty Foot Philosopher*, highlighting the difference between globalisation erasing local culture and local culture being expressed through new cultural forms. This is important for our

DOI: 10.4324/9781003247470-15

journey through Scottish hip-hop as it establishes the idea of being both local and global. And that is important for our critical audience who don't understand how Scottish folks can tell true, resonant stories about their own life experiences through hip-hop – a black cultural artform and global cultural commodity. How can these things be used to express genuine local Scottish culture? A global cultural form like hip-hop does not necessarily equate to homogenisation, appropriation or simulation when engaged with by cultures around the world. Rather, it can provide opportunities for existing local cultures to express traditional, historical and current experiences in new, hybrid ways. As broadcaster and author Vic Galloway explains, this is "real, contemporary storytelling" (2012).

Paul Gilroy's work on the "double consciousness" of black European experience is useful here (Gilroy 1993). Hip-hop is a black music artform. It is also a global music. It is also a local Scottish cultural form. All these things can be true. Gilroy's double consciousness relates to black European experience within the boundaries of European white cultural forms, and within black minority culture at the same time, creating a doubling, an expectation of double meaning, an engagement with and subversion of cultural signifiers. Doubling is significant in Scottish hip-hop culture as it represents an established expectation for double meaning in the form of hip-hop output, but also represents a type of doubling reflected in the duality of Scottish culture being both Scottish and British, individual and part of a larger whole, apparently united and yet dismissed by a larger majority. Indeed, the issue of Scottish national identity and language is one that is central to how we consider hip-hop in Scotland. Recently, singer Iona Fyfe succeeded in challenging Spotify to add Scots as a language for artists uploading music in 2021 (Duffy 2021). Connections have been made between increased Scots language in popular music, the acceptance of self being reflected in culture, and the increase in self-determinacy that comes with devolved government (Hook 2021). These considerations are important because language – the everyday, evolving language used around the country – is central to hip-hop expression. The significance of this is twofold. Firstly, the reflection of overt Scottish language in music – that has historically jarred with Scottish cultural sensibilities – is core to hip-hop expression in Scotland. Secondly, in Scottish rap music we might be able to witness the living, evolution of language as it is happening.

Henry Louis Gates Jnr's (1988) appreciation of the signifyin(g) practices in African American literature is also relevant here. A litany of daily examples of signifyin(g), double-meaning and word play can be found in Scots cultural expressions. Take the wee lady sat in the dentist's chair and the dentist asks, "comfy?", to which she replies "Govan". This short joke emphasises cultural wordplay and double meaning, as well as representing place and space. Here, the word 'comfy', is sonically identical to the Scots pronunciation of 'come from' – 'come fae'. As such, the dentist's question is reframed as "where do you come from?", with the lady's response being Govan, Glasgow. In addition to the meaning subversion here, there is also the signifying practice that the use of Scots language and location infer. This is a secret joke, for those who match its dialect. This signifying and subversion mark a point at which hip-hop culture and Scottish culture converge; where both linguistic practices are aligned.

What's in a Name?

Scottish hip-hop. Hip-hop in Scotland. Hip-hop *from* Scotland. The Scottish hip-hop community. Just *hip-hop*. What are we trying to say with the name? Regarding location-based labels, hip-hop has always been about geography. Forman (2012: xvii) notes, "Rap's lyrical constructions commonly display a pronounced emphasis on place and locality". The Bronx, Brooklyn, Manhattan, Queens, Staten Island, then on to LA, Compton, Long Beach, to Miami, Atlanta, Houston, and on. From macro to micro levels, local areas, conurbations and streets are equally celebrated. I've never been to the Bronx but I have a loose understanding of some of its key geographic locations due to the stories told in rap. 1520 Sedgewick Avenue – Kool Herc's address and the birthplace of hip-hop; Cedar Playground – the nexus for nascent live hip-hop events; the Bronx Little Italy – the scene of Big Pun's tale in *Twinz (Deep Cover 98)*. The psychogeography of the place is mapped out in the stories told in the raps. It serves to communicate, celebrate and historicise local experience, narrating the psychic understanding of the community from which the music emanates. So, geography is important. New York hip-hop. LA hip-hop. Atlanta hip-hop. Hip-hop fans and artists around the world understand the significance of location to the stories being told. We start to define the music by where it was made. I regularly hear Scottish hip-hop artists ask, "why can't we just call it hip-hop?". Well, we can, but back to that thing about labels – human beings need a way of making sense of the world and that way, for better or worse, is by classification. "You are this because you are from here". "You are not this because you are not from there". The binary, the hyphen, the imperial identifier. Thus, we attempt to make a little bit of sense out of the chaos. Does it limit, reduce and fail to fully explain things? Yes. Can we continue with the label on the understanding that it isn't fully fit for purpose but serves a purpose all the same? For now, let's.

So hip-hop has always been about geography. But as Rakim so famously said: "It ain't where you're from, it's where you're at" (Barrier, Griffin & Griffin 1987). And so hip-hop has also always been about ignoring geography, focusing on what you have to think and say, as opposed to where you are from or what you look like. Challenging invisible boundaries drawn along lines of race, class, gender, otherness. It is about geography and it is about *defying* geography. And so it continues, in happy perpetual paradox.

What have we covered so far? Hip-hop is contradiction. It is about geography and it is not about geography. It engages with the local and the global. It shares local stories through a globally established medium. It is hybrid in form, messy, fluid and multi-point in both its origins and destinations. Scottish hip-hop is a marginal, underground sub-culture, that has never had the cultural or financial capital required for it to become overground. It is a collection of people across the country loosely bound together by their love of the music and culture who – metaphorically speaking – reside in a series of underground tunnels and antechambers, leading to the occasional modest overground rudimentary croft and terraced housing block, rendered virtually invisible against the skyline of towers, concert halls, factories and townhouses that make up the widely recognised cultural landscape of Scottish music. Let's meet these people.

Who We Are… Where We Come From…

In the early to mid-1980s in the Plaza Ballroom on Glasgow's Victoria Road, young teens gathered from all over central Scotland to breakdance. Imported from the 'States, breakdancing became a national story across Scotland, as it spread across the rest of the globe. Pockets of young people all over the country were enthralled by it. The films (*Wild Style*, *Beat Street*, *Street Wars*), the music (Grand Master Flash and the Furious Five, Cold Crush Brothers) and the breakers (Crazy Legs, the Rock Steady Crew) inspired and enthused a generation of young folks. These grew into local crews: Glasgow City Breakers, Laser City Crew. Speaking to those who were there, the excitement is evident some forty years later. Graffiti came at the same time and folks developed their own regional styles from Dundee, to Edinburgh to Glasgow. The 2019 documentary *Loki's History of Scottish Hip-Hop*, produced and directed by music producer Sace Lockhart (founding member of ground-breaking hip-hop group Two Tone Committee) explores its beginnings. Lockhart notes that these were radical artists, operating extensively outside the law, committed to changing the spaces and places we move through and inhabit in the city (personal communication December 2021).

Then there are the music pioneers: Two Tone Committee and Sugar Bullet, Dope Inc, Steg G & The Freestyle Master, Big Div, Jay Large, Blackanized, DJ Richie Ruftone … Scottish hip-hop came in waves and these early waves were truly radical, constantly fighting a dual battle of what the public perceive hip-hop to be and what we as Scots perceive Scottish culture to be. By the early 2000s this first wave of hip-hop innovators was joined by new upstarts, Loki, Respek BA, the bEINg emcees, Mog, Scotland Yard Emcees, Pen Pushers, Live Sciences, All Time High, Mad Hat, Stanley Odd, Werd – the list goes on.

What about the demographic of Scottish hip-hop – these are predominantly white men making this music? Well, yes. Scotland is around 96% white (Scottish Government 2021). There are significant contributions from people of colour – Bigg Taj, phenomenal pioneering beatboxer in Scotland; Joseph Malik and AJ Nuttal – leaders of hugely impactful hip-hop-based group Blacka'nized in the late 1990s/ early 2000s; Mista Defy, rapper with Two Tone Committee; Edinburgh's Profisee, to name a few. But in its initial decades, hip-hop in Scotland is representative of wider Scottish music cultures – it is built around a predominantly white, male, working-class experience, participants, and voices.

Where were the women? Shell Toe Mel – eminent b-girl and hip-hop cultural lynchpin in Scotland, notes in Arusa Qureshi's book *Flip the Script* (2021), that there weren't many if any female emcees that she knew of in its early stages. By the early 2000s this was starting to change. Indian-Glaswegian emcee, Soom T was making an impact with Monkeytribe. Eunice Olumide broke through with Northern Exposure. Lyrical powerhouse Empress has proven her dedication to hip-hop culture and lyrical skill. Long-time hip-hop community collaborators Becca Starr and Becci Wallace are increasingly adding rap to their output. Nova Scotia the Truth won the prestigious national prize, Scottish Album of the Year, in 2020, welcoming in a new generation of young female voices.

Contemporary Scotland is refreshingly, increasingly diverse. This brings a new range of perspectives, interpretations and experiences. The cutting-edge, jagged, stuttering production and rap of Iranian-born, Ashtronomik. The underground flow mixed with mainstream potential of Bemz, representing Ayr by way of South London and Nigeria, winning *BBC Introducing Scottish Act of the Year 2022*, and – very importantly – publicly asking the question "What is Scottish Hip-Hop?" in order to address feelings of alienation, outsiderdom and rejection felt by some who make hip-hop in Scotland (Bemz 2021). Paisley's Shogun continuing to build on his impact and recognition across UK rap. Chef, Louis Seivwright, GLUCO, Spawn Zero, CCTV, Skoop Syndicate. These are the vanguard in a growing legion of important new rap voices across Scotland.

Disruptors, Displacement, Paradoxes and Patter: An Analysis of Scottish Hip-Hop

As an introduction to the culture of Scottish hip-hop, Darren McGarvey AKA Loki, makes a compelling first contact. A prolific and impactful artist and figure in both Scottish hip-hop and now wider Scottish culture, Loki has released in excess of eleven full-length albums and a plethora of other projects, collaborations and outputs. His work spans the early 2000s to the present day. Until 2018, his position in Scotland – while very well respected within the hip-hop community and areas of the arts – remained an underground, outlying voice. What then changed in 2018, that allowed Darren, after fifteen years of releasing work, to become recognised nationally and internationally for his searing and insightful creative, cultural, societal commentary? The answer: he put his work in written form. It was recognised as being culturally significant. The book – *Poverty Safari* – won the esteemed Orwell Prize for Literature. He was not necessarily saying things he hadn't already said in rap form or presenting ideas that he wasn't already respected and valued for within his community. But he changed the format and suddenly it was credible; authentic social commentary; culturally valuable. This says a lot about the cultural capital ascribed to hip-hop in Scotland. It amounts to something ringing literally and metaphorically in the ears of rappers around the country: "You canny be saying anything serious if yir rapping it".

Disruptive, defiant and thought-provoking, Loki's work epitomises hip-hop practice. He subverts cultural norms, language form and wordplay in order to take a counter-perspective stance, creating conflict and contradiction. By this means, language becomes playful, socially aware, culturally connective, challenging beliefs and opinions. Take this stanza from his 2018 release *Send for That*, from the song, 'Politics':

Crashed a Vespa in the window of the Yes bar
And woke up on the Death Star
For anybody intae metaphors: there y'are
I'm away tae throw a fucking tenner in the swear jar.

Here, the very British image of the – ironically Italian made – Mod-ish Vespa moped crashing into the window of a Glasgow bar named after its support for Scottish independence juxtaposes Britishness and Scottishness, suggesting the outcome being finding yourself on or in a doomed imperial state – the Death Star. In doing so, Loki synthesises ideas of British and Scottish nationalism, tying them both to the UK's history of imperial expansion and colonialism. He then casually breaks one level of reality, pointing out the metaphorical nature of the previous lines, before humorously swearing about putting money in a jar designed to discourage swearing. This, itself a rebellious act, implies a frustration at the pointlessness of the whole process and perhaps even the whole concept of nationhood itself. This is neither overtly pro-independence nor pro-union. It is designed to challenge everybody. The four lines combine humour, wordplay, a bricolage of cultural imagery, social commentary and individual character.

Continuing the theme of challenge to socio-cultural norms, let's return to women in hip-hop. To say that women in hip-hop culture have not always enjoyed an equal, fair or honest representation is like saying in Scotland it rains a bit – true but not really communicating the scale of the situation. The male-dominated, patriarchal social structure that has been the case in many elements of hip-hop can be seen as a reflection of inequalities in wider culture and society. Regina Bradley dissects gender in hip-hop: "Hip-hop masculinity is aggressive, dominant and flattened while hip-hop femininity is submissive, (hyper)sexual, and silenced" (2015: 182). Although there have been important contributions from women in Scotland, hip-hop music has similarly been a primarily male preserve historically. This dynamic is changing.

Empress has a proven record of dedication and commitment to lyricism, as central to her rap practice. Her 2021 release, the provocative, 'Only Flans' – a play on the content subscription service *Only Fans* – challenges, subverts, and rewrites narratives on her own terms. The accompanying video opens with out-of-focus images of Empress sat on a bed in lingerie, in-keeping with stereotypical imagery for both women in hip-hop and *Only Fans* content. The scene then cuts to her in the kitchen, streaming live to her phone, while she cooks. Waving a large knife, she raps to camera, severed limbs in a pot on the stove, provocatively dressed women behind her. The effect is a bombardment of signifying, multi-layered messages that both confirm and subvert expectations.

Each phrase in the verse is enveloped in double-meaning and signifying practices. Opening with:

Now I'm No Diggity down for no-dignity bound encounters
That ring out wi an ignorant sound. Ye canny keep a good besom down

The first line establishes the level of intertextuality to be expected throughout the song. The phrase "no diggity", references the 1996 song of the same name, making use of the -iggity-style rap of Das EFX, both actions authenticating her work by association with historically credible authentic output. The internal five-syllable rhyme of "no diggity down" with "no dignity bound" allows her to state immediately an opposition to the supposition of female submission. She dismisses this "ignorant" behaviour, completing the rhyming couplet with the subversion of the phrase "you can't keep a good man down", substituting "man" for "besom". This Scots' term, used for women of "disreputable character, also sometimes (a) term of endearment for mischievous young girl" (Scott 2015), doesn't just supplant man with woman. The choice of word also speaks to a challenge to the categorisation of out-spoken women as disreputable. It takes ownership of derogatory phrasing, reframing it on the user's terms, subverting negative cultural stereotypes, to challenge dominant narratives. This one rhyming couplet demonstrates multi-layered dialogue: global, genre-specific and local referencing; hybridity, locality, duality and individuality.

Building to the chorus, Empress highlights the crux of the dilemma between popularity, social media and economic freedom. She notes:

> Cause I can't pay bills off applause even though that's nice
> And I can't keep my fridge stocked off comments and likes
> And I really don't want my name in lights
> Nah I'm talking shite, that's something I'd actually like, an' they better be bright.

These lines emphasise the emptiness of support and a social media fanbase, under the reality of capitalism and economic struggle. She feigns an unassuming, demure response – "I really don't want my name in lights" – playing a modest, feminine role, then smashes that image to pieces with, "I'm talking shite, that's something I'd actually like", demanding that, "they better be bright". This is the demolition of male-dictated female image, and the rebuilding of that image by her own architecture (through a Scottish cultural lens) in its place, centre-stage and fully visible. By these means, Empress gracefully flits between domains – hip-hop, Scottish culture, global culture – in a state of constant provocation, dismissing gender suppositions, rewriting narratives, celebrating female power and sexuality. It is parody and sincere, proposing a new space built from the rubble of deconstructed stereotypes.

Creating new spaces and redefining existing ones is a central part of hip-hop culture. A naturally historicising artform, rap chronicles cultural evolution as it happens. Aberdonian rapper Ransom FA clearly demonstrates this process in his 2021 piece, 'Momentous' A young black Scot, Ransom combines and hybridises images of Scottish and rap cultures, seasoned with African cultural elements that also reflect his Nigerian heritage. The first Scottish rap artist to represent Scotland in BBC Three's programme *The Rap Game*, he has carved out a space for himself in UK grime, building a sizeable audience, consistently representing Scottish accent and culture.

Consider the introductory lines of this song:

> Might throw me a Scottish national party, call me Nicola Sturgeon
> Just a different version, the troops they moving determined
> I put in labour, but now I gotta try conserving
> Stop wasting ma energy, what they do is not concerning
> Far from your average person, king of the North resurgence
> Where I'm from I'm a Don, you don't wanna see the young team lurkin'.

In this short section, a variety of images, perspectives and identities are performed, engaged with and subverted. The Scottish national party phrase speaks to Ransom's profile being on a national level, engaging with a nation. He likens himself to the Scottish First Minister, a leader and national figurehead. The political referencing continues with double meaning of labour/ Labour and conserving/ Conservative. The geographic referencing in the phrase "king of the north" acknowledges his Scottishness, completed with: "where I'm from I'm a Don". This carries the duality of being in-keeping with hip-hop cultural practice of referring to yourself as a "Don" as-in Mafia boss, combined with meaning an Aberdeen football fan. The use of "young team" for youth gang is also specifically Scottish. Thus, Ransom, navigates and guides the listener through a world that is simultaneously UK rap-authentic in its style, delivery and content, while also being Scottish culture-authentic in its referencing, wordplay and language. These dualities continue later in the verse:

> They know me bro, it's the king of the coast
> See me scranning a Sunday roast
> …
> Auntie got the jollof – that was a lot
> Sometimes I feel like I'm losing the plot

Here the word "scranning", meaning to eat, is a decidedly Scottish phrase, combined with the quintessentially British Sunday roast. This is placed adjacent to "auntie got the jollof", introducing family and Nigerian rice dish, jollof. These combinational references serve to further emphasise the hybridisation of culture; the representation of the local and traditional – both Scots and Nigerian – through the conduit of the global contemporary – rap music.

Analysis of the accompanying video provides deeper evidence of the hybrid nature of contemporary culture manifest. Across several scenes that alternate throughout the video, Ransom is seen in black and white wearing a crown, with a woman in sexually provocative clothing, in and around a pristine black Bentley. These images ascribe to mainstream global hip-hop iconography of dominance, affluence and glamour. They serve to cement his national status, his authenticity as a rap artist and his success therein. This is juxtaposed with a scene where he is wearing an Aberdeen Football Club top, wrapped in a Scotland flag. This version of Ransom signposting Scottish culture. These scenes both contrast and complement. They demonstrate difference and the rationalising of the two identities in one constant whole – Ransom. When the jollof line occurs in the song, the image of the rice is bright yellow in colour, set against the rest of the image in black and white, signifying the colour, liveliness and literal flavour of Nigerian culture. The lyrics, style, delivery and visual images all indicate interwoven, hybridised identities from consumed culture, lived culture and cultural heritage.

From Footnotes to Footholds…

That hip-hop in Scotland has remained an underground subculture for forty years while global hip-hop becomes the biggest influence on popular music in decades speaks to the duality of Scottish life and culture. The complexity of Scottish/ British cultural experience is borne out in these dualities. The socio-cultural schizophrenia that comes from being a nation that is both coloniser and colonised – at the same time. The duality of language, of code-switching between how you speak within your community and how you speak to representatives of government and social services. The issues of self-mockery; self-embarrassment; the dreaded "cultural cringe"

(Krusenstjerna 1989). These ideas resonate in the frequencies at which Scottish hip-hoppers interpret and transmit hip-hop culture and Scottish culture. The practices revealed across Scottish hip-hop artists' work recall the subversion and reimagining that J. Griff Rollefson identifies in his work on post-colonialism in European hip-hop (Rollefson 2017). Ironically, Scottish hip-hop's continued underground status is what maintains its potency for protest, challenge and rebellion. It's continued subcultural economy and lack of wider infrastructure is also its superpower – allowing diverse sounds and approaches, never dictated by economic levers.

Hip-hop is identity formation in action. It is the creation and recreation of self that takes place in all of us as we grow, change and express ourselves, made overt and visible. It is the ever-increasing pace with which our life experiences, influences and communities shape who we are and the identities that we project. Hip-hop is hybrid. It takes from all of its surroundings and fuses whatever it comes in contact with into something new, something 'other'. That is to say, hip-hop synthesises, syncretises and subverts. It combines local cultural experience with reinterpretations and repositionings of global cultural experiences and presents them intertwined with the idiosyncratic perspective of the individual. This is the rapid, continual shifting and changing of a globalised, digital, virtual universe and all the multiple, co-present influences that that can allow, interacting with the local, the familial, the traditional, to create new invigorating, innovative hybrid ways of communicating, channelling, challenging and representing lived experiences. This is the power of hip-hop to me. It takes the myriad sources of impetus, interpretation and inspiration, and brings them together into a fluid, constantly evolving new whole. This is neither global homogenisation, nor local imitation of an incompatible culture. It is local reinterpretation, reverse-engineered and reconstructed in each community in which it takes root; global amplification, translation, re-dissemination. Hip-hop is not unique in this. Many contemporary cultural forms demonstrate and evoke these characteristics. However, hip-hop's cultural rules of locality – individual and communal – blended with the global, its vernacular wordplay, signifying and subversive, lend themselves to these outcomes. They allow and facilitate the demonstration of this fast-paced, contemporary hybridisation. This manifests in Scottish hip-hop culture as new and traditional (re)definitions of what it is to be Scottish in the twenty-first century. This is evidenced in the work of Loki, Empress and Ransom FA. In these outputs Scottish hip-hop embodies the living evolution of oral tradition, protest, struggle, celebration; the sounds that keep community voices alive; the new, fresh sounds and perspectives that allow stories to cross generations; the permanently impermanent; one current future in a multiband of constantly splintering and diverging artistic means of expression.

A footnote in the history of Scottish music? The outlier, the peripheral, the marginal? Outside views can yield fresh perspectives. And boundaries shift. Centres move, edges become cores, borders fall, walls collapse. What is a footnote now, may in time become the central text; the campfire around which folks gather as the storyteller tells their tale. Footnotes can become footholds, from which dusty feet may climb and walk new paths.

References

Barrier, E., Griffin, E., Griffin, W., 1987. *I Know You Got Soul*. [lyric] NY: 4th & Broadway.

Bemz, 2021. [Twitter] 2 October 2021. Available at: https://twitter.com/bigbemz1/status/1444396288963907587 [Accessed 19 December 2021].

Boyle, N., 2015. 'The top five Scottish hip hop acts who aren't Young Fathers'. *Time Out* [online]. Available at: https://www.timeout.com/glasgow/blog/the-top-five-scottish-hip-hop-acts-who-arent-young-fathers [Accessed 30 April 2022].

Bradley, R. N., 2015. 'Barbz and kings: Explorartions of gender and sexuality in hip-hop' in J. A. Williams, ed. *The Cambridge Companion to Hip-Hop*. Cambridge: Cambridge University Press, pp. 181–191.

Duffy, E., 2021. 'Iona Fyfe: Singer In Spotify Scots Success'. *The Herald*. [online] Available at: https://www.heraldscotland.com/news/19138686.iona-fyfe-singer-spotify-scots-success/.

Forman, M., 2012. '"Represent": Race, space and place in rap music' in M. Forman & M. A. Neal, eds. *That's the Joint: The Hip-Hop Studies Reader*. 2nd Edition ed. New York: Routledge, pp. 248–269.

Galloway, V., 2012. *The Urban Myth* [Online] Available at: https://www.heraldscotland.com/life_style/arts_ents/13054313.urban-myth/ [Accessed 11 April 2022].

Gates Jr, H. L., 1988. *The Signifyin' Monkey*. Oxford: Oxford University Press.

Gilroy, P., 1993. *The Black Atlantic - Modernity and Double Consciousness*. London: Verso.

Hawthorne, K., 2021. '"It was like: People from Aberdeen shouldn't rap!" Scotland's hidden hip-hop scene' *The Guardian* [online]. Available at: https://www.theguardian.com/music/2021/aug/10/it-was-like-people-from-aberdeen-shouldnt-rap-scotlands-hidden-hip-hop-scene [Accessed 30 April 2022].

Hook, D., 2021. '"Scottish people can't rap": the local and global in Scottish hip-hop', *Popular Music* 40(1) pp. 75–90.

Krusenstjerna, S., 1989. The Scottish arts council grows up? An identity crisis' in D. McCrone & Brown, eds. *The Scottish Government Yearbook 1989*. Edinburgh: Unit for the Study of Government in Scotland, University of Edinburgh, pp. 155–172.

National Museum of Scotland, 2018. *Rip It Up: The History of Scottish Pop* [online] Available at: https://www.nms.ac.uk/exhibitions-events/past-exhibitions/rip-it-up/ [Accessed 19 December 2021].

Pennycook, A. & Mitchell, T., 2009. 'Hip hop as dusty foot philosophy: Engaging locality' in H. S. Alim, A. Ibrahim & A. Pennycook, eds. *Global Linguistic Flows: Hip Hop Cultures, Youth Identities, and the Politics of Language*. New York: Routledge, pp. 25–42.

Qureshi, A., 2021. *Flip the Script: How Women Came to Rule Hip-Hop*. Edinburgh: 404 Publishing.

Rimmer, J., 2016. *Voices for the Voiceless: Scottish Hip Hop in 2016*. [Online] Available at: http://bellacaledonia.org.uk/2016/02/11/voices-for-the-voiceless-scottish-hip-hop-in-2016/ [Accessed 21 December 2021].

Rimmer, J., 2018. '2018 Could be the year scottish hip-hop makes its mark' *Clash* [Online] Available at: https://www.clashmusic.com/features/2018-could-be-the-year-scottish-hip-hop-makes-its-mark [Accessed 20 April 2022].

Rollefson, J. G., 2017. *Flip the Script: European Hip-Hop and the Politics of Postcoloniality*. Chicago: The University of Chicago Press.

Scottish Government. 2021. "Ethnicity" in *Scotland's Census*. [online] Available at: https://www.scotlandscensus.gov.uk/census-results/at-a-glance/ethnicity/ [Accessed 21 December 2021].

Scott, M., 2015. 'Scots Word of the Season: "Besom"', *The Bottle Imp* [online] Available at: https://www.thebottleimp.org.uk/2015/06/scots-word-of-the-season-besom/ [Accessed 21 December 2021].

Discography

Eric B. & Rakim. "I Know You Got Soul" on *Paid in Full* (1987). Island Records.

Empress. *Only Flans* (2021). Self-released.

Loki. "Politics" on *Send for That EP* (2018). Self-released.

Ransom FA. *Momentous* (2021). Self-released.

Films

Loki's History of Scottish Hip-Hop (2019) Directed by Sace Lockhart. BBC.

13

'Indy' Music

Scottish Popular Music and the Constitutional Question

Adam Behr

Introduction: The Roots of the Scottish Independence Campaign

On July 3rd, 1990 a crowd of over 30,000 gathered for a family-friendly festival with a mixed programme of speakers, comedy, theatre workshops and music. The musical offering was broad, not least in terms of its 'Scottishness', from folk doyens like Dick Gaughan through singer songwriter John Martyn to various rock and pop bands. Among these latter, too, there was a range of musical emphases: the overtly Celtic rock of Runrig, the jazz and Latin tinged Hue and Cry, the sophisticated glossy pop of Deacon Blue, and The Shamen, already some distance along their journey from guitar led psychedelia to electronically driven acid house dance music.

The eclecticism on display did not, though, obscure the political thrust of the event at Fallen Inch Field in Stirling. Organised by Stirling District Council and the Scottish Trades Union Congress (STUC), *A Day for Scotland* was infused with a critique of the Conservative government of the day (see Stewart 2004: 277) and momentum towards Home Rule, for a devolved Scottish parliament. Promotional material promised "a positive celebration of Scottish life – which says we must decide our future – no-one else!" (University of Stirling 2020).

Like many political events, *A Day for Scotland* had long historical roots and can be viewed as a stepping-stone rather than a starting point. Agitation for some degree of separation from the UK had been a feature of Scottish politics since the formation of the Scottish National Party (SNP) in 1934. The movement gained salience following the discovery of the North Sea's oil fields at the end of the 1960s.[1] In 1974, campaigning with the slogan "It's Scotland's Oil!", the SNP won six seats in the Westminster Parliament in the February general election and eleven in the year's second election in October. In the 1979 referendum on the creation of a Scottish Assembly a majority of those voting opted for devolution but on a turnout insufficient to meet the threshold of 40% of the registered electorate voting in favour. The SNP's consequent withdrawal of support from the Labour government of the day was among the factors that led to the Conservatives calling for a vote of confidence which Labour lost, precipitating a general election and the advent of the Thatcher administrations. The start of eighteen years of Tory rule in the UK was, then, closely contemporaneous with the formation in 1980 of the Campaign for a Scottish Assembly.

The nexus of political campaigning in 1980s Scotland was, in consequence, multifarious and complex. Opposition to Thatcher's Conservatives masked underlying divergences, not least between those for whom devolution *within* the UK was a destination and those who, like the SNP, saw it as a way station to the ultimate goal of a *separate* nation. *A Day for Scotland* may have

DOI: 10.4324/9781003247470-16

presented a unified front on the day, but the musical variety on offer was evidence of counter-vailing forces in the characterisation of popular music as 'Scottish', countervailing forces which reflected tensions in the broader political trajectory.

Scottish politics has changed substantially since then, as has its relationship to popular music. Since *A Day for Scotland,* to put this another way, popular musical and political cultures have evolved in tandem. Understandings of the former have expanded beyond a Celtic focus and been characterised by a more cohesive music industry presence; the latter has become increasingly focused on constitutional questions. In the rest of this chapter I will examine the relationship between Scottish popular music and the independence movement as the 1990s mix of civic and labour movement politics crystallised into a starker call for departure from the UK, most notably (to date) with the 2014 referendum. My essay is organised in three parts. The first examines the changing meanings of 'Scottish' popular music; the second examines the development of specifi-cally Scottish cultural policies; the third examines the problematic concept of 'national identity'.

Defining Scottish Popular Music

While it is beyond the scope of this chapter to provide a comprehensive account of the last thirty years of Scottish popular music, it is possible to say something about music, national identity and the sometimes messy relationship between the two, as the former is brought into the service of the latter.

The first question is 'what constitutes "Scottish" popular music?', given that the definition of popular music itself is contested territory, comprising elements of folk (a music 'of the people') and commerce (produced for a mass audience, for profit), and rooted in the knotty issue of 'au-thenticity'. I adopt a necessarily broad approach to 'popular' here, taking it to encompass an aes-thetic spectrum of commercially available music across a range of 'pop', 'rock' and 'folk' genres (some more mainstream than others). The role of popular music in the Scottish independence campaign is, anyway, based less on what it *is* than what it *does*. I understand pop here less as a set of aesthetic tropes than in terms of its social use-value for its audiences. From this perspec-tive we can view pop in terms of its social function, as one means by which we forge identities and negotiate the relationships between private and public lives:

> [We] enjoy popular music… because of its use in answering questions of identity: we use pop songs to create for ourselves a particular sort of self-definition, a particular place in society (Frith 2007: 264).

This applies across the numerous genres that we might, generally speaking, deem 'popular'.

> [T]his is not just a feature of commercial pop music. It is the way in which all popular music works… Folk musics, similarly, continue to be used to mark the boundaries of ethnic iden-tity, even amidst the complications of migration and cultural change… It is not surprising, then, that popular music has always had important nationalist functions (ibid. 265).

Scottish music – traditional, folk and commercial – operates along these faultlines of 'cultural change', which is to say that the commercial and the traditional co-mingle in the cut and thrust of everyday consumption and production. As Simon McKerrell (2011: 9) has pointed out, the latter decades of the twentieth century saw "the interdependence of musical repertoire with na-tional identity… reformulated by globalization and the economic pressures on professional mu-sicians". There is, then, no straightforward alignment between musical styles and orientation to a 'Yes' or 'No' vote on Scottish independence. Runrig, for example, as one of the *Day for Scotland* acts, had a distinctly Scottish Celtic aesthetic: the band sang in Gaelic as well as in English as part of its Celtic Rock sound. But this was not a marker of a group stance on the independence question. Lead singer Donnie Munro twice stood for the Labour Party – defeated both times by Liberal Democrats – and spoke in favour of the devolution of more powers to Scotland *within* the union, warning of the "enormous disruption, cost and uncertainty of separation" and criticising the Yes campaign's "determin[ation] to tear us out from the stability of one historically successful union" (quoted in Ross 2014). Pete Wishart, the band's keyboard player in 1990, was, by contrast, a successful parliamentary candidate for the SNP, committed to removing Scotland from the UK. Indeed, while both men had left Runrig by the time of the referendum, their political divergence had been evident long before that. In 1997 Munro (an avowed socialist) warned that if the SNP "willingly hypes up the emotive issues of pride, dignity and the juvenile misappropriation of the Braveheart factor, it will continue to feed the nasty rump of blatant racism of which that form of emotional elitism simply fans the flames". Wishart responded that this was an "unnecessary and vicious" attack. (Quotes from *The Herald* 1997.)

If membership of a Celtic act was no guarantor of support for independence, neither was a mainstream pop sound any indication of constitutional agnosticism. *A Day for Scotland* was not the only, nor even the biggest, Scottish pop event in the summer of 1990 to resonate with questions of identity. *Big Day*, one of the celebrations marking Glasgow's status as the European Capital of Culture, had an audience of around 250,000 across stages around the city and was the biggest live music broadcast to that point by UK television station Channel 4. Both the *Day for Scotland* and the *Big Day* took an ecumenical approach to Scotland's cultural life, although the Glasgow event was less ostensibly political and more overtly oriented towards the commercial music of the day.[2] While its line-up was heavy with Scottish acts, it leant towards the mainstream, including the likes of Deacon Blue, Texas and Wet Wet Wet, who were joined by Americans Michael Stipe and Natalie Merchant, as well as by English troubadour Billy Bragg. Perhaps the most notable expression of national sentiment at the event was Glaswegian-born singer Sheena Easton being booed and pelted with bottles by the audience for, apparently, having adopted an American accent, but the smooth pop of Deacon Blue also served as the launchpad for lead singer Ricky Ross (another avowed socialist) to mount a tirade not just, as might have been expected, against the Tories but also against the local Labour Party, criticising them for the closure of a local steelworks and dedicating his final song to "to the people of Scotland who have been lied to and sold down the river by the Labour Party who don't ask questions on their behalf in Westminster" (English 2015).

Ross, like former Fairground Attraction singer Eddie Reader, who also appeared at the *Big Day*, would go on to become a highly vocal supporter of the 'Yes' campaign in 2014, although in 1990 neither artist had a markedly 'Scottish' sound. What is clear is that Scottish popular music had a deep strand of political engagement well before independence reached the ballot paper.

The Making of Scottish Cultural Policy

The resounding defeat of the Conservative Party by Tony Blair's re-branded 'New Labour' in the 1997 General Election precipitated several significant developments. There was, almost immediately, a second referendum on devolution, with the vote now significantly in its favour. The re-opening of the Scottish Parliament in July 1999 (after nearly 300 years) was marked by a series of musical events in the capital city of Edinburgh. In a programme put together by commercial promoter Unique Events, rock bands Idlewild and Garbage headlined a stage at one end of the city centre's Princes Street Gardens, with the Scottish Chamber Orchestra, Royal Scottish National Orchestra and Scottish Opera playing at the other end.[3] An indoor event at the

Assembly Rooms featured folk and traditional acts like fiddler Aly McBain and the Callanish Ceilidh Band (UZ Arts 1999).

Another early development in New Labour policy was the formation of the Department for Culture, Media and Sport (DCMS).[4] While there had been a precursor to this in the previous administration's Department of National Heritage, the emergence of the DCMS marked a shift of emphasis from 'culture' to 'creative industries' policy.[5] The significance of this was not lost on the music industries, which in both London and Scotland had a growing appreciation of the need to court government (Cloonan 2007: 48).

Following increased lobbying, and the establishment by the DCMS of a Music Industry Forum to foster dialogue between government and the music industries, 2008 saw the establishment of a new umbrella organisation, UK Music, to represent commercial music-making overall. Also formed in 2008 was the Scottish Music Industry Association (SMIA), although unlike UK Music its membership was mainly comprised of sole traders and small-to-medium enterprises (Behr and Brennan 2014: 170). Scotland obviously lacked the lobbying firepower of the London-based major labels, industry bodies and copyright collection societies which underpinned UK Music but its largest live music promoters were also not SMIA members, despite being among the country's most commercially significant music businesses. In consequence the SMIA has relied more heavily on state support, via the arms-length funding body Creative Scotland, than its UK counterpart.

It has, nevertheless, helped to carve out and promote a distinct identity for Scotland's popular music, not least through one of its Creative Scotland supported initiatives – the Scottish Album of the Year (SAY) Award, launched in 2012 as a counterpoint to the Mercury Prize for albums by British and Irish artists, which was, itself, set up as an arts prize in contrast to the more explicitly sales-oriented BRIT Awards.[6] The SAY Award, in explicitly casting its view across genres – seeking to celebrate "the diversity and creativity of music and art in Scotland" (SAY Award 2013a) – reinforced the notion, implicit in the commercially and more politically oriented cultural events of the 1990s, that 'Scottish' music was not tied to a specific aesthetic but defined by geographical boundaries and the multifarious creative urges of the people within them. In this, it aligned neatly – if not necessarily explicitly – with the SNP's goal of presenting Scotland as distinct from the rest of the UK and itself as the face of a 'civic nationalism' marked by cultural liberalism and a lack of ethnocentrism.

This goal was made easier to attain as the political fissures across geographical lines in Britain became steadily deeper. The early years of devolved government in Scotland involved Labour administrations in both Westminster and Holyrood but the declining electoral appeal of New Labour led to the election of a minority SNP government in Scotland in 2007, followed by majority SNP rule in 2011, while at UK level Labour ceded power in 2010 to a Conservative led coalition and there have been Conservative governments since 2015. These voting shifts helped the SNP ramp up perceptions of the political differences between Scotland and the rest of the UK. SNP-led Scotland could be cast as a centre-left, social democratic polity in contrast to the budget-cutting austerity in the UK by the Conservative Party.

Such rhetoric has fed through into cultural matters. In a 2013 speech, for example, Scotland's SNP Culture Secretary, Fiona Hyslop (who attended the first SAY Award Ceremony and proudly posed for pictures with that year's winners, Bill Wells and Aidan Moffat), distinguished her approach to culture from that of her southern counterpart at DCMS, Conservative Maria Miller. Hyslop emphasised culture's *intrinsic* value as a public good; Miller suggested that the arts' case for public support should be based on their *economic* contribution (Behr and Brennan 2015: 171). In practice, however, the differences between the two administrations' cultural policies were not as striking as Hyslop was suggesting. Scotland's arts funding body, Creative Scotland, shares a DCMS-style approach to the creative industries as drivers of economic growth. Indeed,

Creative Scotland's early years were marked by a fracas deriving from confusion between its responsibilities and those of Scottish Enterprise, the public body responsible for business and economic development (Stevenson 2014: 179).

An instrumental account of culture has certainly characterised the overall approach and policy announcements of successive SNP governments, with the "creative industries" listed as a "growth sector" in 2011 (Behr and Brennan 2013: 25), alongside the likes of life sciences, energy and financial services, notwithstanding that music was, in the words of SMIA board member Tam Coyle, "a small potato to these guys" (ibid.). 'Growth' was also uppermost in the SNP government's White Paper outlining a *Guide to an Independent Scotland* (2013) while music received scant mention, despite previous research commissioned by Scottish Enterprise to map Scotland's music businesses (Williamson et al. 2002), and the publication of a *Music Manifesto* (Frith and Cloonan 2010) by the Royal Society of Edinburgh, which expressly sought to place music onto the policy agenda.[7] In terms of music policy the similarities between Holyrood and Westminster (between Creative Scotland and the Arts Council) seem more obvious than political rhetoric would suggest.

Towards a National Identity?

The Scottish independence referendum in 2014 provided a discursive space in which questions of nationality were untethered from specific types of music yet still associated with acts' brand identities. Nationality was already to some extent inscribed in the marketing and branding of popular music in the UK by record companies (which help to shape genre labels) as well as by governments. From before it took power New Labour made efforts to hitch its wagon to the popular cultural concept of 'Cool Britannia' and the associated commercial success of Britpop – Blur made a well-publicised pre-election visit to Tony Blair's office; Oasis's Noel Gallagher was an even more well-publicised guest at Downing Street's first big post-election cultural reception.

Amidst this celebratory atmosphere, however, the question of nations *within* Britain still lurked. Martin Cloonan (1999: 202) and Mark Percival (2010) have both argued that the spotlight of 'Brit-pop' shone primarily on English bands. The 'Brit' in 'Britpop', that is to say, came to be seen as somewhat synonymous with Englishness while Scottish and Welsh bands were more closely associated with their home nations. Non-English musicians played on this as part of the authenticating strategies common in popular music. As Percival (2010: 126) puts it:

> The success of Travis and Stereophonics was often framed by the bands themselves and by journalists in terms of their Welshness or Scottishness, and associated national stereotypes of self-deprecation, Celtic passion/sentimentality and an authenticist appeal to their regional and class origins.

Questions of national identity in pop, though, are more complicated than media or artists' narratives sometimes suggest. There is room for interpretation in the gap between the national labels associated with album prizes like the Mercury (British and Irish) and the SAY Award (Scottish), and the interleaved commercial and personal relationships actually at work. The 'Britishness' of the Mercury Prize winner of 2005 – Antony and the Johnsons' *I Am A Bird Now* – was, for example, widely challenged. The lead singer was British-born but the rest of the band were American and the album was recorded (for a US label) in New York. For the judges, though, the key to the award was that the record "was clearly an expression of a very British sensibility" (Street 2018: 123).

The SAY Award defines eligibility in terms of an artist (or majority of a band) being born in Scotland or having made it their creative base for three years or more (SAY Award 2013b: 3) but since the prize rewards artistic merit (rather than sales figures), judging involves blurring the boundaries between cultural orientation, geographical origin and the logistics of production. The SAY Award's definition of "Scottish Artist", referring to a creative base "*irrespective of nationality*" (2013b: 3, emphasis in original) clearly resonates with a conception of 'Scottishness' rooted in civic rather than ethnic identity. The 'Scottishness' of some of the more celebrated Scottish acts can be as open to question as the Britishness of Antony and the Johnsons. As Cloonan (2007:120) has noted, for instance, with regard to Franz Ferdinand (whose first album won the 2004 Mercury Prize), only one of the band at the time was born in Scotland, its record label and management are English and "in common with all Scottish acts, their royalties (and thus most of their earnings) are collected by UK collecting agencies".[8]

However national identity is ascribed, the fact is that music business infrastructure is weighted towards London. Album prizes and cultural discussions may be able to dance around the niceties of national identities but they can't ignore bluntly economic matters. The impetus for the SMIA lay partly in this divergence. 'Scottish' acts may have featured on the Mercury Prize podium and shortlists, but Scottish record labels were almost entirely passed over – Chemikal Underground remains the only Scottish based label ever to have a Mercury nomination (for The Delgados' *Great Eastern*).

The relationship of cultural ideals and economic reality was at the heart of the referendum debate about the retention or dissolution of the 300-year political union of England and Scotland, but musicians' contributions to the arguments involved not the thorny details of how independence would work for them but were used, rather, as a kind of "experiential marketing" (Street 2012: 88), helping to sell a product (in this case, a political project) by "associating it with an experience" (ibid.).

To this end, the aesthetic breadth of 'Scottish music' came increasingly into play as the question of independence moved from the abstract to the concrete. The National Collective, for instance, was an arts-led movement in support of independence that operated between 2011 and 2014, drawing in participants who ranged from grassroots musicians to established professional performers. Its remit was clearly as musically broad as it was politically tight; its activities included a touring *Yestival* in the summer of 2014, designed to "showcase the grassroots cultural movement for Scottish Independence", and a *Soundtrack to Independence*, hosted online, on which eclecticism was key. The call for contributions spoke of a "diverse independence sound" and explicitly welcomed "submissions from any genre – rock, pop, rap, folk, electronic, experimental" (National Collective 2013).

The point here was to project a sense of momentum and mass appeal for the political project rather than to provide a musically consistent offering. The range of musicians signing up to support the Collective was correspondingly broad, from rappers to folk fiddlers, and included – from the line-up of the 1990 events – Ricky Ross and Hue and Cry's Pat Kane, as well as SAY Award winners Aidan Moffatt and RM Hubbert (National Collective 2014). The scale of activity even provided something of a bridge between grassroots and commerce. Singer songwriter Gerry Cinnamon broke into the mainstream after releasing a pro-independence single, 'Hope Over Fear', and headlining a rally in Glasgow's George Square hosted by Scottish Socialist politician Tommy Sheridan.

Sheridan's involvement, like that of Ricky Ross, also indicated the success of the 'Yes' movement in wrapping the constitutional question in broadly left-wing, progressive clothing. Notwithstanding the wide divergence of opinion on what the politics of an independent Scotland might actually look like, there was a broad sense, among the musicians at least, that it would mark a break from the deregulatory, economically liberal trajectory of the UK, and, in particular, from the austerity of David Cameron's coalition government.

The progressive case for a 'No' vote was thus hampered by its alignment, on the ballot at least, with the Conservative preference for the Union. Among the unionist interventions was an open letter from celebrities based in England to Scottish voters that spoke of "our bonds of citizenship with you, and… our hope that you will vote to renew them" (*The Guardian* 2014). The signatories included musicians with a history of supporting the Conservatives (like Cilla Black and composer Mike Batt) as well as those who leant towards Labour (like Pink Floyd's David Gilmour) and those of no obvious party orientation at all. The extent to which the independence question became conjoined in popular perception with progressive arguments was illustrated by the fact that even the most celebrated of musicians were not immune from the emotional tide of the 'Yes' movement. When David Bowie's message on receipt of a Brit award in February 2014 included the plea "Scotland, please stay with us", the response was vituperative. Angry messages from independence supporters proliferated on social media – "Wrap it, you out of touch has-been!" – while the Brits show itself was denounced for being out of touch with the "real concerns" of musicians and fans. "Ironically", wrote Stuart Braithwaite of Scottish band Mogwai, "cringe-fests like the Brits are one of the biggest adverts for cultural independence you could muster" (McNabb 2014).

If Bowie and those in support of maintaining the constitutional *status quo* ultimately prevailed at the ballot box – the result was 55–45% in favour of 'No' to independence – the efforts of the National Collective campaigners were not completely in vain. The movement for a 'Yes' vote, the arts at its vanguard, lost primarily on economic grounds – the successful 'No' vote was dubbed 'Project Fear' for its emphasis on the practicalities of setting up an independent Scotland. But the Yes campaign was successful in changing the general terms of political and cultural engagement with the Scottish polity, precipitating a collapse in Labour and Conservative support and ushering in an era of SNP hegemony in both the devolved Scottish parliament and among Scotland's representatives at Westminster. The broad swathe of support for independence among Scottish musicians may not have been a direct cause of this political shift but it was, at the very least, illustrative of a drift in national sentiment within the arts away from historic attachment to the union and towards a separatist vision for Scotland. The belief that Scotland had its own national identity was now shared by artists, bohemians, musicians and many on the left who would previously have baulked at being called 'nationalists'.

Conclusion

At the time of writing Scottish public opinion is still evenly divided on the question of Scottish independence but there is no doubt that one effect of the 2014 referendum debate was to push nationalism closer to the centre of British as well as Scottish politics. The Conservative campaign in the 2015 General Election, for example, made much of the risks to Britain of a Labour government being beholden to the SNP for its parliamentary majority, and David Cameron's subsequent decision to hold a referendum on the UK's continuing membership of the European Union opened up a discursive public space for an aggressive English nationalism. The constitutional questions already dominating Scottish politics were further enflamed when a majority in Scotland voted to Remain in the EU while the narrow victory across Britain overall was for the Leave campaign.

Expressions of musical identity are, in the end, the result of developments in the political and economic as well as cultural spheres. Devolution has meant both a more distinctive Scottish political forum and a more clearly organised Scottish commercial music sector. Scottish musicians' journey from a left-wing sensibility, oriented around the Labour movement, to 'civic nationalism', framed as a progressive response to right wing governments in Britain, has changed the ways in which musical identity in Scotland is articulated. 'Scottish' popular music, already partly detached from generic considerations, now rests on claims to embody the concerns of 'the Scottish people' rather than on the way it sounds.

Notes

1   See Maxwell (2009: 121).
2   Though it did campaign around and fundraise for homeless charities.
3   The line-up of Garbage was largely American, save for its singer and frontwoman Shirley Manson.
4   'Digital, Culture, Media and Sport' from 2017.
5   See Behr (2015) for an overview of this shift internationally, and Cloonan (2007: 39–66) for details of how it played out in the UK under New Labour.
6   The BRIT Awards were formerly the BPI Awards until being re-branded in 1989, and are run by the British Phonographic Industry.
7   The mapping of Scotland's music industries was, itself, subject to tensions about what constitutes a 'national' music economy when representatives of the UK's copyright collection societies disputed their lack of input into the Scottish focused report (Williamson et al 2011: 463–464).
8   Later line-ups of the group did include more Scottish-born musicians.

References

Behr, A. (2015) 'Cultural policy and the creative industries', in Shepherd, J. and Devine, K. (eds.) *The Routledge Reader on the Sociology of Music*. London and New York: Routledge, pp. 277–286.

Behr, A. and Brennan, M. (2013) *Scotland on Tour: Strategies for Promoting the Scottish Music Industry*. University of Edinburgh/University of Glasgow/AHRC/Live Music Exchange.

Behr, A. and Brennan, M. (2014) 'The place of popular music in Scotland's cultural policy', *Cultural Trends*, 23 (3), pp. 169–177.

Cloonan, M. (1999) 'Pop and the nation-state: Towards a Theorisation', *Popular Music*, 18 (2), pp. 193–207.

Cloonan, M. (2007) *Popular Music and the State in the UK: Culture, Trade or Industry?* Aldershot: Ashgate.

English, P. (2015) 'The big day 1990: Stars look back on legendary gig that was Scotland's biggest live TV event', *Daily Record*, 3 June. Available at: https://www.dailyrecord.co.uk/entertainment/music/music-news/big-day-1990-stars-look-5813320 [Accessed 04/10/2022]

Frith, S. (2007) 'Towards an aesthetic of popular music', in S. Frith, (ed.) *Taking Popular Music Seriously*. London: Routledge, pp. 257–273.

Frith, S. and Cloonan, M. (2010) *A Music Manifesto for Scotland*. Edinburgh: Royal Society of Edinburgh.

Maxwell, S. (2009) 'Social justice and the SNP', in G. Hassan, (ed.) *The Modern SNP: From Protest to Power*. Edinburgh: Edinburgh University Press, pp. 120–134.

McKerrell, S. (2011) 'Modern Scottish Bands (1970–1990): Cash as authenticity', *Scottish Music Review*, 2 (1), pp. 1–11. Available at: http://www.scottishmusicreview.org/index.php/SMR/article/view/22 [Accessed 04/10/2022]

McNabb, S. (2014) 'Scottish independence: Yes voters hit out at Bowie', *The Scotsman*, 21st February. Available at: https://www.scotsman.com/news/politics/scottish-independence-yes-voters-hit-out-bowie-1544422 [Accessed 04/10/2022]

National Collective (2013) 'Project: Soundtrack to independence', *NationalCollective.Com*, 31st October. Available at: http://www.nationalcollective.com/2013/10/31/project-soundtrack-to-independence/ [Accessed 04/10/2022]

National Collective (2014) 'Over 1,300 artists sign letter in support of yes vote', *NationalCollective.Com*, 7th September. Available at: http://www.nationalcollective.com/2014/09/07/over-1300-artists-sign-letter-in-support-of-yes-vote/ [Accessed 04/10/2022]

No author (1997) 'Argument mars the Runrig party', *The Herald*, 20 May. Available at: https://www.heraldscotland.com/news/12326266.argument-mars-the-runrig-party/ [Accessed 04/10/2022]

No author (2014): 'Celebrities' open letter to Scotland – full text and list of signatories' *The Guardian*, 7th August. Available at: https://www.theguardian.com/politics/2014/aug/07/celebrities-open-letter-scotland-independence-full-text [Accessed 04/10/2022]

Percival, M. (2010) 'Britpop or Eng-pop?' in A. Bennett, and J. Stratton, (eds.) *Britpop and the English Musical Tradition*, Farnham: Ashgate, pp. 123–143.

Ross, C. (2014) 'Scottish independence: Ex-Runrig star Donnie Munro speaks out', *Press and Journal*, 12 September. Available at: https://www.pressandjournal.co.uk/fp/politics/scottish-politics/342384/scottish-independence-ex-runrig-star-donnie-munro-speaks-out/ [Accessed 04/10/2022]

SAY Award (2013a) *www.sayaward.com* Available at: https://web.archive.org/web/20121127173925/https://www.say-award.com/ [Accessed 04/10/2022]

SAY Award (2013b) *Format and Eligibility Guidelines: Coversheet'*. Available at: https://web.archive.org/web/20130730160020/ http://www.sayaward.com/wp-content/uploads/2013/04/Format-Eligibility-Coversheet.pdf [Accessed 04/10/2022]

Scottish Government (2013) *Scotland's Future: Your Guide to an Independent Scotland.* Edinburgh: Crown Copyright.

Stevenson, D. (2014) 'Tartan and tantrums: Critical reflections on the creative Scotland "stooshie"', *Cultural Trends*, 23 (3), pp. 178–187.

Stewart, D. (2004) *Challenging the Consensus: Scotland under Margaret Thatcher, 1979–1990.* PhD thesis. University of Glasgow.

Street, J. (2012) *Music and Politics.* Cambridge: Polity Press.

Street, J. (2018) 'Reflections on the Mercury Music Prize: An interview with Simon Frith', *Popular Music*, 37 (1), pp. 119–129.

UK Music (2008) Press release, 26th September. Available at: https://web.archive.org/web/20081222230502/http://www.ukmusic.org/page/news-6 [Accessed 04/10/2022]

University of Stirling (2020) 'A day for Scotland: 30 years on', *University of Stirling Website*, 14 July. Available at: https://www.stir.ac.uk/events/calendar-of-events/2020/august/a-day-for-scotland-30-years-on/ [Accessed 04/10/2022]

UZ Arts (1999) 'Opening celebrations - New Scottish Parliament', *UZ Arts.Com* website. Available at: http://www.uzarts.com/new-scottish-parliament [Accessed: 09/06/2023]

Williamson, J., Cloonan, M. and Frith, S. (2002) *Mapping the Music Industry in Scotland: A Report.* Glasgow: Scottish Enterprise.

Williamson, J., Cloonan, M. and Frith, S. (2011) 'Having an impact? Academics, the music industries and the problem of knowledge', *International Journal of Cultural Policy*, 17 (5), pp. 459–474, DOI: 10.1080/10286632.2010.550682

PART III

Futures and Imaginings

Simon Frith

In the 1955 British General Election Conservative and Unionist parties won 50.1% of the Scottish vote; the Scottish National Party won around 0.5%. In the 2015 General Election the SNP won 50% of the Scottish vote; the Conservative, Labour and Liberal Democratic parties won just one Westminster seat each. By then Scottish voters had voted clearly for devolution—a Scottish Parliament was established in 1999—and more narrowly against independence (in 2014). Following the 2021 Scottish Parliamentary elections there is, at the time of writing, a majority of pro-independence MSPs.

Various explanations can be given for the transformation of Scottish political culture: de-industrialisation and the effects of Margaret Thatcher's economic policies, for example, or secularisation and the declining political significance of Protestant and Catholic identities.[1] But historians agree that the increasing belief in an independent Scotland also involved an imaginative leap that was driven as much by cultural as political activists, by painters and poets, playwrights and film-makers, story-tellers and songwriters.[2]

It could be argued, indeed, that Scotland has always been an imaginative project. Its greatest literary figures, Robert Burns (1759–1796) and Sir Walter Scott (1771–1832), were enthusiastic Romantics. Hence their interest in Scotland's folk culture, their delight in finding old songs that seemed to express an essential Scottish sensibility. Their influence was long lasting. The first Burns Supper was organised as early as 1801, a few years after his death. Over the following centuries Burns Night suppers became the most celebrated rite of Scottishness around the world. Burns's songs are equally treasured. In 1959 the bicentenary of his birth was marked by EMI with the release of *His Immortal Memory*, Burns songs and poems performed by Kenneth McKeller, Duncan Macrae, Ian Wallace, Stuart Gordon and the Jimmy Shand Band. In 2009 Rough Trade marked the 250th anniversary with a deluxe edition of *Eddie Reader Sings the Songs of Robert Burns*. Stylistically these records reflect quite different commercial takes on Scottish folk music but they share an assumption that Burns's articulation of Scottish identity is timeless.

In December 2020 the Aberdeen *Press and Journal* reported on another cultural anniversary:

He is one of the world's most famous composers – and Ludwig van Beethoven was born in Germany 250 years ago this month.

As the creator of such works as the Pastoral and Eroica symphonies, the opera Fidelio, the Moonlight Sonata and Ode to Joy, time has not diminished the impact of his work or its popularity throughout the world.

Yet, while the anniversary is being commemorated with many different events, albeit with social distancing, few people will be aware of the links which Beethoven had to many poignant and evocative Gaelic songs – or the fashion in which he joined forces with acclaimed author and poet Sir Walter Scott.

DOI: 10.4324/9781003247470-17

Between 1809 and 1820 Beethoven was commissioned by the Edinburgh music publisher George Thomson to compose new versions of a large selection of Scottish melodies. Thomson employed Scott to write uplifting lyrics to replace the Gaelic verse and successfully established the Scottish song as a parlour concert favourite throughout Europe.

Burns and Scott have different cultural legacies: Burns has a supper, Scott a railway station. As a poet and songwriter Burns is renowned for his use of the Scots vernacular. He is celebrated as the plain and convivial 'man of the people'; the Scot as the canny commentator holding forth at the bar. Sir Walter Scott, by contrast, is regarded as a bit of a toff, whose gift to the Scottish Tourist Board was tartanry and whose contribution to the history of Scottish music was to make it respectable enough for the bourgeoisie.

The inspirational effect of Robert Burns is obvious in a project like Ronnie Gurr's *Burnsong,* staged annually from 2007 to 2014. This involved a weekend writing retreat in Galloway at which eight selected songwriters could work both individually and collaboratively. One successful result was the Burns Unit, a band featuring such different musicians as King Creosote, Emma Pollock, Future Pilot AKA and Karine Polwart. It could be argued, though, that Scott's romantic fictions did as much as Burns's Ayrshire poems to shape what is meant by musical Scottishness. Romances feature "improbable or marvellous events, a poetic or atmospheric emphasis, a plot defined by wandering, quest, homecoming, or discovery of lost or secret origins". A romance can thus be distinguished from a novel, "a picture of real life and manners, and of the times in which it is written". In his historical novels, however, as Roger Hansford suggests, Scott resolved the tension between the fabulous and the real in the figure of the minstrel. He

employed the figure to give his romances antiquarian appeal yet make them thoroughly contemporary for consumers… [the minstrel was]… talented in literature and music, a good entertainer, and excelled at chivalry and creativity in the romantic arts.

(quotes from Hansford 2017: 12, 68–69)

Under Scott's early nineteenth-century influence "songwriters combined the role of knight and troubadour into one single persona" and enabled drawing-room singers to take on this idealised role in their own performances. And such a performance ideal was not confined to nineteenth-century singers. The singer as "knight and troubadour" is a familiar image in contemporary Scottish popular music too, if in modern dress, as are balladic tales of "wandering" and "homecoming".

Such lyrical romanticism is not peculiar to Scottish popular music, of course, but the legacy of Burns and Scott is not simply to provide Scotland with romance in its own accent but to do so in a distinctly literary and geographically self-conscious way, as in *Ballads of the Book*, for example, the record released by Chemikal Underground in 2007 in honour of Scotland's first state-sponsored national poet, the Scots Makar Edwin Morgan. The album featured a series of collaborations between Scottish musicians and Scottish writers, such as Aidan Moffat with Ian Rankin and Emma Pollock with Louise Welsh.

Scottish song celebrates above all the pleasures of story-telling. If the Irish have, in their own account of themselves, the gift of the gab, the Scots have the blessing (and curse) of an imagination that willingly rides a roller coaster between the fabulous and the familiar, the mundane and the appalling.

In this section we discuss these issues in three essays.

In the first essay Simon Frith considers the rich seam of Scottish literary fiction about popular music. The writers he discusses vary in their musical interests but each explores the ways in which Scottish identities are formed by music and Scottish music is shaped by identities.

In the second essay we transcribe a conversation between Martin Cloonan and singer/songwriter Alasdair Roberts who, among many other things, muses on traditional music, Burns, ideas of Scottishness and the musical intertwining of the political and the metaphysical.

In the third essay, Diljeet Bhachu focuses on Scotland's increasing cultural diversity and the political and aesthetic consequences for our understanding of 'the Scottish voice'. What does it mean today to 'sound' Scottish? Who is allowed (or not allowed) to be Scottish? Culturally? Musically?

Soon after these essays were completed Fergus McCreadie's album *Forest Floor* was short-listed for the 2022 Mercury Music Prize. McCreadie is a jazz pianist, inspired by Keith Jarrett; he is part of the jazz world. At the same time, however, as Hugh Morris noted in *Jazzwise*,

> McCreadie is rooted in the Glasgow scene, and in Scottish identity. On *Forest Floor*, he borrows 'The Unfurrowed Field' from Lewis Grassic Gibbon's *Sunset Song*, a celebrated Scots text that depicts rural communities coming to terms with mechanisation.

For McCreadie, jazz "is kind of a folk music in itself". For Morris,

> *Forest Floor* circles around a kind of pastoral melancholy of ridges, glades and hills … a kind of unspoilt world that can only really exist in the imagination. It's a far cry from Ewan McGregor's Renton dunking his whole body into an overflowing public toilet in *Trainspotting*.[3]

Music made in Scotland is, it seems, necessarily a response to the ways in which the country has been shaped by literary imagination.

Notes

1 Old religious/tribal differences do still shape one form of Scottish popular music. Sectarian songs continue to be sung on the football terraces despite such performances now being treated as a criminal offence. See, for example, McKerrell (2012) and Millar (2016).

2 In a 1999 interview with *disClosure* magazine the literary historian Cairns Craig thus suggested that following the failure of the 1979 referendum on devolution, the energy previously put into political activity was channelled into culture. The consequent cultural vitality "gave Scottish people the sense of confidence in themselves and in their own identity that produced the political changes we are now going through" (quoted in Tranmer 2016: 133).

3 https://www.jazzwise.com/features/article/fergus-mccreadie-interview-jazz-is-kind-of-a-folk-music-in-itself
The phrase "a far cry" also recalls the title of a famous book by another Scottish writer, Muriel Spark's *A Far Cry From Kensington*, published in 1988.

References

Hansford, R. (2017) *Figures of the Imagination: Fiction and Song in Britain, 1790–1850,* London/New York: Routledge.

McKerrell, S. (2012) 'Hearing Sectarianism: Understanding Scottish Sectarianism as Song', *Critical Discourse Studies* 9(4), 363–374.

Millar, S.R. (2016) 'Let the People Sing? Irish Rebel Songs, Sectarianism, and Scotland's Offensive Behaviour Act', *Popular Music* 35(3), 297–319.

Tranmer, J. (2016) 'Popular Music and Left-Wing Scottishness', *Études écossaises* 18, 133–149.

14

The Fiction of Scottish Music

Simon Frith

Introduction

This chapter examines the stories told about popular music in Scottish literature. The literary tradition in Scotland is unusual in the way it has been imbricated in popular culture—in the continuing idolatry of Robert Burns, for instance. One of the early acts of the Scottish Parliament was to create the position of an official National Poet, the Scots Makar. As I have already noted, the appointment of the first Makar, Edwin Morgan, was celebrated with an album of literary/musical collaborations, *Ballads of the Book*. Morgan had already worked with jazz saxophonist Tommy Smith (on the projects *Beasts of Scotland* and *Planet Waves*) and with the rock band Idlewild (on the album *The Remote Part*—reciting a newly written poem, 'Scottish Fiction', over the title track). It is also not uncommon for Scottish writers to make music themselves. The poet Don Paterson was in the jazz folk group Lammas; the crime writer Ian Rankin wrote and performed songs with Doll By Doll's Jackie Leven; and the novelist Doug Johnstone, whose book *The Ossians* I discuss below, was drummer in the Fence Collective band, Northern Alliance.[1] Here, though, I'm less interested in these kinds of occupational overlaps than in how Scottishness has been shaped imaginatively by the interplay of literary and musical sensibilities.

I'll begin, then, with *Dirt Road*, the 2016 novel by Scotland's finest male contemporary literary author, James Kelman.[2] In *Dirt Road*, Murdo's mother has died and neither he nor his father, Tom, can cope; both find it hard to talk without a woman's mediation. Tom decides to take the boy to visit his aunt and uncle, now settled in the American South. Murdo is an awkward and unhappy boy, a gifted musician but tightly curled in on himself and only able to stretch out when he is wearing his accordion. In the States he finds himself drawn into the world of *zydeco*, music-making which, like traditional Scottish playing, is not about self-expression but just means being a musician with other musicians.

> And that was them. It was there in the song and the playing of the song. There was nothing other, not anyplace. He was there in it and didn't have "to feel like he was" because he was; and not "feel like a musician" among other musicians because he was one. He was just Murdo and this was Murdo. So what? It didn't matter anything else, he would play whatever, anything; and just say whatever, whatever he felt like saying; he was a musician and so what, that was all. He knew it and had done for such a long long while and was so weary weary but on ye go, ye just go on, that is that, picking yourself up, here he was. Whoever else was there that was them, it was up to them (Kelman 2016: 335–336).

On stage, with the band, Murdo realises he is not anyplace. He speaks Scottish with his accordion, the notes and phrases and rhythms he uses, just as Kelman writes Scottish in the words and phrases and rhythms he uses. But what they express, in the music, in the fiction, is not Scottishness as a geographical or even historical identity but as a more sublime sense of belonging.

The comic and the uncanny

My introduction to the fiction of Scottish music was a BBC Scotland drama series, *Tutti Frutti*, which was shown on television in 1987, the year I moved to Glasgow. *Tutti Frutti* was produced by Andy Park, whose career we outlined in the introduction, and written by John Byrne, playwright, artist, designer and illustrator (for Gerry Rafferty's album sleeves among other things). It starred Robbie Coltrane, Emma Thompson and Maurice Roeves as members of a rock'n'roll band, The Majestics, and Richard Wilson and Katy Murphy as their manager and his assistant. The series followed The Majestics on their Silver Jubilee Tour and made the band's squabbles and demanding fans seem at once comic, brutal and disturbing. The series ends with the band's final concert, at the Glasgow Pavilion: guitarist Vincent Driver, "the iron man of Scottish rock", drenches himself in vodka and sets himself alight.

What fascinated me about *Tutti Frutti* was not so much what it said about Scottish popular music as what it said about the place of Scottish popular music in the Scottish literary imagination. *Tutti Frutti* seemed to me rather more authentic than, say, David Hare's sentimental and self-satisfied 1975 musical, *Teeth 'n' Smiles*, which also dramatised the performance of a failing rock band, or Howard Schuman's entertaining but cliché-ridden 1977 TV drama series, *Rock Follies*, which starred a female rock trio seeking fame and fortune.

Tutti Frutti was not about thwarted idealism or the tragic conflict between integrity and exploitation; it was about popular culture as something both banal and appalling, comic and uncanny. It was Scottish in two ways. On the one hand it was a strand in the exuberantly guilt-ridden Scottish literary tradition that runs from James Hogg's *The Private Memoirs and Confessions of a Justified Sinner* (1824) through Robert Louis Stevenson's 1886 story *The Strange Case of Dr Jekyll and Mr Hyde* to Jenni Fagan's fantastical 2021 novel, *Luckenbooth*. On the other hand it understood popular music as the ideal site for an artistic exploration of Scotland as a particularly *unsettling* kind of place.

Alan Warner's novel *Morvern Callar* (1995) begins like this.

> He'd cut His throat with the knife. He'd near chopped off His hand with the meat cleaver. He couldn't object so I lit a Silk Cut.

Warner's heroine, Morvern Caller, works in the stockroom of a supermarket in a Scottish port. Her boyfriend has just killed himself and her response sets the tone for the subsequent action: matter-of-fact, opportunist, emotionally free of fuss. She takes trips to pass the time; meets people and passes on. The novel is a dazzling display of surface realism, vivid but ungraspable. It describes the unrelenting flatness of experience (Camus's *L'Étranger* is an obvious model) but over this Warner lays a continuous soundtrack: Morvern's own compilation tapes, her boyfriend's records, the jukeboxes in pubs, the music at parties and on the radio in cars; the dance tracks on the beach and in clubs and raves. Morvern's tapes (one to listen to as she cuts up and hides her boyfriend's body parts; one for a camping trip) are wonderfully strange (Berio and Bill Laswell, The Inkspots and This Mortal Coil, Miles Davis and the Cocteau Twins) because for Morvern the music doesn't stand *for* anything it just is.

> Lanna chose one of His records. It was Prince doing The Future. Our hands were the fingery movements of voices that set the theme, weaving in and out then splitting up, shooting out

half the theme just to remind you. Thighs and middle were the throbbing you hear cushioning it all. Feet chose to move as you felt: to the percussion or the broken up words, then Lanna and me did a daft little waltz to the orchestra bit that sounded jiggled about. Our eyes looked at each other and we tried to do a tango (Warner 1996: 74).

Morvern Callar is not a sociological novel. It's not about how a young Scottish woman of a certain class in a certain place at a certain time listened to music or how it shaped her life. Rather, it's as if the songs Warner was listening to (as a young Scottish man of a certain class in a certain place at a certain time) are inscribed in his text. The novel is not about the music that drives it; it is the story that Warner heard *in* this music. From this perspective, popular music is understood as a literary kind of storytelling. This is also illustrated, if in different ways, by Ian Banks's *Espedair Street* (1987) and Doug Johnstone's *The Ossians* (2008).

Espedair Street is narrated by Daniel Weir (Weir, D., as he was listed on the school register), a rock star in the 1970s (songwriter and bass-player for Frozen Gold), now, at 31, a super-rich recluse living in a vast nineteenth-century gothic folly in central Glasgow. Banks starts his story this way:

> Today I decided to kill myself. I would walk and hitch and sail away from this dark city to the bright spaces of the wet west coast, and there throw myself into the tall, glittering seas beyond Iona (with its cargo of mouldering kings) to let the gulls and seals and tides have their way with my remains, and in my dying moments look forward to an encounter with Staffa's six-sided columns and Fingal's cave … (Banks 1990: 1)

The book reads in part like an authentic rock memoir. It describes convincingly both Weir's childhood and teenage years growing up in Ferguslie Park, the most deprived area of Paisley, and Frozen Gold's progress from local to global success, from the moment Weir joins as a seventeen-year-old in 1973 to its dissolution in 1980. But for Banks such rock realism necessarily involves something out of the ordinary and *not in a good way*. Weir himself is 6ft 6. He has a stutter; he recurringly describes himself as a hunched-over gangling ape. The band's guitarist is killed during a show when the set collapses onto him; the band's singer is murdered by a religious fanatic, enraged by her on-stage performance of her own crucifixion. In his seclusion Weir's only companion is McCann, a B-movie version of a Glasgow hard man.

As literary fiction *Espedair Street* is driven by Weir's guilt ("the constant bassline of my life") at having lost his sense of place. He describes writing a new song as he walks with his memories through Paisley:

> I walked and remembered, and I found I was humming a new tune, to the beat of my steps. And heard new words combine to fit the tune. And the words said
> I thought this must be the end
> And never again we'd meet
> It just that I hadn't reckoned on
> Espedair Street.
> It's the wrong side of the wrong side of the tracks
> The dead end just off Lonely Street
> It's where you go, after Desolation Row
> Espedair Street.[3]
>
> (Banks 1990: 229)

Later he adds that

> It wasn't really Espedair Street or Ferguslie Park or anywhere you could point to on a map; it was somewhere of a different sort, an amalgam of places and feelings and times, and a place only I knew about (ibid. 238).

In the end Weir goes looking for old love. He finds her in Arisaig, a village on the West Coast of the Highlands. Weir cuts his rock star Silver AmEx card in two to use as a wedge to steady a table in the community bar. A happy ending as he takes his part in the performance of good neighbourliness? Perhaps and perhaps not, though the novel certainly describes a familiar theme in Scottish song: the anxiety of leaving home and the even bigger anxiety of going back to it again.

The Ossians, like *Tutti Frutti*, is organised around a tour. It is the late 1990s and 4-piece Edinburgh indie rock band The Ossians are beginning to attract record company and media interest. The book describes their tour of Scottish seaside towns (ten gigs in fourteen days) leading up to their showcase appearance in King Tuts in Glasgow. Johnstone's description of bad gigs and worse venues is entertaining and convincing and if neither the plot nor the characters are particularly interesting in themselves, Johnstone's take on Scottish music is illuminating. Early on in the book, front man Connor explains to a journalist where the group's name comes from: "a third-century Scots Gaelic poet" whose work "was discovered by a guy called James Macpherson in the eighteenth century".

> Most people thought Macpherson made it up, and he was discredited as a fake. It's typical of Scotland that our oldest history and literature might not even exist ... Everywhere you look, Scotland is made up of stupid myths and romantic ideals, most of which are fake or, more likely, a mixture of falsehoods and reality. Tartan and shortbread for tourists. Fucking Brigadoon.

> "Sounds like you hate Scotland".
> "Not at all". Conor was getting more animated now.

> I fucking love being Scottish. But it's that whole corny Jekyll and Hyde thing, isn't it? The dual nature of Scotland, blah, blah, blah ... it's a terrible fucking cliché these days. But clichés are clichés because they are true. I just thought Ossian was another side to that. People reinventing an early history of Scotland to give them something to be sentimental about. I see us as part of that schizophrenic heritage.

> (Johnstone 2009: 32–33)

At the end of the book, reflecting on the mess he's made of his band, on his reckless use of drink and drugs and violence so that he could play "the battered victim", Connor realises that

> He'd wrapped this whole thing up in a flag. From the band's name, which now seemed like a puerile joke, onwards, he'd been banging on about looking for the real Scotland, a tangible nation, something he could call home at least. But he'd missed the point. He hadn't even been able to read more than thirty pages of that book of Ossian's poems, what the fuck did he know about the history of this sorry little country anyway? It wasn't a matter of inventing. Or denying some romantic, made-up ideas about nationhood or homelands or worrying about borders or the fucking English, it was just about getting on with life (ibid. 257).

Historical fictions

In a 2018 piece for *Vice* (written as a commentary on the *Rip It Up* exhibition at the National Museum of Scotland), Assa Samaké-Roman asked "how political is Scotland's pop music *really*?"[4] The answer depends, of course, on what is meant by 'political'. In day-to-day terms people in Scotland listen to much the same music as people in the rest of the UK, and Scottish musicians have the same ambitions and draw on the much same cultural resources as musicians elsewhere.[5] It is striking in all the novels that I discuss here how few of the records name-checked are actually by Scottish artists. On the other hand, the Scots do spend rather more time thinking about Scotland's relationship to England than the English spend thinking about the Scots, and this does have political effects.

Describing one of Scotland's best-loved pop songs, Jeremy Tranmer notes that

> The narrator of [The Proclaimers'] 'Letter from America' wonders what happened to his compatriots who were forced to leave Scotland for North America as a result of the Highland Clearances of the eighteenth and nineteenth centuries ("I've looked at the ocean / Tried hard to imagine / The way you felt the day you sailed / From Wester Ross to Nova Scotia"), before lamenting the impact of their departure on local communities ("Lewis no more / Skye no more / Lochaber no more / Sutherland no more"). The expression "Lochaber no more" had historical and cultural resonance. It was first used in the ballad "Farewell to Lochaber" written by the poet Allan Ramsay in 1724. It recounts the tale of a soldier leaving Scotland to fight in a distant land. The theme of exile was behind John Watson Nicol's 1883 painting *Lochaber No More*, in which a Highland couple could be seen on a ship with their belongings (Tranmer 2016: 140).

In the next chorus the focus shifts from nineteenth-century rural clearances to twentieth-century urban clearances, the effects of the Thatcher government's industrial policies on ship building, car making, the steel industry and mining. ("Bathgate no more/Linwood no more/ Methil no more/Irvine no more".)

'Letter from America' was released in 1987 and, in the years that followed one sort of protest, against Thatcherism and then the poll tax, morphed into another, for independence. In 1990 there were two large-scale live music events. The Big Day, held across four stages in Glasgow on June 3, was a free pop concert in which performances were punctuated by speeches against the poll tax. A Day for Scotland, held at Fallen Inch Field in Stirlingshire on July 14, combined music, politics and family fun. Headliners such as Runrig, Hue & Cry and The Shamen were joined by folk luminaries such as Dick Gaughan and Hamish Henderson. A day of face-paint and sunshine included comedy acts, beer tents and theatre workshops, with a running theme of national pride. Billed as 'a Festival for Our Future', "this was a key event … in linking popular culture and politics in the campaign for a Scottish parliament".[6]

The best fictional account of the evolution of Scottish music and politics since 1990 is Kirstin Innes's 2020 novel, *Scabby Queen*. This is, formally, a fictional version of the rock biography, and Innes adopts a currently widely used way of accounting for someone's life: through an oral history.[7] The story is told through the words or recollections of the people who knew the star at the different stages of her career. For a novelist this is a useful device. Innes can take on many voices. Her heroine is always present but never known; we see only her through other people's eyes.

Scabby Queen tells the story of a singer, Cliodha Campbell (1967–2018). Her musical career takes off in 1990 when she has an unexpected hit with an anti-poll tax song, 'Rise Up', which she performs on *Top of the Pops*, and ends, with her suicide, in 2018. The book provides a sweeping, subtly fragmented satirical history of both popular music and popular politics. (Innes has particularly good fun skewering music journalism.) As cultural history *Scabby Queen* is not an exclusively Scottish book but Innes is a self-consciously Scottish literary writer.

The book's epigraph comes from Robert Burns's 'The Northern Lass', which is the title of Clio Campbell's album of Burns songs, and it is also to the point that Campbell, like Burns, grows up (with her mother) in Ayrshire. Burns becomes the link between the various points in her musical/political career. Her godfather Donald Bain, a Scottish islander and the fiddle-player in her father's folk band recalls her childhood visits.

> In the van, driving back and forth from the seaside, they would sing, favourite tunes from their own youth and Burns, always Burns. Malcolm [Clio's father} created simple harmonies for Cliodha's sweet soprano to pull against the more prosaic of Rabbie's songs she'd learnt by rote at school. They taught her Gaelic lullabies, reminded her of songs they'd sing when she was a baby. It was important work, Donald felt; it was keeping the island part of her alive (Innes 2020: 137).

After her death, Radio Scotland re-plays an interview Campbell gave the station's folk show in 2007, following the release of *Northern Lass*. Asked why she wanted to do a Burns album, Campbell says

> Because, you know, he was a deeply political artist. And the messages he was preaching—egalitarianism, equality—they're messages we need to hear today. But he was also working class, so I thought, well, where are the artists of today who are doing what he did. And it occurred to me to look at what the younger rappers and grime artists coming out of South London were making, and to involve some of them on some of the tracks, both rapping Burns's lines and laying down some of their own thoughts.

The interviewer, Jim Arbuthnott, suggests this might be considered controversial.

> But why would people need reassurance. Jim. Surely we're not that precious about the work of a man who died two hundred years ago that we can't let a woman and some non-white men sing his songs? (ibid. 212–213)

Robert Burns always was an international as well as a national poet. He began writing in the context of European romanticism and his songs have long had a global presence (see Grant 2018). As Clio Campbell suggests, Burns idolatry in Scotland is a way of avoiding questions—questions in which Burns himself was interested—about tradition and modernity, the popular and the people.

Finding one's voice

The English writer Jonathan Meades has suggested that among other European countries "Britain offers the fewest opportunities for awe, the fewest experiences that may be infected by sublimity. It is that lack that has squashed the romantic sensibility".

Rather "we have invented a substitute appropriate to our scale-model environ", the *picturesque*, a way of "seeing in English". Not all of Britain can be seen this way—Meade excludes "Glasgow's quasi-Baltic skyline", for example—but his account of the picturesque certainly includes the Scottish Highlands,

> whose wilderness and grandeur are never quite wild enough, quite grand enough to discourage the notion that they are, at base, pretty and scenic and unthreatening and the stuff of tourist posters. And such places, once discovered—or invented—by the romantic imagination were tamed by the idiom of humankind's architectural intervention.
> In the Highlands the picturesque can thus be found, for example, in "the lavishly baronial auld alliance castles of Pitlochry", in their "bogus unity between structure and landscape"
> (Meades 2021: 23, 25).

This is to return to Connor's question at the end of *The Ossians*. Could it be that Scottishness—and hence Scottish popular culture—is, in fact, defined by an English sensibility, by an English way of seeing? This is particularly tricky question for Scottish folkies for whom authentic Scottish popular music is measured less by its popularity than by class resistance: the people *vs* the property owning/capitalist oppressor. The issues here are well charted in Corey Gibson's study of Hamish Henderson, a key figure in the post-war Scottish folk revival.

In 1952 Henderson launched the Edinburgh People's Festival as a riposte to the 'elite' Edinburgh International Festival (first staged in 1947). The People's Festival programme was designed "to restore Scottish folksong to the ordinary people in Scotland, not merely as a bobbysoxer vogue, but deeply and integrally". Henderson attacked the BBC for neglecting "ethnic song" in favour of cultivating "popular taste" and suggested that "firmly entrenched in all key positions of administration, religion and the organization of culture, the elect deny just as long as they are able that anything so vulgar as popular culture exists". Even worse than the elect's studied ignorance of popular culture was its attempt, "once folk song and folk art could no longer be denied", to take possession of them. Hence the distortion of folk song by art singers and the creation of kitsch. In "improving" the songs he collected, Burns was therefore "counterfeiting the anonymous folk voice", making it not universal but sentimental. (Quotes taken from Gibson 2015: 165–175.)

Later in his career, reflecting on the cultural and commercial effects of the folk revival, Henderson shifted his position. He now understood folk as a kind of historical consciousness, a continually developing "living form" that had developed by cross-fertilising with literary poetry, producing, for example, Ballad-Scots as "a flexible formulaic language" and a form of resistance to the "fatty degeneration" of folk commercialism. In this respect "Scots contains English and goes beyond it" (ibid. 187–189).[8]

But then in the 1950s Henderson had also discovered Jeannie Robertson and "the oral literature and song of the Travelling People" which, he decided,

> was, probably, not only the most substantially ancient but also the most vital of all Scotland's various, towering folk traditions—traditions which are of crucial national importance here at home, and matchless gems in the crown of international folk music.
>
> (quoted in ibid. 191)

For Henderson, Jeannie Robertson was not just a "tradition bearer". The Travelling People also lived "socialism in practice", were an exemplary folk "underground", nomads who stood against the state and, indeed, against modernism. The Stewart Family, likewise, may have been a tiny band but also had "a rich and varied repertoire". Their "lifestyle and their culture were affirmation of a major strand in Scotland's history, the way Scotland was, is, and will be". (Quoted in ibid.193.)

Half a century later, in 2014, Aidan Moffat, who had come to fame as the singer in Arab Strap, set out on his own folk tour of small Scottish venues. The tour was filmed by Paul Fegan who captures Moffat's meeting with the most successful of the Stewart Family, Sheila, by then aged seventy-nine and a ballad singer of international renown. In the words of the blurb for the resulting film, *Where you are meant to be*, "Moffat believes Scotland's oldest songs are ripe for re-working against a contemporary urban back-drop. [Sheila] Stewart does not".[9]

Knowing one's place

In a 2021 interview promoting his new novel, *Kitchenly 434*, Alan Warner explains

> I wanted to write about rock music but it's hard to write about—few have done it well and so I was looking for a weird tangent to come at it from. In a freakish way, this is my most

autobiographical novel: all Crofton does is hang out on his own in the house, listen to old records and read books.[10]

This could be said of many Scottish novelists it seems. Both Carl MacDougall's *Stone Over Water* and Gordon Legge's *The Shoe*, for example, are organised around their narrators' engagement with music and books; both are faultless in the way they give pop sensibilities literary form. This is McDougall on the 1960s:

> She liked Esther and Abi Ofarim singing 'Cinderella Rockefella'. It was Number One in the hit parade for three weeks and while her parents were on holiday she lay on top of me cooing and purring the words, which I found embarrassing.
>
> She complained when Marmalade reached Number One with 'Ob-la-di, Ob-la-da' relenting when she learned they were a Scots group whom we had seen performing in Invercullen Town Hall as Dean Ford and the Gaylords, reverting when she heard *The White Album*: 'The Beatles sang it better', she said. 'I don't know why they didn't release their own version as a single'.
>
> 'Jumping Jack Flash' pleased her; Engelbert Humperdinck's 'Man Without Love' and Tom Jones's 'Delilah' annoyed her. 'That song really annoys me', she said.
>
> Louis Armstrong sold more records than anyone that year with a song called 'Wonderful World'. Judy was singing the bit about seeing babies cry and watching them grow. I was reading *Portnoy's Complaint*. 'That's nice', she said. 'What is?' 'Watching babies grow (MacDougall 1990: 124).

And this is Legge on the 1980s:

> 'I don't believe the first three singles you bought were the first three Roxy singles', Richard shook his head. 'No fucking way'.
>
> 'They were. The second and third were bought on the day of release. Swear to God'. Mental smiled with pride. Archie's first record was *Twenty Fantastic Hits Volume II* (bought mainly for 'Jean Genie' and 'Blockbuster'), and Davie's was 'Moon River' by Greyhound. 'I've always had great taste', continued Mental. 'I might not have the same range of appreciation as you, but my taste is immaculate'.
>
> 'I didn't like "Mr Blue Sky". Honest'. This point was really important to Richard. 'I'll have to run', said Davie. 'Cheerio lads'.
>
> 'See you', said Richard. 'I'll get in touch about the golf and the football'.
>
> 'Are your clubs at your ma's?' asked Davie.
>
> 'No, they're in Dostoyevsky's room. Were you wanting to see them?'
>
> 'No. No. It's okay. See you'. Davie left (Legge 1989: 60–61).

Both writers follow the ways in which friendships and identities are shaped by pop culture; both writers satirise Scottish masculinities defined by musical tastes and arguments. And both writers have a comically acute sense of the locality of taste. Their characters are not defined by their Scottishness in terms of nation or history but in their sense of place in particular neighbourhoods, social structures, families and friendship groups, and by the dreams that emerge from such places. The finest music fiction from this perspective is David Keenan's magnificent *This Is Memorial Device* (2018). The story of this band from Airdrie, active from 1983 to 1985, is put together by journalist Ross Raymond from interviews, archive material, and memoirs; it includes a discography, an index, mini-bios of all the relevant characters—"the cast of misfits, artists, drop-outs, small-town visionaries", and, as Appendix B, *A Necessarily Incomplete Attempt to Map the Extent of the Post-Punk Music Scene in Airdrie, Coatbridge and environs 1978–1986*. In the words of the (real) *Times* reviewer, in its range of voices and obsessions, of regrets and excuses, the book captures "the utter seriousness, the all-consuming belief, the sacrifice to art, the veneration of ideas that was as true for a shonky band in Airdrie in 1984 as it was for David Bowie in 1967, or Man Ray in 1915, or Gustav Mahler in 1884".[11]

Conclusion

The bohemian dreamers in Keenan's novel are all asking the same question: where do I belong? It is the question asked by the protagonists in all the novels I have discussed and while this makes for many interesting and contrasting versions of Scotland my conclusion is that 'Scottishness' is not, in fact, defined by these answers but by the emotional urgency of the question. To be Scottish is to be *unsettled*—unsettled by the ever-unfolding relationship between Scotland and the rest of the UK, unsettled by the relentless push and pull of leaving the country and staying. Music matters to Scottish writers because it is a way of resolving these tensions, the most pleasurable path towards a balance between fatalism and exhilaration.

Notes

1 In 2008 Northern Alliance released *The Ossians*, performances of the songs in the book.
2 Until Douglas Stuart won with *Shuggie Bain* in 2020, Kelman was the only Scot to have been awarded Britain's Booker Prize for fiction (with *How Late It Was, How Late* in 1994). Interestingly, both novels are written in Glaswegian.
3 A real street in Paisley.
4 https://www.vice.com/en/article/zmkdva/why-scotland-has-a-reputation-for-making-potent-political-pop
5 In the afterword to her 2021 novel *1979*, set in Glasgow, the Scottish crime writer Val McDermid lists "the forty-track rotation I listened to when I was researching, prepping and writing *1979*. They were all released in the late 1970s". Only three of the listed tracks are by Scottish acts: The Skids, Rezillos and Simple Minds.
6 Quoted from the advertisement for an event organised to celebrate the concert's 30th anniversary. See https://www.stir.ac.uk/events/calendar-of-events/2020/august/a-day-for-scotland-30-years-on/ The concert itself had been promoted by the Scottish Trades Union Congress and Stirling District Council.
7 Innes has been involved with one such book herself, a biography of The Arches—see Bratchpiece and Innes 2020.
8 This argument had resonance for ballad collectors in the USA. For a good fictional account of the travelling "consciousness" of a Scottish ballad see Sharyn McCrumb's *The Song Catcher* (2001), which traces a song, 'The Rowan Tree' (which McCrumb wrote herself), from Islay to North Carolina in the 1750s and then down the generations to the present day. It is now being hunted by a big-name contemporary Appalachian folk singer, Lark McCourry.
9 The film is well worth seeing if only for the sight of one of the editors of this volume in full fan mode at the front of the Barrowlands crowd at the tour's final concert.
10 *Kitchenly 434* is, one could say, Warner's English book, a combination of P. G. Wodehouse, *Country Life* and prog rock. (Quote from *The Observer* 14.03.21: 37.)
11 Quote taken from the publisher's blurb on the book's cover.

References

Banks, I. (1990) *Espedair Street*, London: Abacus [1st edn.1987].
Bratchpiece, D. and Innes, K. (2021) *Brickwork. A Biography of the Arches*, Glasgow: Salamander Street.
Gibson, C. (2015) *The Voice of the People. Hamish Henderson and Scottish Cultural Politics*, Edinburgh: Edinburgh University Press.
Grant, M. J. (2018) 'Distant voices, Scottish lives. On song and migration' in S. McKerrell and G. West eds. *Understanding Scotland Musically*, London: Routledge, pp. 159–174.
Innes, K. (2020) *Scabby Queen*, London: 4th Estate.
Johnstone, D. (2009) *The Ossians*, London: Penguin [1st edn. 2008].
Keenan, D. (2018) *This Is Memorial Device. An Hallucinated Oral History of the Post-Punk Scene in Airdrie, Coatbridge and Environs 1978–1986*, London: Faber & Faber [1st edn. 2017].
Kelman, J. (2016) *Dirt Road*, Edinburgh: Canongate.
Legge, G. (1989) *The Shoe*, Edinburgh: Polygon.
MacDougall, C. (1990) *Stone over Water*, London: Minerva [1st edn. 1989].
McCrumb, S. (2001) *The Song Catcher*, London: Hodder and Stoughton.
Meades, J. (2021) *Pedro and Ricky Come Again*, London: Unbound.
Tranmer, J. (2016) 'Popular Music and Left-Wing Scottishness' *Études écossaises* 18, pp. 133–149.
Warner, A. (1996) *Morvern Callar*, London: Vintage [1st edn. 1995].
Warner, A. (2021) *Kitchenly 434*, London: White Rabbit.

15

An Interview with Alasdair Roberts on Being a Scottish Songwriter

Martin Cloonan

Interviewed by Martin Cloonan 16 June 2022

Introduction

Alasdair Roberts (www.alasdairroberts.com) is one of Scotland's leading contemporary folk singers and songwriters, whose professional career now spans over twenty years. Born in Germany to a German mother and a Scottish father, he was raised in Callander, Perthshire, before moving to Glasgow as an adult. His first band, Appendix Out, released its first single, 'Ice Age' in 1996, and its first album, *The Rye Bears* a Poison in 1997. Roberts' first solo album *The Crook of My Arm* was released in 2001 and since then he has released fifteen albums, the last of which, The Old Fabled River, was released in 2021. He has also been involved in numerous collaborative projects, of which perhaps the most prominent is the Furrow Collective.[1]

Let's start at the beginning and how you came to be a musician in the first place. I know that your late father Alan was also a musician and a key influence, but what other important ones were there?
Well, that was probably the main one.

I was born in Germany in 1977, because my mother's German. My father was Scottish. He died in 2001.

And around the time I was born and maybe for a few years before that my mother, Annegret her name is (everyone calls her Peggy) and my father Alan, they ran a booking agency in Germany and so they booked a lot of Scottish, Irish and also some English folk bands because it was very popular in Germany at that time, the sort of 'Celtic' music, for want of a better word.

So probably some of my earliest musical experiences would have been being taken around folk festivals and clubs in Germany when I was very young but probably before I was able to remember, because we moved to Scotland when I was about two and a half. But I feel like it must have seeped into me somehow.

I have two sisters as well so I think with three young children my father thought that he needed a more lucrative career, because the music business wasn't. But he would still play music in the house when I was growing up, mostly at the weekends.

He was involved in haulage and importing stuff. Before the booking agency he'd been a long-distance truck driver. That's how he and my mother met – she and a friend were visiting Britain, hitch-hiking and he picked them up in his truck at Scotch Corner and gave them a lift

 DOI: 10.4324/9781003247470-19

to Glasgow! The next day he took her to the Scotia Bar, which was kind of the centre of his social and musical circle at the time.

My father started a company importing German beer in the 1980s when he moved back to Scotland. He's responsible for introducing Fürstenberg beer to Scotland. That kind of went well for a while, until later in the 1980s when he was bought out by Guinness, Guinness took over Fürstenberg and my dad's business was fucked basically.

But he played for fun at home at the weekends and we would play together. He played guitar, banjo, mountain dulcimer, accordion and sang a bit too.

So that was a big influence. He was the first person to teach me about guitar, when I was in my early teens and I started to develop an interest in the guitar. The first song he showed me was 'House of the Rising Sun', maybe because it has so many chords in it, and it involved some fingerpicking. There were acoustic guitars in the house because he had a few.

The one that I still play regularly… I mean all my acoustic guitars were inherited from my father. I don't actually know that much about acoustic guitars because I was lucky enough to have inherited these ones. I've never had to go and buy one, so I wouldn't really know how to begin to find what I was looking for because I've always been used to these ones.

One he bought in Cologne in the late 1970s was a K Yairi, a Japanese Martin copy, which is now my regular touring guitar. And there are others which were made by friends of his, a friend from Dumfries, Les Brown, and a friend from Glasgow, Alec Houston, in the early 1970s.

His guitar style was like picking finger style. Not exclusively but he did a lot of finger style. He'd grown up in Callander and he moved to Glasgow in the mid-1960s, from Callander – which is the town where I grew up too – and got involved in the music scene then, in the mid- to late 1960s.

He was actually influenced a lot by his girlfriend at the time, Cathy, whom I never met. Cathy was the sister of Alec Houston, the guy who made a couple of the guitars that my dad had. She actually became my dad's first wife. They split up. It was a very short-lived marriage. It was already kind of over by the time that my dad met my mother.

Cathy was quite into music and particularly the American folk revival and my dad got quite interested in that and they would play Carter Family songs, Doc Watson and stuff like that, old timey kind of Appalachian music, together. So my dad's guitar style had that in it.

A few years ago Alec sent me an old recording he'd found of a BBC session from about 1969 that my dad and Cathy had done – not BBC Radio Scotland but whatever came before it. My dad was mostly playing autoharp and Cathy guitar, and they were singing Appalachian songs in close harmony. It was fascinating to hear.

Later he started playing more Scottish folk music.

He played a lot with Dougie MacLean, very well-known these days. I suppose Dougie had been in the Tannahill Weavers when he was very young, like seventeen. And my mother and my father had booked the Tannahill Weavers to play in Germany. That must be how my dad met Dougie. He was kind of adopted by my family because my parents were a bit older than him. When we were kids, Dougie was in our house so much that my sisters and I thought that every family had a mummy, a daddy and a Dougie! But my dad played with him and I think that's where he developed his great skill in accompanying traditional fiddle tunes and so on.[2]

You've just described being born into a musical family, but how would you describe the music that you now make?
I will get to that but I just wanted to speak maybe a bit more about the other more sort of formal learning that I had.

When I started getting into the guitar, I learnt about the finger style and learnt about things like open tuning from my father and then when I was very young we lived in Stirling for a while and one of our neighbours was a guy called Laurie Hamilton and his family and my family became quite friendly.

He was a jazz guitarist, I guess he would have played with people like Bill Wells in that kind of central Scotland scene of the 1980s.[3] And later Laurie and his family were living in Bannockburn so when I was fourteen or fifteen I had a couple of years of guitar lessons from him, travelling there once a week. It was good in terms of learning scales and just being a bit more rigorous about left hand fingering and stuff, a bit of musical theory and a bit of kind of fancy jazz chords which I don't really use but I'm interested in a bit of chromaticism and colour, so that kind of helped in that regard I suppose.

I also had some piano lessons but I didn't really stick to that very rigorously.

But before I had any formal music lessons, from when I was a young child I was drawn to music. In the early eighties I had, like, wee Casio or Yamaha keyboards and would sort of improvise songs and so on. Then in about 1986 a school friend of mine, Douglas, and I decided to form a band. We called it The Chartbusters! It was a kind of primitive synth-pop duo with silly songs based around a very basic Yamaha keyboard with pre-set drum sounds. At that time Douglas was one of the few people I knew who was so interested in music. The garden of his family's house backed onto the primary school playing fields so at lunch breaks he and I would go to his house. I remember watching his VHS copies of *The Great Rock 'n' Roll Swindle* and *Purple Rain*, which both seemed quite illicit and shocking to me as, like, a nine-year-old. I think The Chartbusters played one gig, outside Douglas's house, but to no audience. Well, maybe a couple of local kids.

Back to the previous question, how *would* you describe the music that you now make?
I try not to narrow it down, I try not to define it too much.

I had this project called Appendix Out which made three albums when I was in my late teens/early 20s and then I abandoned that name and then I started making records under my own name and it got a bit of attention. At first people were calling me a folk singer or a folk musician and I didn't really feel comfortable with that at that point, not because I didn't have any respect for traditional music, it was more that I felt that I hadn't really *earned* that title, I hadn't really done my sort of apprenticeship or something in music to obtain that designation.

I remember once I had an album, *Farewell Sorrow*. I think it was *The Herald* newspaper got in touch about doing an interview and they wanted to present me as a folk musician. Then we did the interview and I kept asserting that I wasn't a folk musician and they decided not to run the interview in the end, because they couldn't really figure out what to do with me or how to categorise me, I suppose. But that album was probably one of the earliest ones of mine where the influence of folk or traditional music was more obvious.

But nowadays I'm more comfortable with the term 'folk musician'. It just stops people asking! It's folk music I suppose, generally folk music. I sing traditional songs and ballads, but I also write new songs which can be inspired by traditional idioms or songs, among other things. On one level it's definitely born out of that traditional music world.

It seems like you've grown into the title of being a folk singer, so my follow up question to that is what does it mean to be a folk singer in the modern, digital, age?
I don't really know because obviously my roots in it are from before that age, I'm in that age now I suppose. I'm just trying to figure out the transition, maybe.

So is it just a matter of carrying on what you were doing in a different environment?
Yeah I suppose so.

When I started making records – this is true of any kind of music I suppose – folk music, traditional music, but when I first starting going into studios it was before digital recording had taken off and so it was all tape and stuff. So I'm not like radically opposed to digital recording. I do sort of really prefer analogue recording but I'm also grateful for the ease of being able to, like, record at home and so on. I've made records at home and stuff which I wouldn't really have been able to do twenty-five years ago to the same kind of standard, although I was kind of recording at home when I was sixteen or seventeen on a cassette four track. Nowadays I use a Zoom digital multi-tracker that has, like, twenty-four tracks instead of four, but I never need to use that many tracks!

In terms of making folk music I kind of think that I think about it a lot less than people who maybe aren't musicians.

People like me!
Than music lovers for example. Or maybe it's just because in the early stages of my musical life I thought those kind of things through and through, so have internalised the thinking now to the point that I don't consciously think about it anymore, although it's possibly always still somewhere in the back of my mind.

For example, at [this year's] Leigh Folk Festival I'm on the same bill as Evan Parker[4], playing in the same venue on the same day and I've got a friend who was sort of emailing me about it recently and making a deal of it like – "How are the folkies gonna cope with that?". I don't really see those divisions in that way. Sound is sound.

With Scottish folk music, traditional music, wider UK folk music, there's an enormous repertoire of songs to choose from. So when you're planning a project or a record and bringing material together, how do you go about choosing what songs to record and the percentage of new songs etc.?
I tend to kind of separate in my head, I tend to compartmentalise, like traditional songs and other songs, although there's obviously a blurred line between them.

For example, I would tend to make a record of entirely of self-written songs and then maybe a record of all traditional songs. I don't necessarily want to mix them up. I don't know why that is. It's probably just being anal. Maybe it's just not wanting do each type of song a disservice.

I just made a record, well I recorded twelve traditional songs. It varies. The main criterion is that it has to be a song that I can kind of relate to or get my head round.

Also in terms of finding traditional songs. I like finding interesting melodies or unusual melodies. I also like to find unusual versions of songs, songs that are quite well-known but there might be some variant that's not very well known that shines a new light on that song. Or rare songs that no one really sings any more.

Some of the songs that I've just recorded are songs that I've been playing for years, maybe ten years some of them, but never really felt ready to record until now and then having this recording session booked was the impetus to try and kick them into shape.

Then maybe sometimes I'll become interested in a song and then work on it and look for other songs which kind of somehow complement it. So I can work on a few.

For example, on the new record there's a song called 'The Wonderful Grey Horse' which is from a nineteenth-century broadside, a fantastical story about a horse that's existed since the beginning of time and has countless riders and has been through all these amazing adventures, battles with Alexander and Scipio. I learnt it from a recording of an Irish singer, Paddy Tunney, but it's ultimately from an eighteenth- or nineteenth-century broadside which was published in Glasgow but versions of it were probably being printed all over the place. And I also really… there's a longer version but I trimmed it down because it was too long!

But then I suppose that led to an interest in that idea of songs featuring allegorical animals. There's a song from Prince Edward Island in Canada, eastern seaboard of Canada, called 'Dri-mindown', a song of Irish origin about a mythical cow. Then there's a Jacobite song called 'The Bonny Moorhen'. On the record there's a kind of triumvirate, or a triptych of animal allegory songs.

I wondered if you could say something about your own songwriting and what inspires you and in particular, in the context of this book, whether Scotland – its people, its landscape, traditions, politics, etc. – informs your songwriting

Ye---ah. I think to answer that I have to go back to the previous question about song selection because I think when I first started singing traditional songs I wouldn't give so much thought to ideas of Scottishness, I was more interested in the universality that I saw in certain songs, particularly in the big ballads, "muckle sangs", because I was always attracted to songs that seemed to have archetypal themes which could maybe have happened anywhere, regardless of language or Scots. Songs with a sort of universality, as I supposed. Maybe I fancifully took them as sort of emanations of the 'collective unconscious', in a Jungian sense, although I don't really see it that way now.

A lot of those songs seemed to be preoccupied with mortality, a bit gruesome and there's also the supernatural, which appealed to me.

I feel that as I've aged I've sort of been there and done that and got over that. It feels like a young man's game, a young person's game, that preoccupation with death and the macabre.

I think I have become increasingly conscious of some ideas of Scottishness. For example, with the twelve songs I've just recorded, nine of them are Scottish.

And I think the record I made with David (McGuinness) and Amble (Skuse), *What News?*, features eight Scottish ballads, so that has become more important to me somehow.

For example, the School of Scottish Studies, their resources have been important to me for the last ten years or more, particularly the sound archive, as I tend to learn by ear.[5]

One review I read of you said that you had one foot in traditional Scottish music and one foot in indie rock. I wondered if that was a characterisation that you would agree with and – if so – what it means?

The record label I work with, Drag City, has a lot of music that could fit that description. But it also releases quite a wide range of music.

Maybe when I was younger, when I was in my teens I was very into what you could call indie rock, American bands like Pavement and Sonic Youth and also bands on Drag City. I don't really listen to much of that kind of music nowadays, but it's definitely a big part of my musical history.

One of the things about folk is that it is often political and I got to know you better when you joined the Steering Committee of the Janey Buchan Collection of Political Song.[6] So I wondered to myself if I regard you as a political songwriter and I answered myself that I *do* think you are, but in a somewhat understated way and certainly not in a didactic way. So I wondered about your views on that and on politics and folk in Scotland.

I have written some songs that are more overtly political than others, but I think you're right, it tends to be quite understated.

Maybe I should be more outspoken!

Maybe I'm just not bold enough, sometimes I think that. But I stylistically like to be elliptical and ambiguous. So I like to pose questions rather than offer answers or to profess to offer answers that I don't have.

That sounds very wise!

So, yeah because I don't have the answers I'm not going to pretend that I do, I'm not going to be didactic, I'm not gonna preach or anything. But I do have my ideas and thoughts about things, but I'd rather provoke thought than preach.

I read in *The Quietus* in 2015 that you said that you regarded yourself more as a metaphysical or spiritual artist rather than an overtly political one. Is that still the case?

That sounds a bit pretentious doesn't it! (laughs)

Maybe, that's true but I think that you can have an interconnection of all those things, they are kind of interconnected.

One of my favourite songs is Robert Burns' 'Song Composed in August', 'Now Westlin Winds', of which Dick Gaughan does the sort of definitive version I think and that kind of brings together all these things – it's got romantic love and it's got love of nature and this political aspect and kind of metaphysical and political intertwining.

I try and aim for that with some of my songs. I wrote a song, 'Composed in December', which was kind of in tribute to Burns' 'Song Composed in August' because I felt like it was aiming for that sort of blend of the political and the metaphysical.

I like the idea that you mentioned before about trying to look at more universal things, rather than narrowly political stuff. Sometimes folk gets referred to as "the music of the people", but the problem with "the people" is that they are divided on lots and lots of issues, for example, Brexit. So I wondered if you had any thoughts on whether folk music *is* the music of the people?

(Pause, laughs). In a way, but it's interesting that a lot of those early collectors, for example English collectors like Cecil Sharp, were very not 'of the people', in the sense that they were quite middle-class or upper class, and had quite a narrow conception of popular culture.

People like Sharp did a lot of great work in collecting songs, in England and Appalachia, but then in a way it arguably produced a very bourgeois construction of what working class musical culture is. I suppose quintessentially it kind of tends to be focused on a very rural and agrarian kind of music rather than industrial folk music. And it's telling what people like Sharp chose not to collect or include, as much as what they did focus on.

And similarly in Scotland, for example, in the School of Scottish Studies not very much of their collecting work seems to have happened in Glasgow or Dundee. There is a bit in Edinburgh and Aberdeen probably mostly because there were Travellers living in and around Aberdeen, and their musical and traditional culture is of course very rich. But I don't see a lot of attention paid to sort of industrial folk music in the twentieth-century folk revival.

Well, there was the Polaris and sort of anti-nuclear stuff, but that's not really urban in that way although I think a lot of those songwriters and activists were city dwellers.

You are a Scottish artist who has always worked internationally, so I have some questions about your working career. Appendix Out got to release their first single on Will Oldham's Palace Records after you gave him a demo tape at one of his gigs. Could you say something about that and how you came to go for someone based in the States rather than the UK?

Well, I was a fan of Will's music. I think that was in the very early days of his career of releasing records. I heard the first Palace Brothers' single on John Peel which I used to listen to all the time in my bedroom in Callander. The song was 'Ohio River Boat Song' and I didn't realise at the time that it was a kind of Americanisation, or localisation by Will of the Scottish 'Loch Tay Boat Song', although my dad and Dougie had actually recorded a version of that song. My dad heard it through my bedroom door and asked me who it was singing the 'Loch Tay Boat Song' – that's how I found out. Anyway, by the point Will had put out two or three records I heard he was playing in Glasgow, he was actually playing at the Plaza which doesn't exist anymore… it's now a block of flats.

But he was actually opening for, well Palace was opening for Teenage Fanclub. So I went along, I think I was only seventeen, so I wasn't really supposed to be there, because it was eighteen or over. I went with my girlfriend who was sixteen. This was the summer of 1995.

I'd been doing a few tapes. I'd just bought a four track with the proceeds of my job, my fist proper job working as a waiter in a Chinese restaurant after I left school. But I used to spend a lot of my free time in my bedroom recording and I made some demo tapes and gave them to various people and sent them out to the *Melody Maker* demo review column. And it got quite a good review in the *Melody Maker* demo column.

So after that I got a few phone calls from people from publishing companies and record labels saying "Can you send us your demo tape". And I did and nothing came from any of that (laughs).

But then a couple of months after I gave this tape to Will I got a postcard saying "We'll put out a single". The first two songs on the tape, they put out as a single. So that was an exciting time. I was seventeen and it came out when I was eighteen. (That was) just through being a fan of his music and we're still in touch to this day.

You mentioned Drag City earlier on, a label based in Chicago and I wondered if you could say a few words about your relationship with them, how it came about and what it's like?
Well it came about through that first single because Palace Records… Will was releasing music on Drag City and Palace Records, Will's label, was kind of a subsidiary of Drag City. He put out his and his friends' own sort of weird stuff.

So after the single they said we'll do it when the time's right, because I kept sending them demos and stuff and then I think once the possibility of a good album being made had been reached then they were willing to go along with it.

So I started making albums on Drag City (laughs).

As you do!

Anyone looking at your career would be struck by the number of collaborative projects you've been involved in and I've seen you quoted before as saying that collaboration is *extremely* important to you. So could you say something about why it's important and how you select people to collaborate with.
I think it's maybe important in a sense because a lot of my early formative music making was done alone. Although I played with my father quite a lot and he taught me the importance of musical sharing and so on, and of listening.

I spent a lot of time alone playing music so when I finally did… when I moved to Glasgow and I got the chance to play with more people I found it was exciting and I really thrived on it so… In a way I'm very used to playing alone and working and I'm quite happy to do that. But it becomes something else when other people are involved too.

I suppose it's like part of a learning process. You've chance to learn from other people and have fun, just to learn about other musical mindsets and other approaches, other ways of doing things that you might not have considered.

And when it comes to collaborating with people from different cultures, you know I've worked with Norwegian musicians recently and French musicians and although I don't have deep knowledges of those kind of cultures and traditions, it's a way of coming to understand them a bit better through music.

Are there any artists you find particularly inspirational and – in terms of this book – particularly Scottish ones?
I suppose there would be a lot of the traditional singers that continue to inspire me.

Obviously Dick Gaughan is a big kind of hero of mine musically.[7] Sadly he has been unwell recently.

A lot of them would probably be long gone folk singers. I'm trying to think of people nowadays.

I really like the group Burd Ellen.[8] It's a duo, Debbie Armour and Gayle Brogan, a Scottish duo kind of doing interesting things with traditional songs. They're really good.

Is there anything else you'd like to say about making music from a Scottish base? Anything I should have asked you?
There's lots of different things we could have talked about music- it's a kind of wide topic!

In terms of Scottishness I notice that nowadays there's a lot more debate around the Scots language, a lot more awareness of Scots as a language distinct from English. But it also seems to wind certain people up, you know like people on Twitter, people writing in defence of Scots as a language and then a lot of people writing saying it's not really a language or I don't understand what you're saying.

If I listen back to some of my earlier recordings of traditional songs… we're talking about when I was in my early 20s, I think even I, if I listen now I think I was maybe Anglicising them some how and I try to be… I feel like I'm much more conscious of that nowadays, wanting to preserve the distinct kind of Scots tradition, the Scots language aspects of songs rather than sort of softening it down or something.

If I went back and re-recorded the first album of traditional songs that I did, I would do it very differently in terms of that kind of linguistic aspect.

I guess that might be characteristic of a broader sense of confidence in Scottishness which followed the setting up of the Parliament, the feeling that Scotland has a lot to be proud of and it shouldn't be hiding or Anglicising its culture. It stands in its own right.
Yeah, exactly.

Yeah, it's definitely that and I also think that maybe in the part of Scotland that I grew up it maybe wasn't particularly rich in Scots language in the same way that somewhere like Ayrshire or Aberdeenshire would be, but maybe that's because historically it would have been a Gaelic speaking area, 200 years ago. All the place names are Gaelic around there. And back then the choice would be… people would go to school and be made to speak standard English while you would have the Gaelic beaten out of you. I mean, maybe my great- or great-great grandparents' generation. So I think it's partly that.

I think that when I was younger, when I was a teenager and so on, I had some sort of negative… my view of traditional Scottish culture was shaped by the fact that I'd grown up in a very sort of touristy part of Scotland as well and I was next door to a former woollen mill which was now a shop which sold woollen things and tartan and it was all 'tartan and shortbread'. And you'd walk in there and they'd be playing the kind of the cheesiest kind of music that a tourist would think of as traditional Scottish music. And those kinds of associations kind of put me off when I was (young).

Later in my late teens and early 20s when I discovered what are arguably more kind of authentic Scottish traditions, the singing of Jeannie Robertson, or Lizzie Higgins, The Stewarts of Blairgowrie, all of whom would be on my list of Scottish musical heroes that you asked me about earlier.[9]

Sheila Stewart, for example, until I discovered *those* kind of traditions and cultures in Scotland then I associated it with the more kind of tartan and shortbread image which had been presented to me by growing up in a touristy area in Scotland. There wasn't a lot going on musically where I grew up in terms of traditional music, although that might have changed now. I think there was one duo who played in the local pubs – it was a good fiddler but then an accordion player who played his instrument through a huge amplifier with a built-in drum machine which drowned the fiddler and everyone else out.

Anything else you'd like to say?

I'd also like to list Norman Kennedy, who's a great Scottish singer. He's from Aberdeenshire, but he also spent a lot of time in the Hebrides, I can't remember where, and sang Gaelic as well. But he left Scotland in the sixties to live in America. He went to the [1965] Newport Folk Festival and it blew his mind. He decided that he didn't want to live in Scotland anymore.[10]

I think he felt under-appreciated in Scotland and when he moved to America his work was very appreciated and valued as a musician, but also as a weaver which was his main kind of trade. He now runs a weaving school, the Marshfield School of Weaving, in Vermont. He was awarded a National Heritage Fellowship by the US National Endowment for the Arts in the early 2000s, but never received similar recognition for his work his native country, which seems strange to me because his work is so Scottish. He's getting on a bit now. I don't know whether he sings much anymore because he must be approaching ninety I would say.

I don't know how to best say it, but sometimes I feel like that within Scotland I don't necessarily think that my own work is that much appreciated in the way that it is more outside Scotland and I wonder why that is, if it's because it doesn't really conform to these expected kinds of notions or displays of Scottishness. It's probably been about six or seven years, for example, since Radio Scotland have played my music even though in that time I've released several albums, including albums of Scots ballads. But Radio Scotland won't play it.

Maybe in terms of establishment conceptions of Scottish traditional culture I'm still a bit of an outsider in a way. Or maybe those ballads are just considered too long for radio play!

Maybe it's because I'm half German and they can smell it (laughs). Just kidding!

You always seemed like the definitive Scot to me!

It's almost like there's some competition in Scotland to be the most Scottish. You know if you're not quite Scottish enough….

I think that the first time I came across your music was when I was in Canada and someone mentioned you in terms of great music in Scotland

I feel like I'm a bit of a secret in Scotland, maybe apart from in Glasgow because I've lived here for so long.

I tend to get to get a more enthusiastic reception elsewhere.

I think that's a great place to stop the interview! Thanks.

Notes

1   See http://www.thefurrowcollective.co.uk
2   Multi-instrumentalist Dougie MacLean is one of Scotland's most revered singer-songwriters, the author of 'Caledonia'.

3 Laurie Hamilton's son, Steve, became a distinguished jazz pianist, a member of Bill Bruford's Earthworks and the Billy Cobham Band among many others. He continues to perform regularly with Scottish singer Eddi Reader.
4 Improvising saxophonist Evan Parker is a legendary figure in the history of European free jazz.
5 See https://www.ed.ac.uk/information-services/library-museum-gallery/cultural-heritage-collections/school-scottish-studies-archives
6 See https://www.gla.ac.uk/schools/cca/research/music/archives/psc/
7 Dick Gaughan is described by the Scottish Traditional Music Hall of Fame as "Scotland's most passionate troubadour" – see https://projects.handsupfortrad.scot/hall-of-fame/dick-gaughan/.
8 See https://www.burdellen.com/.
9 Jeannie Robertson (1908–1975) and Lizzie Higgins (1929–1993) were singers from Aberdeen, the latter from a traveller family. The Stewarts of Blairgowrie were also a traveller family; their best known singers were Belle (1906–1997) and Sheila (c1935–2014).
10 See https://www.thetraditionbearers.co.uk/norman-kennedy/.

16

Re-thinking 'Scottishness' – Who, and What, Sounds Scottish?

Diljeet Kaur Bhachu

As a person of colour, I'm sure many would automatically assume that I wasn't Scottish and that is something all people of colour living in Scotland have probably experienced at some point in their lives (Arusa Qureshi, freelance writer and editor).[1]

Introduction

Against the backdrop of the (contested) notion of a culturally inclusive, anti-racist Scotland (Peterson 2020), this chapter explores the possible futures of the idea of 'Scottishness' in the context of the popular music industries. I draw on my multiple perspectives – as a South Asian Arts producer, a music industries higher educator, an equalities advocate and activist, and a practising musician of South Asian heritage – to unpack what 'Scottishness' means in society and the arts sectors. I also invited people of colour within the Scottish music industries to share their views and experiences of participating in this ecosystem.

I ask: What is Scottish music? What does it mean to 'sound' Scottish? Who is allowed to be Scottish, in society, and in our music industries? How do we move forward with these messy notions of Scottishness?

First, let's try to understand what Scottishness might have meant until now.

What Is Scottish Music?

As discussed across this book, Scottish music is many things. It is an umbrella under which folk, jazz, classical, DIY, commercial, instrumental and lyrical works and practices co-exist. Yet for many – certainly in terms of popular music – it can also be defined through a lineage of bands and artists, their sound-worlds and their reception over recent decades.

As Sushil Dade, who goes by stage name Future Pilot AKA, recounts, there are many names synonymous with the label of 'Scottish music':

> Bands from The Poets, through to Alex Harvey, through to, you know, The Pastels, through to Orange Juice, through to where we are now, Mogwai, Sacred Paws. I mean there's hundreds of them, so that is … you know …there's evidence of the sonic fruits Scotland can create.[2]

DOI: 10.4324/9781003247470-20

Dade connects these artists and bands to Scottishness through the reputation garnered by their work: a collection of critically acclaimed musicians who demonstrate Scotland's potential. Glaswegian singer-songwriter Kapil Seshasayee echoes this, focusing on the position of certain bands and artists as ambassadors for Scotland.

> I would define it [Scottish music], from experience, as "music typical of acts which have served as ambassadors for Scottish music". This can encompass indie bands like Frightened Rabbit, 1980s acts like The Proclaimers or trad bands like Lau, whose international success has a strong influence on what a 'Scottish' act can sound like.[3]

Other artists are, then, drawn to emulate the sonic palettes of internationally successful bands in the hope of tapping into their market power. In this way, bands and artists synonymous with Scottish music become taste-makers, setting up parameters for what 'successful Scottish music' looks or, rather, sounds like. This type of external recognition could be seen as parallel to how the UK and US view Ravi Shankar and Bhangra music as defining Indian music. Seshasayee reminds us that:

> … there are many kinds of Indian styles of music but Ravi Shankar / Bhangra tend to be the ones defined as representative because they've had the most international success, especially in the west.

This is to erase a diverse ecosystem of musical practices and forms of expression simply because they are not the dominant sound or style. There are many bands and artists from Scotland, spanning the history of popular music, who are hugely successful – world renowned even – but not immediately characterised as Scottish. This seems to be the case regardless of genre, accent, time and place – from hip hop to noise rock, Scottish or Americanised, the 1950s or now, successful in Scotland or world-famous. So what actually is (or isn't) Scottish music? Kapil Seshasayee:

> This presents challenges of all sorts to acts who sonically or aesthetically don't fit the mould of acts which typically 'break through' within a territory.

David Pollock, writing about the Rip It Up exhibition in 2018, suggests that working class roots are one common thread among Scottish pop's exports[4]. Wood (2012), Tranmer (2016) and Samaké-Roman (2018) suggest politics as another. Drawing on Mäkelä and Whittall, Wood (2012: p.197) argues that "certain musical traits come to be understood as being 'Scottish'" through the "political and cultural rhetoric that surrounds the music's creation and reception". From this perspective, national identity has little to do with the music itself but, rather, is defined by the baggage and labels that have been attached to the musical idioms or instruments that are used. 'Scottishness' is constructed.

In attempting to define Scottish pop music through its politics Assa Samaké-Roman (2018) concedes that "trying to squash decades of music from one country into a neat category feels a bit silly". In saying this, though, Samaké-Roman foregrounds the role of singing with a Scottish accent as a way of "leaning in" to an idea of Scottishness. This echoes Wood's theory that 'Scottishness' is ascribed as opposed to existing inherently (2012: p.197).

Samaké-Roman (2018) goes on to describe the formation of national pride in Scottish music through a history of both political music and politically vocal musicians. Politics are, she suggests, a significant part of Scottishness. Wood (2012), similarly, describes a desire for positive and useful ideas of Scottishness that relate to a politicised national identity. She suggests that language and accents are a strong part of this Scottishness, alongside instrumentation, ideas of authenticity and links to Scottish traditional music. Tranmer (2016) details politicised expressions of Scottishness by Scottish pop artists and musicians in recent decades – around both the 1979 and 2014 Independence Referendums, for example, describing the growing confidence in Scottish identity through a focus on the cultural sector. An artist-participant in Netto's (2008: p.58) research reflected on the effects of Scotland's mission to be viewed as its own country with its own identity in the wider context of the United Kingdom: this was to prioritise space for those who are seen to represent 'Scottishness'; others will have to wait to be given a platform.

So, Scottishness is constructed from many different elements, yet there are recent instances of artists being excluded from this identity simply because of their accents.

(Being and) Sounding Scottish: The Politics of Scottish Accents

Speaking about her English accent after winning the 2020 Scottish Album of the Year award, Shaheeda Sinckler, AKA Nova, said, "For some people, the accent's just really important […] They didn't see me as a Scottish artist" (Hawthorne 2020). In contrast, *Glasgow Guardian* editor-in-chief Holly Jennings commented that same year on the fact that not all big Scottish names who make it do so with a broad Scottish accent – Americanisation has had a strong hold on popular music from Scotland and it doesn't seem to raise any eyebrows (Jennings 2020). In recent times, KT Tunstall, Emeli Sandé and Lewis Capaldi have all done extremely well without adopting a Scottish accent while singing and without their Scottishness being called into question. It could be said that 'local' accents are deemed to be more important in other genres (like hip-hop) but the question this raises for me is that of race. Is it just harder to see past an accent when the artist isn't white?

A few years ago I was approached in a search to find a Scottish South Asian female vocalist for a high profile project. I sent a demo of myself singing a song in my natural voice, explicitly not Americanising my vocals but also refraining from a mock broad Scots voice. The response made clear that the organisers didn't read this performance as having any kind of Scottish accent, because it wasn't a strong accent. I was asked to resubmit but 'sound Scottish'. Reflecting back on this, I can't help but wonder why my original demo wasn't perceived as Scottish enough. There could have been many things at play here. Perhaps they wanted a stereotypically broad accent. However, given that the response came from fellow Scots, I'd expected a more nuanced approach. And now, more aware of how racial biases work, I can't help but wonder whether, in knowing that I was of South Asian heritage, my unaltered voice was never going to be heard as Scottish enough.

> It has definitely been challenging finding a space for myself in Scottish music (Kapil Seshasayee).

For Scots with heritage in other places, experiences of being in Scotland – especially when formative years are spent here – have a complicated relationship with belonging. A sense of dual identity is a double-edged sword. On the one hand, having multiple heritages is enriching. On the other hand, many people who grow up with multiple cultural identities find they lack a sense of belonging in either their countries of residence or their ancestral homes – they are viewed as foreign in both places (Netto 2008: p.54). In an interview with the *Alloa and Hillfoots Advisor* (Smith 2021), rapper Bemz suggested that "The onus is usually on the traveller to somewhat assimilate when they leave their culture and enter another" but also acknowledged that having a Scottish accent makes it much easier for people of colour to fit in in Scotland, compared to those arriving from other countries. Being the 'other' is difficult both in terms of finding a place of belonging, and in being welcomed. Emphasis on fitting prescriptive definitions of 'Scottishness' can present barriers to those who don't fit them sonically or aesthetically.

A 2021 episode of the Accentricity Podcast explored some prominent Scottish singers' decisions to sing either with or without their Scottish accents.[5] The contributors – Justin

Currie, Aidan Moffat, and Dave Hook – describe their different relationships with, and views on, Scottish accents in song. Each made different decisions regarding accents, with varying levels of thought behind those decisions – some conscious, others not – but all arguably successful in what they did. While there is space for pride in Scottishness via accents for artists who have grown up noticing the complete absence of Scottish accents in popular music, this cannot be used to exclude those without Scottish accents: to be proud of Scottish accents does not mean those who don't have a Scottish accent can't also be Scottish and be proud of it. There is space for a pride in a broader idea of Scottishness in which ancestry is not the defining factor in qualifying as Scottish but, rather, being here, working here, contributing and investing in Scottish society, is what makes us so. It should also go without saying, that we can be proud of the wide range of accents that can be found across this country.

In a linguistic analysis of Scottish accents in popular music, Krause and Smith (2017) outline characteristics of Scottish accents and how they differ by regions and class culture. Songs featuring two prominent Scottish singers were analysed, and the singers were asked about their views on singing with a Scottish accent, including their perceptions of whether they thought they were actively using an accent in their own singing practice. The decision to sing with or without an accent raises questions about authenticity – what is an authentic, naturally Scottish singing voice? Krause and Smith considered practices of emphasising particular vocalics that sound more stereotypically Scottish, and whether singers – or indeed speakers – leant into these in order to achieve a more Scottish sound. Tranmer (2016: 138) notes a turning point in the 1970s, when the punk movement encouraged people to retain their accents as a statement of authenticity amidst widespread adoption of mid-Atlantic voices in popular music. Tranmer highlights The Proclaimers' use of Scots language in their lyrics and Runrig's promotion of Gaelic as overtly left-wing political acts.

Returning to the critique faced by Shaheeda Sinckler in relation to her accent and, in particular, to the emphasis within hip hop on authenticity, why was she not deemed Scottish enough? At what point does our right to national identity become policed by accent or skin colour instead of the place we call home?

This leads me onto my next discussion – who is allowed to be Scottish?

Diversifying Scottishness

Wider societal definitions of Scottishness have changed – at least in how this country is perceived from the outside. In the decade between the 2001 and 2011 Scottish Census the number of Scots of migrant backgrounds grew substantially – increasing by over 400% in the case of Scotland's Black communities, and with Polish communities becoming the second largest minority group (Simpson 2014). Overall, one sixth of all residents in Scotland identified as having heritage elsewhere, including the rest of Britain and internationally (Ibid). Fast-forward ten years, and on the eve of our next census, it is anticipated that Scotland is even more diverse now (Walsh 2017: 12).

Politics over the last decade or so have seen Scotland position itself as an open and inclusive nation, accepting of people from all parts of the world, and adopting them as New Scots. However, this is not reflected in the experiences of people of colour in Scotland. Racism is still rife. Marcus Nicolson (2021) reported in *The Conversation* that young adult migrants in Scotland felt that "as people of colour and without a Scottish accent they were unable to claim this identity". Participants in Peterson's (2020) research felt that Scottishness was synonymous with whiteness – that to be Scottish is to be white. Peterson's article details several examples of overt racism – micro-aggressions, verbal assault, repeated 'othering'. This is a reality that is ongoing for Scots with heritage in other places, whether they have recently come to Scotland or are the second or third generations (or more) born in this country.

Racism in Music

The music industries do not exist in a vacuum. They reflect society in many ways. Therefore, if society is still rife with inequalities, so are the music industries. If the playing field was more level, the sector would be more diverse. The *Music Blueprint* report (Creative and Cultural Skills 2011) found that 93% of the UK music industries is white (pp.12–13). A follow-up workforce analysis in 2018 found that the Scottish creative industries (encompassing visual arts, performing arts, literature, design, craft and heritage, alongside music) was 96% white, sitting above the UK average of 88%. A recent report by Black Lives in Music highlights UK-wide issues in music industry funding structures, racism relating to physical appearance, inequalities in music education, and a race pay gap (2021).

Music Education

Racial bias runs deep in education – it shapes how some pupils are discouraged or excluded from pursuing their interests because of stereotypes about family support or whether they would succeed. This doesn't only happen along lines of racialisation. Classism, gender-based discrimination, homophobia and ableism also have a significant impact on how young people experience music education in Scotland, and this extends to popular music education. A report commissioned by Intercultural Youth Scotland found that young Scots from ethnically diverse backgrounds do not feel represented by curricula, and that some teachers still demonstrate racial bias in how they treat pupils (Guyan 2019).

In my own educational experience, the inclusion of musics from the Global South was tokenistic. There was an over-emphasis on notation and reading, and the only popular music studied was made by white musicians. The closest I got to studying the music of my own cultural heritage in my formal music education was a university module that delved into The Beatles' *Revolver* – and even then it was all about George Harrison and barely about Ravi Shankar. Yet I had a rich musical life outside of school where I acquired all of the skills that would help me in a popular music context – learning and playing by ear, singing and self-accompanying, improvising, memorising.

Obviously times have somewhat changed, but while there is now a process for the Scottish Qualifications Authority to provide assessors for pupils performing musics from non-Western European traditions in performance exams, curricula still focus on music from the Global North, largely due to its measurability. In my own music education, there was an implicit message that the skills I learnt from my own musical-cultural heritage were not welcome. Racism in the primary school classroom tempered any confidence I might have had to be my whole (Indian) self. To have it pointed out by peers at the age of seven years old that I didn't look like anyone in my favourite pop groups (and therefore couldn't participate in their tribute acts) immediately sent a message that I didn't belong in pop music. Turning to a Western classical music education, I was encouraged to read notation instead of learning pieces by ear. I've been told that my musical instincts are 'wrong' when deciding how to shape phrases in a Mozart concerto, when at no point had the teacher and I discussed what kind of interpretation we were each trying to achieve. There was no room for creativity – an essential part of pop music.

Aspiration and support play a huge part in any musician's journey. Music education is a key site for creating and nurturing aspirations of musical lives for young Scots. Musicians and music teachers often cite their music teachers as the inspirational figures who enabled them to pursue musical lives (Bhachu 2019). While pop and rock music have been present in Scottish music curricula since at least the late 1980s (Byrne and Sheridan 2000), it remains the case that because of the criteria for entering teacher education the majority of school music teachers in Scotland are trained within the Western European framework. Music teaching is overwhelmingly white, although this is slowly changing. There is, in short, some way to go before all Scottish pupils feel represented by who is teaching them and what is being taught. While pop musicians have long thrived without the input of formal music education and music in schools, if we are to see a more diverse sector, it must do more to support those who rely on school music to develop their practice. Intercultural Youth Scotland consulted with young people of colour in 2020 (*Mapping the Young Person's Journey*), finding that there are differences in cultural expectations with regards to young people's pathways after compulsory education, some of which are gendered, and that culturally aware careers advice is also a necessary part of providing better support for all of Scotland's young people.

Responding to #BlackOutTuesday

In the two years since the murder of George Floyd, we have witnessed an unprecedented surge of interest in anti-racism work, a surge that has reached Scotland. I say 'interest' because there has (sadly but unsurprisingly) also been a drop in commitment as it stopped being trendy. Part of the increased impact of the Black Lives Matter movement crossed into the music and entertainment industries, and a number of Scottish organisations participated in calls for change.

The PRS Foundation's *Power Up* programme is "an ambitious, long-term initiative which supports Black music creators and industry professionals and executives, as well as addressing anti-Black racism and racial disparities in the music sector".[6] Creative Scotland is named as a partner of the project, which in its first iteration supported artist TAAHLIAH and industry professional Sami Omar in pursuit of their projects – two out of a total forty supported projects from across the UK.

Returning to the statistics mentioned earlier in this chapter, the Scottish music industries are overwhelmingly white. While there has been a growing number of Scottish artists of colour achieving national and international success in recent years, it continues to be the case that industry bodies are not representative of Scotland's increasingly ethnically diverse music industries. This extends to music education. I am often the first person of colour my students encounter, and while education is not the only pathway into the music industries, I can count on one hand how many students of colour I've taught in music higher education in Scotland in the past decade.

Re-thinking (and Future-Proofing?) 'Scottishness' in the Music Industries

'Scottishness' should be about enabling artists to create their own unique voices and to be given the platform and support to develop this… to be as creative as you can be in whatever field you operate in, that is 'Scottishness' (Sushil Dade).

Scottish music is already many things: music by indie bands who gain international recognition; songs sung in Scots, Gaelic, or with a Scottish accent; music made in Scotland. It is not yet synonymous with music made by artists who visibly have roots elsewhere in the world, although this is slowly changing. With more data emerging every year on the diversity of the creative industries, there are notable attempts at diversifying programming, including more artists of colour, women, disabled artists, being more inclusive generally.

However, efforts to be more inclusive must be made with care – it is easy to fall into the trap of tokenistic representation. This not only stops any real change from happening, it can be damaging for artists of colour: we are seen only as racialised people, and not as individual artists.

It is true, though, that the Scottish music industry is still predominantly white and, particularly among the older generation in the industry, there may still be some outdated and problematic viewpoints that need weeded out. That being said, I'm positive that there are enough of us taking things forward and trying to change the entire landscape that someone's Scottishness would never be a question in the future (Arusa Qureshi).

Of course this chapter isn't going to solve the problem of racism in the Scottish music industries, but what I can do is offer some insights that might make us think about how we understand 'Scottishness'.

There Is a Problem Here

Tackling inequality starts with acknowledging that it exists. The Scottish creative industries often give the impression that we are a collectively left-wing, inclusive bunch. The reality is that not everyone is a good person. There are misogynists, racists, transphobes, ableist people and a whole host of other bad people who uphold inequality. This exists across all parts of the music sector, irrespective of genre, style or context. By recognising the problem, we might begin to critically think about how to address it.

In 2017, I co-founded the Scottish-Asian Creative Artists' Network (ScrAN), emphasising the plurality and diversity of Scottish-Asian artists' identities and arts practices. This was partly in response to frequent questions as to whether I performed 'Indian' music – despite growing up in Scotland at a time when access to specialist South Asian arts training was minimal. Assumptions like these come from lazy thinking. I was just as often mistaken for an international student when I was doing my doctorate: that was more conceivable to people in Higher Education than that there was a UK-born and raised South Asian woman in the music department.

When I first started working as a South Asian arts producer for Glasgow Mela, through ScrAN, I realised that we were missing entire sections of South Asian culture and diasporic communities. There was no nuance. Men were musicians, women and children were dancers, and the people on stage were typically upper-caste, non-disabled, straight and cis-gendered (there were some exceptions, although they typically weren't South Asian). We now question who gets to be a South Asian artist. Historically, communities from the northern Indian and Pakistani regions of the Panjab have dominated UK South Asian cultural representation, but society has changed, and so must representation. I find parallels here in how the wider music industries need to make space for a more pluralistic and diverse notion of Scottishness. Just as South Asian arts programming requires more space for diaspora artists who don't fit the typical mould of South Asian arts programming, Scottish arts programming requires more space for artists who have historically not been included in definitions of Scottishness. Glasgow Mela has since featured a stage dedicated to performers of South Asian heritage who do not necessarily work with traditional or popular South Asian arts practices.

There Is No Single Scottishness

Brown (2020: 14) describes the pluralistic nature of Scottish identities in the present day. Scotland has been multilingual for centuries, with its strong traditions of Scots and Gaelic alongside English. Thinking more broadly about the pluralities of Scottish music, and going back to the idea of 'musicians who become ambassadors', there is definitely a marked shift in who makes Scottish music and what that music sounds like. Arusa Qureshi highlights hip hop and R&B as possible markers of Scottish sound, shifting away from a tradition of "white indie pop bands" and making room for the variety of musicians and music this country has to offer.

While we can undeniably be proud of those [white indie pop] bands that put Scotland's music industry on the map, I think there's so much variety in terms of genre and artist that it's impossible to pigeonhole Scottishness as one thing … To me, the most exciting music coming out of Scotland at the moment is made by women and non-binary artists, especially in hip hop, pop and R&B. I'm sure hip hop and R&B in particular wouldn't traditionally be linked to Scotland but the scene is growing and bold new voices are crucially being given the support they deserve (Arusa Qureshi).

Conclusion

Scotland and Scottishness are constructed by the people in this country. Borders do not exist until we draw them, and identity-markers do not exist until we ascribe such value to them. We must therefore be prepared to move with society and let go of our attachment to a singular definition of 'Scottishness'. Only then can we be ready to support and promote the richness of what all of Scotland's musical talent has to offer.

Notes

1 Via email interview, 9th November 2021.
2 Via zoom interview, 13th November 2021.
3 Via email interview, 15th November 2021.
4 https://www.independent.co.uk/arts-entertainment/music/features/scottish-pop-music-rip-it-up-story-national-museum-scotland-mogwai-orange-juice-calvin-harris-a8406376.html.
5 https://www.accentricity-podcast.com/transcripts/2021/3/2/singing-voice-speaking-voice.
6 https://prsfoundation.com/powerup/

References

Bhachu, D. (2019) *Facilitating Musical Learning in Scottish Primary Schools: An Interview Based Study of Generalist Primary Teachers', Primary Music Specialists' and Community Music Practitioners' Views and Experiences.* Doctoral Thesis submitted to the University of Edinburgh. Available Online: https://era.ed.ac.uk/handle/1842/36622

Black Lives in Music (2021) *Being Black in the Music Industry.* https://blim.org.uk/report/

Brown, I. (2020) *Performing Scottishness: Enactment and National Identities.* London: Palgrave MacMillan. https://doi.org/10.1007/978-3-030-39407-3

Byrne, C., & Sheridan, M. (2000) 'The long and winding road: The story of rock music in Scottish schools'. *International Journal of Music Education,* 36(1), 46–57. https://doi.org/10.1177/025576140003600106

Creative and Cultural Skills (2011) *The Music Blueprint,* online http://blueprintfiles.s3.amazonaws.com/1319716452-Music-Blueprint-Web_26_7_11.pdf

Guyan, K. (2019) *The Perceptions and Experiences of Black, Asian and Minority Ethnic Pupils in Scottish Schools.* Edinburgh: Intercultural Youth Scotland.

Hawthorne, K. (2020) 'I'm an alchemist': Nova, the unknown MC with the Scottish album of the year, *The Guardian,* online. https://www.theguardian.com/music/2020/nov/02/nova-shaheeda-sinckler-scottish-album-of-the-year-award-re-up

Intercultural Youth Scotland. (no date) *Mapping the Young Person's Journey.* Report available online: https://www.interculturalyouthscotland.org/reports

Jennings, H. (2020) 'Singing in Scots: When did we get so American?' *The Glasgow Guardian,* online https://glasgow-guardian.co.uk/2020/11/01/singing-in-scots-when-did-we-get-so-american/

Krause, M. and Smith, J. (2017) '"I Stole It from a Letter, off Your Tongue It Rolled." The performance of dialect in Glasgow's Indie Music Scene', in C. Montgomery, and E. Moore, (eds) *Language and a Sense of Place: Studies in Language and Region.* Cambridge: Cambridge University Press, 215–233. https://doi.org/10.1017/9781316162477.012

Netto, G. (2008) 'Multiculturalism in the devolved context: Minority ethnic negotiation of identity through engagement in the arts in Scotland.' *Sociology,* 42(1), 47–64.

Nicolson, M. (2021) 'Immigration: how Scotland sees itself and how migrants actually experience it', *The Conversation,* online https://theconversation.com/immigration-how-scotland-sees-itself-and-how-migrants-actually-experience-it-173187?utm_source=twitter&utm_medium=bylinetwitterbutton

Peterson, M. (2020) 'Micro aggressions and connections in the context of national multiculturalism: Everyday geographies of racialisation and resistance in contemporary Scotland'. *Antipode*, 52, 1393–1412. https://doi.org/10.1111/anti.12643

Samaké-Roman, A. (2018) 'Why Scotland has a reputation for making potent, political pop', *Vice,* online https://www.vice.com/en/article/zmkdva/why-scotland-has-a-reputation-for-making-potent-political-pop

Simpson, L. (2014) *How Has Ethnic Diversity Changed in Scotland?*, Manchester: Centre for Dynamics of Ethnicity, Manchester University.

Smith, I. (2021) 'Blackout Tuesday – one year on: Scottish black artists share their stories'. *Alloa and Hillfoots Advertiser*, online https://www.alloaadvertiser.com/news/weekender/19356302.blackout-tuesday---one-year-scottish-black-artists-share-stories/

Tranmer, J. (2016) 'Popular music and left-wing Scottishness', *Études écossaises*, 18, 133–149.

Walsh, D. (2017) 'The changing ethnic profiles of Glasgow and Scotland, and the implications for population health'. *Glasgow Centre for Population Health*, online https://www.gcph.co.uk/assets/0000/6255/The_changing_ethnic_profiles_of_Glasgow_and_Scotland.pdf

Wood, N. (2012) 'Playing with "Scottishness": Musical performance, non-representational thinking and the "doings" of national identity'. *Cultural Geographies*, 19(2), 195–215.

Coda
The World of Scottish Music

Simon Frith

In Scotland 2014 was the *Year of Homecoming* when VisitScotland "welcomed the world to take part in a unique celebration of all that the country has to offer". Five years earlier, in 2009, VisitScotland had co-organised *Homecoming Scotland*, a series of events designed to attract "people of Scottish ancestry" to the home country culminating in *The Final Fling*, an event to be promoted by Glasgow's DF Concerts in the Scottish Exhibition and Conference Centre (SECC). The original idea seems to have been to feature the homecoming of the biggest Scottish names in pop and rock, artists who had achieved global fame, but, as DF knew from their experience booking acts for T in the Park, to bring such acts together for a single concert was both logistically and economically problematic and the final concert line-up (across three stages) primarily featured bands who were still regulars on Scotland's local live music circuits: Deacon Blue, the Skids and Hue and Cry; the View, Teenage Fanclub and Idlewild; Mike Scott of the Waterboys and Eddi Reader.[1]

The idea of 'homecoming' was obviously important for the Scottish National Party which had, for the first time, formed a Scottish government in 2007. It gave new meaning to the description of Scottish music as world music: Scottishness, it seemed, extended beyond the country's geographical boundaries into a global diaspora. But the 'homecoming' events did not just involve ideological arguments about Scottishness, they also reflected the new government's determination to develop a stronger, more independent music economy in Scotland itself. This was a cultural policy designed to bring economic returns.

In a small country, music-makers have to look outwards for sales of records and tickets sufficient to sustain their careers. State music policy begins, then, with the promotion of musical exports. Such policy involves two strands: developing what one might call 'unique musical selling points', sounds that are not made by anyone else; and enabling local musicians to compete in global genre economies (in the rock market, for instance).

Both these strategies can be traced in Scottish popular music history. Bagpiping, for example, has long been marketed as distinctively Scottish music-making with an appeal to an economically significant global market. Lismore (founded in 1973) and Temple (founded in 1978) are examples of Scottish independent record companies which established themselves by selling pipe-band and traditional Scottish folk music to the North American Scottish diaspora. The labels were the driving force in creating the Scottish Record Industry Association at the end of the 1980s and exploring ways of developing a broader Scottish music business. One suggestion was that Scottish composers and publishers should break away from the London-based Performing

DOI: 10.4324/9781003247470-21

Right Society and create their own rights licensing agency, and for a couple of years the SRIA produced a Scottish record sales chart, hoping to influence Scottish radio play policy.

The difficulty of forming a Scottish licensing agency (modelled on the Irish Music Rights Association which was launched in 1988) was that Scotland, unlike Ireland, was not a state—copyright law was a matter for Westminster. And, meanwhile, although the SRIA chart did reveal that Scottish sales of Scottish acts were under-weighted in the UK hit parade—Scottish acts generally did better in Scottish shops than in English or Welsh ones, as one might expect—it also suggested that record buying habits in Scotland weren't that different from UK patterns generally. While it was possible to sell distinctive Scottish music to tourists and expatriates, it was hard to discern a distinctively Scottish taste in the UK rock or pop or dance markets other than a bit of local boosterism.

In 1994, in order to fill a hole in Glasgow Royal Concert Hall's new year schedule, Colin Hynd staged the first Celtic Connections, a series of concerts by mostly Scottish folk-inflected musicians. The economic and cultural impact of Celtic Connections (and the number of non-Scottish performers) grew steadily and since 2006 (when Colin Hynd was replaced as director by Donald Shaw, a founder member of the commercially enterprising Scottish folk band Capercaille) the event has developed as a trade fair as well as a concert series, as a setting for Showcase Scotland through which deals can be made between a global network of (loosely defined) 'world music' promoters, agents, venues and record companies.[2]

A kind of sonic uniqueness is still being marketed here but labelled 'Celtic' rather than 'Scottish' and the global audience is a self-defined 'roots' diaspora. And it may be that this confusion of Scottish/Celtic music is not so new. In his interview with Martin Cloonan above Alasdair Roberts remarks that:

> around the time I was born [1977] and maybe for a few years before that my mother Annegret … and my father Alan, they ran a booking agency in Germany and so they booked a lot of Scottish, Irish and some English folk bands to Germany because it was very popular in Germany at that time, the sort of Celtic music, for want of a better word.

Thirty-five years later, the Hebridean group Skerryvore announced the fifty dates on their 2022 August-December touring schedule (thus following in the path of Runrig, who had begun a similar journey from the Isle of Skye in 1973, as documented in the 2021 film, *There Must Be A Place*). Skerryvore would be performing in Scotland, England and Ireland, in Denmark, Germany and the Netherlands, in Canada and, above all, in the USA, where in addition to club and campus gigs they were booked into various cities' Festivals of Irish Music.

The band was formed in 2004 on the Isle of Tiree by Daniel and Martin Gillespie (a graduate of the RCS Scottish Music course). It began as a 'West Coast Ceilidh Band', soon became known in its publicity as "The Boy Band of Traditional Scottish Music" and is now described by Wikipedia, accurately enough, as a "Scottish Celtic Rock Band" (its current line-up combines bagpipes, accordions, whistles and fiddle with rock guitar, bass, drums and vocals).

Just like Alasdair Roberts' parents, then, Skerryvore have used the opportunities opened up by the labelling of the folk tradition of Scottish music as 'Celtic' and the Gillespies have also taken note of developments in international pop and rock commerce. In 2005 they began promoting Oban Live, an annual weekend of music in Mossfield Stadium; in 2010 they staged the first annual Tiree Music Festival; in 2019 they established Apex Music International, which offers musicians a range of services: a tour booking agency, event management, expertise in making visa applications and organising tax waivers, advice on marketing and merchandise.

Scotland's place in the world, 'Scottishness', is defined here by a lived sense of locality. The Oban and Tiree events celebrate the Scottish West Coast, draw on Highlanders' and Islanders' understanding of their musical identity: traditional music, Gaelic song, ceilidhs, community gatherings, pub partying, pop songs and rock'n'roll, a kind of celebration of sociality that, like its Irish equivalent, has an appeal which is both local and global. To put this another way, its global appeal lies in its distinct local sensibility.

When we started researching Scottish music policy, in the 1990s, the most common complaint was that in order to have a successful career Scottish musicians and entrepreneurs had to move to London. The result was, it was argued, a musical brain-drain. Scotland's problem was that it didn't have the infrastructural resources to enable music-makers to develop their talents at home. The initial policy focus was on recording facilities (this fed into the SAC's recording support budget) and record companies. By the end of the decade, however, it was understood that Scottish labels would never have the majors' promotion, distribution and talent investment clout. The sensible Scottish development strategy was to enable locally made music to be licensed to the big players in the global music industry (this fed into the SAC's funding support for Scottish bands and their managers to play at Austin's annual South by Southwest showcase). And this was not just a strategy for record making. As Kenny Forbes shows in his chapter, T in the Park could only develop as Scotland's very own international festival by, in effect, licensing itself to the majors in the global live music business.

From this perspective what Scottish musicians and businesses most needed were local managerial, legal and accountancy services, rehearsal spaces and promotional resources (the facilities described in Emil Thomson's chapter on DD8 Music in Kirriemuir and, indeed, offered by Apex Music International). The focus was no longer on developing a Scottish recording industry but on the sustenance of a range of music businesses,[3] and in 2008 a new industry body was established, the Scottish Music Industry Association, SMIA, funded by Creative Scotland with the object of "strengthening, empowering and uniting Scotland's music industry" as a whole.[4] For all its rhetoric, however, the SMIA, is limited politically. It is an industry body funded not by the industry but by the state; much of its work involves lobbying its own funders for more funds to undertake more lobbying! Its best-known activity, determining the annual Scottish Album of the Year, is, in the end, designed for just the same purpose (and with as little effect) as the SRIA's record sales charts: to promote new releases on Scottish record labels. The SAY awards, like the SRIA charts, are largely of parochial interest and have little or no impact on the UK-wide media or music sales, particularly given the changing nature of Scottish media ownership and its declining marketing importance.

So far in this chapter we have been considering the place of Scottish music in the world. We turn now to another kind of music policy: bringing the world to Scotland, using music to attract not just tourists but also investors, businesses, upmarket migrants. What is on offer here is not only what is unique to Scotland—its history and geography—but also what makes its cities as vibrant and modern, as *global*, as cities elsewhere. One object of the Glasgow International Jazz Festival, for example, was to enable citizens of Glasgow to enjoy the very best of international jazz. As Jill Rodger notes in her interview above:

We're not funded by them [Glasgow City Council] anymore, but that was always [our remit] bringing people [performers] to the city, it was always for the citizens of Greater Glasgow. 65% still, roughly, of [our audience] is Greater Glasgow based. We've never had a huge international audience. So if you're just programming Glasgow bands who are also playing other venues all year round it doesn't become so much of a festival.

And as Martin Cloonan has explained,

> Both the SECC and the Hydro stand as examples of public investment in popular enter-
> tainment in the modern era. These were initiatives designed not to help local musicians but
> to attract internationally renowned acts—and thus tourists—to the city. The message to be
> given was that Glasgow was a cool place to visit, or work, or live. They can attract the best
> acts in the world to a venue within easy travelling distance from the city centre. Edinburgh
> (Glasgow's closest rival) cannot make such a claim—it does not have such a venue or even a
> suitable space on which to build one—and so first the SECC [opened 1985: first concert by
> UB40] and now the Hydro [opened 2013: first concert by Rod Stewart] became, for better or
> worse, *the* Scottish venues for arena-sized acts to play and for arena-sized audiences to attend
> (Behr et al. 2016: 17).

Meanwhile, in 2003, Edinburgh welcomed MTV Europe's annual award show to Leith.
Edinburgh's councillors, as Gavin Reid documents, believed that the event would have immediate economic benefits for the local community but the policy-makers were equally convinced
of the MTV event's "symbolic benefits". It would help to establish Edinburgh as a vibrant and
ambitious modern European city, a tourist destination and "a global brand with a rich waterfront in Leith". The MTV Show would be a unique opportunity for "place promotion" and
provide "priceless celebrity endorsements" from the featured superstars. For Henry McLeish,
former Labour First Minister, "there [was] no way of quantifying the effect of the rest of the
world looking at Scotland in such a new light" (Reid 2007: 486–488).

Scottish state support for MTV had little to do with the promotion of Scottish music or the
support of Scottish musicians; it was conceived, rather, as a way to give Edinburgh a new kind
of commercial status, to help make it "the most prominent Northern European city by 2015".

What we have described in this chapter (and, indeed, throughout all the chapters in this
book) are two ways of thinking about Scotland in the world: in terms of the global place of local
music and in terms of the local place of global music. The question remains: for Scottish musicians and audiences what is meant, if anything, by "our music"?

Alasdair Roberts again:

> I think that when I was younger, when I was a teenager and so on, I had some sort of neg-
> ative… my view of traditional Scottish culture was shaped by the fact that I'd grown up in
> a very sort of touristy part of Scotland as well and I was next door to a former woollen mill
> which was now a shop which sold woollen things and tartan and it was all 'tartan and short-
> bread'. And you'd walk in there and they'd be playing the kind of the cheesiest kind of music
> that a tourist would think of as traditional Scottish music. And those kind of associations
> kind of put me off when I was (young).

'His music' as a teenager was indie rock, as it was for teenagers the world over, just as, nowadays,
his music is just as much 'at home' in Canada as in Scotland. For almost all Scottish musicians,
their musical place is found in the relationship between Scotland and somewhere else—Ireland
for many folk performers, North America for jazz, blues and country players, England and
the USA for rock, punk, indie and rap artists, Europe in the club and classical worlds. Music-
making is not by its nature a matter of nationalism. It is a way of being in the world as a Scot,
which may mean performing Scottishness (like Jimmie MacGregor or Skerryvore) or not (like
Sheena Easton or Calvin Harris), but which necessarily involves a kind of constant probing into
what it means to be Scottish.

This is the sensibility shared by Alex Harvey and Bobby Gillespie, by Lulu and Edwyn Collins, by the Reid brothers in the Proclaimers and the Reid brothers in Jesus and Mary Chain, by Alasdair Roberts and Aidan Moffat, Sharleen Spiteri and Shirley Manson, Laura Macdonald and Fergus McCreadie, by someone from Young Fathers or Stanley Odd and by Loki and Shaheeda Sinkler. Music made in Scotland is music about being Scottish but being Scottish is neither a fixed nor simply a geographical identity.

Notes

1 I was commissioned by DF to write an essay on Scottish music for the *Final Fling's* glossy programme. It soon became clear from the constantly changing brief that the concert was going to be less starry than originally planned and the ticket sales less buoyant. As far as I know the programme did not appear.
2 Showcase Scotland is produced and managed for Celtic Connections by Active Events, a contemporary folk and roots music agency originally established in Scotland in 1990. It also manages Showcase Scotland Expo, which aims "to forge relationships with overseas music trade events and to lobby for showcase opportunities for Scottish based artists".
3 This was one of the emphases of our 2003 *Mapping the Music Industry in Scotland*.
4 SRIA was dissolved in 2010.

References

Behr, A., Brennan, M., Cloonan, M., Frith, S. and Webster, E. (2016) "Live concert performance: An ecological approach", *Rock Music Studies* 3(1), 5–23.
Reid, G. (2007) "Showcasing Scotland? A case study of the MTV Europe Music Awards Edinburgh03", *Leisure Studies* 26(4), 479–494.

Afterword
Music in a Future Scotland

How do you see Scottish popular music (and your own career) developing over the next decade?

ARIELLE FREE, DJ, *broadcaster and record producer*
https://www.ariellefree.com/
In the next decade I think we will start to see Scottish artists really become centre stage and accelerate to become huge globally recognised super stars.

With the recent success of Lewis Capaldi, the hunt is already on for the next big Popstar from Scotland.

It also has one of the strongest dance and electronic music scenes in the UK at the moment. So the world is already watching and they will start to really celebrate the talent Scotland has to offer.

The beauty of platforms like TikTok can catapult artists to number 1 selling artists in the blink of an eye, just look at LF System. Thanks to TikTok their hit 'Afraid to Feel' went viral and stayed at the number one spot in the charts for eleven weeks, beating Calvin Harris's record of the longest number one for a dance track. I think this means the artist now has more power and the opportunity to truly be the gate keepers of their own destiny.

As a music making broadcaster I can only hope that as my production skills increase that I'll be able to start making more and more music across the board, as well as starting to produce for other artists and DJ's.

The future I believe is bright for Scotland and its musical talent. The next ten years are going to be some ride!

ARUSA QURESHI, *journalist, editor and author of 'Flip the Script' (404 Ink)*
https://www.arusaqureshi.com/
The Scottish music scene is vibrant and varied, encompassing talent of all backgrounds and disciplines who work in a range of genres. One of the biggest threats facing the future of music in Scotland is in the rolling back of progress made in areas such as diversity and inclusivity, for example when it comes to equality on line-ups, safe spaces and community outreach, because of overarching concerns like the effects of the pandemic and rising costs. On the other hand though, the collective desire to tear down existing hierarchies and structures, and remove gate-keepers is only getting stronger and I believe that we'll keep seeing some of the most incredible, boundary-pushing work coming through from the margins and on grassroots levels in the near future. Hip hop in Scotland, for instance, is thriving and the scene continues to grow in size and popularity. While Scotland does have this significant legacy and history with hip hop, I hope to see more support and resources for women and gender minorities so that the Scottish hip hop

scene matches what is happening more widely in the UK for women in terms of success in hip hop and grime.

BRIGHDE CHAIMBEUL, *piper from the Isle of Skye, youngest ever winner of the BBC Radio 2 Young Folk Award.*

https://www.brichaimbeul.com/

The thing that strikes me about Scottish popular music is its potential for huge diversity in regard to genre. Scotland's music scene has a really wide breadth of sound and influences and I think we see the seeds of this through events such as the Sound of Young Scotland Award.

Recently I have seen a boost in appreciation for Gaelic and tradition coming through in music which has gained popularity, though not in its most traditional sense but certainly an appreciation for its roots and way of life and, more specifically, its instrumentation and even form.

There's certainly space for Scottish tradition to take its place in popular music in whatever form; for me it is about surpassing barriers, connotations; not to be limited by labels and boxes.

CAROLINE SEWELL, *Regional Officer for Scotland and Northern Ireland, Musicians' Union.*

https://musiciansunion.org.uk/

The Scottish music industry will continue to navigate the biggest challenges it has ever faced over the coming years. Several existential crises including Brexit, Covid-19 and the cost-of-living crisis will continue to bear down in particular on those in low paid, precarious work – which is most of our industry. Bigger questions loom – the prospects of Scottish independence and re-joining the EU and what this might mean for the industry. Are they invitations for further precarity, or a means of escape from successive, out-of-touch Conservative Governments, and a route back to hassle-free touring in the EU?

There is much to be angry about. There is much to rally against in defence of what is important – this is where the resilience of this innovative sector will come into its own.

On a positive note, the moral compass within the sector is finding its magnetic north as the industry becomes increasingly aware of the inequalities that must be overcome within popular music. Through initiatives such as Keychange[1] and the work of organisations such as Musicians' Union (among others) we are beginning to see an industry that is more inclusive, diverse, and more representative and so too are the attitudes that shape it.

GILL MAXWELL, *Executive Director, Scottish Music Centre.*

https://www.scottishmusiccentre.com/

Will our songwriters and musicians keep on producing, recording and performing quality original music worthy of world-wide attention in the next ten years? Hell yes.

And what's encouraging is the open-minded, collaborative blurring of boundaries across those working in folk/trad, pop, indie, jazz, hip hop, electronica and contemporary classical, creating new fusions and building new audiences.

Investment in talent development through publicly funded projects (for example, Showcase Scotland/Showcase Scotland Expo, MusicPlus & Hit the Road, Made in Scotland, Wide Days and Celtic Connections) assists our music sector in identifying talent at a very early stage and enables a range of showcase and international exchange projects. Very welcome, but investment in *backstage skills, small business and entrepreneurial* support at an early stage will become ever more important in helping stabilise our infrastructure and ensuring our artists make the most of their talent. Why? Because the post-pandemic, post-Brexit landscape for our industry looks bleak and challenging, imperilling the future of crucial grassroots venues in Scotland

and beyond and negatively impacting the ability of all but our most-established artists to tour- and find new audiences- in Europe. Without touring circuits, income, jobs and livelihoods are endangered.

We're rich in creative talent, we must ensure it can flourish and earn its living in the coming years.

MEGAN MACDONALD, *accordion player in Eabhal, a free-ranging folk group and HEISK, an all-woman six-piece dance band, session musician and teacher.*

https://www.eabhal.com/

https://www.heisk.co.uk/

We see such a high standard across the board within the music scene in Scotland, and I love being a small part of that! There's always something new and exciting to listen to or check out.

Within the traditional and folk music scene here, we are seeing lots of development in live presentation and production. This year I've seen acts such as Niteworks and Elephant Sessions elevate their show with some seriously impressive lighting. These acts have already taken this genre to bigger stages at festivals that wouldn't typically have traditional music on their line-up. I think that working with the production side of shows would open that option up to more traditional music-based acts.

It would be great to continue to build a wider audience for traditional music in the not-so-obvious tour destinations in Scotland. My band, Eabhal, had an album launch tour this summer and part of that was through a project called Scotland on Tour, which matched venues with artists with this idea in mind. This makes live music more accessible and helps artists to grow their audiences. This is an already thriving scene, but projects such as this would continue to develop and grow the touring element of the sector.

Note

1 Supported by the Creative Europe Programme of the European Union, Keychange is a global network working towards a total restructure of the music industry in reaching full gender equality.

Notes on Contributors

Bob Anderson is a lecturer at City of Glasgow College and an affiliate staff member of the University of Glasgow, UK. His PhD thesis provides a thirty-year social history of Glasgow's popular music scene, a scene in which, as a drummer, he has been an active participant.

Adam Behr is a Senior Lecturer in Contemporary and Popular Music at Newcastle University, UK. He researches the connections between popular culture, politics, the music industries and cultural policy.

Diljeet Kaur Bhachu is a musician, activist, educator and researcher based in Glasgow, UK. She co-founded the Scottish-Asian Creative Artists' Network to promote the plurality and diversity of Scottish-Asian artists and their practices. She works at the Musicians' Union.

Alistair Braidwood runs the Scottish cultural website *Scots Whay Hae!* and hosts a podcast and radio show of the same name. His PhD is in Scottish Literature, and he reviews for and contributes to a variety of publications about Scottish culture, literature and music.

Martin Cloonan is the Director of the Turku Institute for Advanced Studies (TIAS) at the University of Turku, Finland. He is also coordinating editor of *Popular Music* and sometimes sings in public.

Carla J. Easton is a singer/songwriter based in Glasgow, UK. She has released three solo albums and collaborated on many others. She is co-director of the film *Since Yesterday: The Unsung Pioneers of Scottish Pop*, a celebration of Scotland's forgotten Girl Bands.

Kenny Forbes is a Lecturer in Commercial Music at the University of the West of Scotland, UK. His research interests mainly focus on live music memories. His PhD from the University of Glasgow investigated the 'legendary' reputation of the Glasgow Apollo theatre (1973–1985).

Simon Frith is Emeritus Professor of Music at the University of Edinburgh, UK.

Dave Hook is an Associate Professor in Music at Edinburgh Napier University, UK. His research focuses on hip-hop, rap lyricism, identity, culture and performance, through practice. He is a member of alternative hip-hop group Stanley Odd.

Seán McLaughlin is Programme Leader for the BA (Hons) in Popular Music at the University of the Highlands and Islands, UK. He has degrees in Popular Music, Musicology and Education. He is an active musician, producer and songwriter.

Graeme Smillie is a lecturer at the University of the Highlands and the Royal Conservatoire of Scotland (UK). His research focuses on widening participation and institutional learning cultures in performing arts education. He is also an active touring and recording musician.

Emil Thompson studied for a doctorate in music at Newcastle University, UK. He lives in the Kingdom of Fife and is a musician and piano tuner. He has recently worked with ex-forces veterans producing original songs. Emil also holds an MFA in Art, Society and Publics and enjoys stone carving.

John Williamson is a lecturer in Music at the School of Culture and Creative Arts, University of Glasgow, UK.

Index